The Reminiscences

of

Rear Admiral Henry L. Miller

U.S. Navy (Retired)

Volume II

U.S. Naval Institute
Annapolis, Maryland
1973

Preface

Volume II of the Reminiscences of Rear Admiral Henry L. Miller, U.S. Navy (Retired), comprises a series of five tape-recorded interviews with Admiral Miller during the period from 27 April 1971 to 19 August 1971 - while he was on active duty and before retirement on 31 August 1971. These interviews were conducted by John T. Mason, Jr. for the Oral History project of the U.S. Naval Institute. Several of them were held at the Naval Institute, others at the Admiral's home at the Naval Air Test Center and one on the Admiral's barge as we cruised in Chesapeake Bay.

This volume begins with Admiral Miller's account of his command of Carrier Division three in the Far East at a crucial time in the development of the Vietnamese War. Other highlights include his three years in Command of the Naval Air Test Center at Patuxent and his two years as Chief of Information, U.S. Navy Department (Chinfo). Historians will find much in this volume of interest and value.

Admiral Miller has seen the original transcript and has made corrections to the text. Later he examined the re-typed version. A comprehensive subject index is attached for the benefit of users.

Certain documents are included in an appendix - again for the convenience of the user.

Interview No. 5 with Rear Admiral Henry L. Miller, U. S. Navy

Place: U. S. Naval Institute, Annapolis, Maryland

Date: Thursday morning, 19 August 1971

Subject: Biography

By: John T. Mason, Jr.

Q: Admiral, it's certainly great to see you this morning. This chapter is to be one of very great significance. Many of the others have been, but this is perhaps of paramount significance in terms of what goes on today. You're going to deal with your period from June 1962 to August 1964 when you served as assistant chief of staff for plans on the joint staff of the commander-in-chief, Pacific.

Adm. M.: I'll go back to the beginning and get everything into perspective. In eighteen months following World War II, the French reconquered Indochina. First, in South Vietnam, it was easy because they didn't have any strong government or strong feelings. The North Vietnam government was headed up by Ho Chi Minh. At that time his government of North Vietnam was militarily and politically very weak, so he did not confront the French with a problem at that time. However, in December of 1946 he started fighting the French.

This was the start of his show-down with the French. The U. S. and French supported Bao Dai, who was the Emperor of South Vietnam. This was in effect supporting colonialism.

Q: Of all of Indochina, wasn't he?

Adm. M.: Yes. Diem, at that time, was not committed in South Vietnam. As you recall, in February of 1954, the Big Four Geneva Conference was held on Korea and Indochina. There were many recommendations made, but Ho Chi Minh was bound and determined that he was going to throw the French out. In May of 1954, the French suffered a big defeat at Diem Bien Phu. In June of 1954, Diem was appointed premier by the French and by the former Emperor Bao Dai, who was then living in Paris. In September of 1954, the French turned over control of the government, the police, and other units there in South Vietnam to Diem, and in October of 1954, President Eisenhower said that American aid would be given directly to South Vietnam, but he hinted that perhaps the government needed some reforms. He backed up his support for South Vietnam by appointing the former Army Chief of Staff, General Collins, as a special ambassador to South Vietnam. Following that, he appointed General O'Daniel as Chief of the U. S. Mission to South Vietnam to train the South Vietnamese Army. That was in 1955. In October of 1955, Diem, as president, declared South Vietnam a republic.

From about this period on, there were lots of small skirmishes started, but really the guerrilla warfare, as such, didn't get too active until 1959.

Q: Was Diem accepted universally as president, when he made that change-over?

Adm. M.: Well, actually, Diem was the dictator and for some of the factions in South Vietnam, certainly he wasn't acceptable, but in the main, at that time, he was accepted by the majority of the people. He ruled with an iron hand. I don't think that was too bad. Somebody had to lead the country, and he took charge.

The guerrilla activity was on the rise throughout 1959 and 1960, and in May of 1960, the Chief of the Military Assistance Advisory Group, who was General O'Daniel, was authorized to detail American military advisers to certain units of the Vietnamese Army, and, also in May of 1960, the United States increased its military assistance to the government of Vietnam.

Q: Was all of this done at the request of President Diem?

Adm. M.: Yes. President Diem made these requests in conjunction with the Chief of the Military Assistance Advisory Group there, who made studies on the military aid that was needed at that time.

H. L. Miller # 5 - 308

Also, we became a little bit more involved in 1960 when we put a few U. S. Special Forces teams into Vietnam to help the Vietnamese special forces get their training.

Q: Under whose aegis were the Special Forces? Were they under military commanders?

Adm. M.: Our Special Forces were supposed to be under the Chief of the Military Assistance Advisory Group (MAAG). Also, in October 1960, President Eisenhower assured Diem that the U. S. would continue to assist South Vietnam. And all during this time, Diem was trying to get the country pulled together. He was having a difficult time. You just don't build a country overnight. So in November of 1960 there was an attempted coup that really didn't work out, but you could see that trouble was coming.

Q: Admiral, for the sake of clarity, by that time had there been a line of demarcation in terms of ideology? Was it clear that the North Vietnamese under Ho Chi Minh were Communist-oriented?

Adm. M.: Yes, I believe the lines were clearly drawn between the ideology of the government of North Vietnam and that of South Vietnam. This was at the high levels. The people really didn't care who was running what, as long as they had something to eat, a place to sleep, and clothes on their bodies - just a few clothes. Additionally, in South Vietnam - and this was highlighted later on - there was always a rift between the Buddhists and the Catolics. Diem was a Catholic. His brother, Ngo Dihn Nhu, was a Catholic, and his brother's wife, Madame Nhu, was a catholic. The Buddhists all felt that he favored the Christians over the Buddhists, and the Moslems - the few that there were - felt the same way. There were other sects also involved and irritated.

At this time, in 1960, our own CIA began training the South Vietnamese Rangers in certain details of guerrilla warfare, and the plot thickens, you might say, because in 1961 the Chief of the Military Assistance Advisory Group (MAAG) was authorized to detail advisers to many lower command post levels - these are U. S. advisers that I'm talking about - and to all the battalion headquarters. So, with this, the MAAG was asking for more and more military advisers from our own Army to be sent to Vietnam. As far as the Navy and the Air Force advisers were concerned, we had very few U. S. Navy and U. S. Air Force advisers, but these eventually began to build up, too.

Then, in May of 1961, President Kennedy said that consideration was being given to the use of U. S. forces, if necessary, to help the Republic of Vietnam. I presume that he said that to scare Ho Chi Minh and to more or less warn that if he expanded the so-called guerrilla war at that time, we may step in and hurt them badly.

Q: At that time, did Ho Chi Minh have the public backing of the Communist Chinese and the Russians? Had that been made apparent?

Adm. M.: Yes. By 1961 the lines were fairly drawn on who was supporting whom. Russia and China were supporting Ho Chi Minh, at that time, but not at the levels that were obtained later. Still he had their 100 percent support. Also in May 1961, Ambassador Nolting arrived in Saigon. He spoke French very fluently. I thought he was a great ambassador. He got along with Diem and Diem's government very well. He had good communications with Diem. And, also in May 1961, Vice President Johnson made a trip to Vietnam. He promised more military and economic aid to Diem. Diem told him he would like to have increased aid, but no U. S. combat troops, just advisers.

Then, later on, in October of 1961, the former chief of staff of the Army, General Maxwell Taylor, who was then retired, arrived in Saigon as a special adviser to President Kennedy. He came to take a look at the situation and to make specific recommendations. He said that at the time - and this keeps coming up - the Diem government needed reforms in administration, the way they did business, etc. With that, on 19 October, Diem declared a state of emergency in South Vietnam. They had various factions who were privately scheming for power. He knew that there were groups that would like to overthrow the government, and perhaps he used this also as a lever to get more military and economic aid from the United States, because the following month President Kennedy said that the U. S. would bolster up and increase their aid - military aid - to the government of Vietnam, but no, repeat no, U. S. combat forces.

Q: This continued to be the attitude of Diem also, didn't it?

Adm. M.: Yes. Diem said, give me the guns, the tools, the food, and my people will fight the war. Now, a little change in philosophy came in December of 1961, and here you might say the plot thickens again, because we put two U. S. Army helicopter companies in there with about 400 U. S. Army personnel, and these helicopter companies were supposed to be used for transportation for the various Military Assistance Advisers around the country, also in case of necessity, to bring supplies or ammunition to outlying units in trouble and to determine what kind of tactics to use with the armed helicopters. When I say "armed", the crew was inside the helicopter, manning the machine guns.

And in December of 1961, the Secretary of Defense, at a conference at CinCPac, was being apprised of the situation by the

Chief of the Military Assistance Advisory Group, who said he estimated that one-fourth of the people in the Republic of Vietnam supported the Communists, one-fourth were on the fence, the other half were for the government of Diem. That was, remember now, the end of 1961.

Q: And I presume that was based on composite reports from CIA, the ambassador, and what-have-you?

Adm. M.: That's right. It was a report from the country team that consisted of the ambassador, the Chief of the Military Assistance Advisory Group, the head of the CIA, the head of the economic aid program, and the head of the United States Information Agency in Saigon. Those people comprised the country team and I imagine it was their consensus that half the people were for the government, one-fourth for the Communists of North Vietnam, and the other was on the fence, they didn't know which way to go and they didn't care really because what they wanted was food, clothing, and shelter.

Q: This is sort of a footnote question. Considering the high rate of illiteracy in South Vietnam, this quarter of the population who supported the Communists, were they largely the educated ones or what were they?

Adm. M.: I really don't know. I can't remember that question coming up.

Q: I'm thinking in terms of leadership and potential leadership. Were the people in that classification Communist-oriented or not?

Adm. M.: I think the educated class - most of the educated class - were for the government.

Also in December of 1961, the total strength of the Military Assistance Advisory Group was about 4,000. This included a fixed-wing company and headquarters of our own Army, our own advisers there. From the beginning of 1962 to the end of 1962, you might say the strategy and the build-up came for the military assistance that we were putting into Vietnam. In January 1962, we put 16 C-123 aircraft in there for combat airlift. Also in January of 1962, we put two more Army helicopter companies in Vietnam. In February of 1962, we started the strategic hamlet program. The strategic hamlet program was much like the forts that were built around the USA in the early days to keep the Indians from killing all the white men, but additionally the strategic hamlet held a great many people who would go out and till the soil or plant rice or pick rice every day, plus a defense unit. They were linked with little villages close by by radio, so that if they were attacked they'd call the strategic hamlet and a force would help them.

There were times when the Viet Cong attacked and burned some of the strategic hamlets, but the strategic hamlet program, in the main, was copied from the program that Brigadier General Thompson of the UK started in Malaya. You recall, the strategy they used to clean the guerrillas out of Malaya. It took quite a while, but they were very systematic and successful in doing it.

Q: And it was a strategy that was learned through painful experience!

Adm. M.: That's right. This was some of the strategy that we were using at the time.

Q: How did we latch on to this strategy? Was Thompson in Saigon?

Adm. M.: Thompson was a special adviser to President Diem, and we talked to him at CinCPac headquarters. The chief of the Military Assistance Advisory Group talked to him. All of our people talked to General Thompson because he was a master at it and knew his business. Perhaps we didn't agree with him 100 percent, but in the main we liked his strategy. In 1962 we continued to build up the Military Assistance Advisory Group in Saigon and outlying areas.

Q: By considerable numbers?

Adm. M.: Yes, Sir, you could see the build-up coming along because just after we started the strategic hamlet program we brought General Paul Harkins in as the Chief of the Military Advisory Group and they changed his title to Commander, U. S. Military Assistance Command, Vietnam. His short title was CoMUSMacV.

Q: This was a significant development, was it not? It was a public recognition of the fact that we had considerable force there.

Adm. M.: Yes, and it was recognition of the fact that we had troubles in Vietnam and we were getting more and more U. S. involvement in Vietnam. Again, there were Vietnamese people who didn't like the way Diem was running the government and other things that probably Madame Nu was doing, so in February of 1962 two planes from the Vietnamese Air Force bombed and strafed the Presidential Palace. They didn't do much harm, but this was an indication that there was dissatisfaction among many groups there and they were showing their displeasure.

Also, in March of 1962, they wanted some more helicopters. The Army was rapidly running out of helicopter support, so the Marines brought some in from Okinawa. So, here come the Marines, now, getting involved. There were 400 men and 16 helos, and they put this helo group of Marines down in the Mekong Delta. The build-up continued and, in May of 1962, we put 20 more C-123s into Vietnam for combat airlift. This was the U. S. Air Force becoming more involved. About this time, Ho Chi Minh, in a private interview, said that it would probably take him ten to fifteen years to take over the government of the Republic of Vietnam. In 1959 he said it would only take him one year, so you can see Ho Chi Minh was having his troubles, too.

Q: Largely based on the heavier involvement of the U. S.?

Adm. M.: Yes, the heavier involvement of the U. S. and better training of the South Vietnamese forces.

Q: Does this speak well for the strategic hamlet idea?

Adm. M.: Yes, it shows that the South Vietnamese knew they had a fight on their hands and they were learning very fast that they had to pull together all the various units to defend themselves.

In July of 1962, a SecDef conference was held at CincPac headquarters. That was the first one that I attended since I had reported in to CinCPac in June of 1962.

Q: Had there been previous ones?

Adm. M.: Yes, there had been previous conferences in Saigon and at CinCPac headquarters, but at this particular one in July of 1962...

Q: The date of it was July 23.

Adm. M.: That's right...general agreement was obtained on the additional amount of military assistance to be provided to the government of the Republic of Vietnam and also for Thailand, because we had problems in Thailand that in the northeastern part of the country were closely allied to the infiltration in Vietnam. Additionally, of course, Laos, because the various factions in Laos were fighting each other.

Q: Admiral, who was present at that conference?

Adm. M.: Normally at the SecDef conferences at CinCPac, the Commander-in-Chief, Pacific, Admiral Felt, was there, also his component commanders, the Commander-in-Chief of the Pacific Fleet, the Commander of U. S. Air Forces, Pacific, and the Commander of U. S. Army Forces, Pacific, with, perhaps, a few of their principal advisers and a goodly number of Commander-in-Chief, Pacific, staff, plus the Chief of the Military Assistance Advisory Group in Vietnam with quite a supporting cast from there, including Army, Navy, and Air Force heads of departments, you might say, of his staff. And the Commander Fleet Marine Forces Pacific Fleet.

Q: Was the Ambassador there, also?

Adm. M.: The Ambassador was there, the USIA man, the CIA official, the head of the economic aid program in Saigon, and from Washington we had the director of the staff of the Joint Chiefs of Staff, who was then Vice Admiral Herb Riley. We also had various members of the staff of the Joint Chiefs plus the special assistant at that time for counterinsurgency who was then Major General "Brute" Krulak. We also had the CIA man at times from Washington, plus others from various departments of the government.

Q: And the prime figure, the Secretary of Defense?

Adm. M.: Oh, absolutely. The Secretary of Defense and some of his special assistants. At one conference we had Secretary of State Dean Rusk...

Q: That was the later one, in October?

Adm. M.: Yes. These were all high-level conferences and lots of business was done, presentations made, agreements made on the spot, and we kept a record of all the actions and milestones that were laid out at these conferences.

Q: Will you be specific about the conference in July? I mean, can you re-create some of the conversation, some of the points made?

Adm. M.: In general, the total strategic hamlet program was agreed to. One of the communications links in the strategic hamlet program was radios and we needed to get radios and put them into the strategic hamlets plus the villages. So, 6,000 hamlet radios were authorized for Vietnam, 2,300 for Thailand, because they were starting the same defensive actions.

It was also agreed that more and more of the training of various groups in Vietnam would be concentrated under the chief of the Military Assistance Advisory Group. The whole military assistance program for Vietnam and for Thailand was laid out at this particular conference - the construction program for airfields, for better ports in both Vietnam and Thailand. Of course, not to the extent that it was done later on, but this was preliminary. We knew that we had to have more of a junk force. The Junk Force was a group of units of junks that were piloted by the South Vietnamese to keep the North Vietnamese infiltration from the water, out of the Republic. We knew that this effort had to be expanded.

Q: This had been in operation for some time?

Adm. M.: This was just really getting started - the Junk Force. It was agreed that we had to have better communications. The supply of transmitters and receivers, radars, and other links that were needed in Thailand and Vietnam had to be expanded.

Q: Admiral, may I ask how adept were the Southeast Asians proving to be in the operation of this electronic equipment?

Adm. M.: The electronic equipment we gave them to use was very easy to operate. It didn't take much instruction, more or less the push-button type. However, we knew they couldn't fix them. But the communications worked pretty well with the various villages and hamlets.

It was also agreed at the July 1962 conference on the general build-up that was needed at that time to take care of the insurgency in Vietnam.

Q: What was the prevailing attitude at the conference? Was Secretary McNamara optimistic, and the others, or was it a discouraging picture?

Adm. M.: Surprisingly enough, everybody felt that with a modest expansion of the military assistance program we would be able to take care of the Viet Cong. As a matter of interest, the number of attacks in the first six months of 1962, these are attacks on hamlets, villages, etc., was 188, in comparison to the war at present time, this was nothing, but it was an indicator of what we had to do. It pointed the finger at us to provide the supplies and training for the defense of the Republic of Vietnam with their people. They had to be able to defend the various villages against the Viet Cong. So, you might say the conference in July was optimistic. We felt that a modest build-up of our advisers, Army, Navy, Air Force, and Marine Corps in Vietnam plus more guns, airplanes, helicopters, junks, and other small boats for the Vietnamese Navy, plus a little better organization would do the trick. At that time, the Vietnamese Air Force leaders and the Vietnamese Navy leaders weren't given much attention by the government of Vietnam or by our own Chief of the MAAG. They felt that the big problem was more or less an Army ground problem. They found out later that they needed more Air Force and Navy help in supporting the troops and also in preventing infiltration from the sea, also carrying the fight along the rivers and canals there by boat. All this came later.

Q: Admiral, may I ask something? General Krulak was very much impressed with the great importance of the economic assistance program in the villages. How much did that enter into the discussions at the conference in July.

Adm. M.: Not too much because we were primarily concerned at that time with defense of villages and helping the people to defeat the sporadic attacks of the Viet Cong that were being made at that time. We were concerned with the economy but the emphasis at the July conference was on defense.

Q: As I understand Krulak, he felt that this aid program, being a humanitarian sort of thing, added a new dimension to warfare of this kind. It was an integral part of it.

Adm. M.: Naturally, people have to eat. You just can't have them holed up in a strategic hamlet all day. People have to go from that hamlet to the rice paddies and get their food, and do other things. Naturally, at a conference of this kind, laying out an over-all program for the Republic of Vietnam and Thailand, we had all the people concerned look at the over-all plan. This included the economic aid people, the CIA, the USIS, ambassadors from both countries, and other appropriate people. We looked at a balanced program, but we still had to put more dollars into the defense of the strategic hamlets.

Q: Was General Taylor present at this particular conference?

Adm. M.: No, General Taylor was not at that July conference. He was at the following one in October.

Also, it was agreed that there'd be more Army helicopters to put into the country for sector surveillance. Additionally, some of those small OV-1 airplanes the Army had, plus the Caribou aircraft and the Mohawk aircraft. The Army was looking at sector surveillance of the country to bring the Vietnamese more intelligence on the whereabouts and the actions of the Viet Cong around the country. However, those particular aircraft were not the type that one needed to bring back intelligence. There had to be camera coverage from various altitudes plus other means of surveillance.

Q: How effective was camera coverage proving to be in jungle areas?

Adm. M.: Pretty poor, because you just can't see under the thick foliage. This brought up another program that was eventually used - the defoliation program. Along the rivers, the Viet Cong could lie there and pick off anybody that came in his canoe or boat anywhere along the river, so we used chemicals to defoliate large areas along the banks of these rivers, first, to experiment and see what it would do, and secondly, if it was successful, to do it on a large scale.

Q: This was not entirely a new technique with us, was it? Had we not used it in World War II in the Pacific, on some of the islands?

Adm. M.: I don't recall using it in any of our Pacific war, and I was in most all of that.

Also at that conference, it was agreed that the chief of the Military Assistance Advisory Group would take over the training of the Civil Guard in the Republic of Vietnam, plus the Civilian Irregular Defense Group. It's very difficult to distinguish between these various civilian groups that the Vietnamese government had. The CIA was training the Civilian Irregular Defense Group, but all of these were now put under the Chief of the Military Assistance Advisory Group to get some continuity and standardization in their training.

Q: Were the natives who were part of these groups volunteers?

Adm. M.: There were a certain number of volunteers in these groups. They weren't considered as part of the Vietnamese armed forces, and they didn't get the salary, either, of the Vietnamese armed forces.

Well, that was the July conference, and following that, in September, I made a trip throughout the Far East and Southeast Asia...

Q: That was a good introduction to your new job!

Adm. M.: Oh, yes. I made that trip, as I told you earlier, with General Taylor, just before he became Chairman of the Joint Chiefs of Staff. Following that, on 8 October [1962], we had another Secretary of Defense Conference at CinCPac headquarters. Now, when I was with General Taylor in Saigon getting briefed by General Harkins, General Harkins made the statement that if we would give him all the necessary tools to fight this guerrilla war plus the other things that were needed to train the Vietnamese armed forces and the civil guards and the other units, including police, so that he could get the offensive going, he felt, if he got all these things, he could have the offensive going by the end of 1962, and, if so, then the war would be over by the end of 1963. One year.

Q: And how did his peers, General Taylor and you, evaluate this statement?

Adm. M.: It really surprised me because I thought from the way it looked to me it would take a lot longer than that to really clean up the country, and I told Admiral Felt when I got back that General Harkins had made this statement and he was going to make this statement at the October conference, which he did.

Q: That conference had already been set up?

Adm. M.: Yes, Sir, and he did. Well, with that, Mr. McNamara, the Secretary of Defense, using General Harkins' statement as a basis, directed that the U. S. plan for a three-year wrap-up period. He said, "I'll give you three years to end the war and to plan for all the necessary guns and tanks and planes and training that is needed, then to plan as we go along to scale down our effort in Vietnam, until at the end of that three-year period the Vietnamese, officers and enlisted, would be trained to fight their

H. L. Miller # 5 - 326

own war, run their own show, and get us out of the country."

Q: So it really was an early statement, then, of the Nixon program for South Vietnam, the Vietnamization?

Adm. M.: Yes, Sir. In other words, General Harkins said give me these things and I will get the offensive going, get the Vietnamese inspired, and the war will be over by 31 December 1963. Mr. McNamara said, I'll give you three years. So his timetable was supposed to be over by 31 December 1965. Now, when he made the statement for General Harkins to scale down his efforts, he said, I think you can bring a thousand U. S. advisers home by Christmas of 1962 - that same year - plan for all this, then start easing people out, but keep the effort going for the three years. We really did pull about a thousand people out that December, but we shouldn't have. We needed all we could muster right in Vietnam.

Q: You said that General Maxwell Taylor was present at that October conference. What do you recall was his particular contribution?

Adm. M.: He really didn't contribute much. He wanted to change the organization and command relationships of the U. S. military command in Vietnam vis-a-vis CinCPac. You see, the command-in-chief, Pacific was in charge of all U. S. forces in the Pacific,

H. L. Miller # 5 - 327

and Maxwell Taylor wanted to pull out the U. S. military forces in Vietnam from the direct command of CinCPac. So, I think he contributed a good internal services fight - that was about all.

Q: How did Admiral Felt feel about all this?

Adm. M.: Admiral Felt didn't like Maxwell Taylor interfering with his organization a bit.

Q: Was he optimistic about the outcome of the Vietnam fracas?

Adm. M.: You mean Maxwell Taylor?

Q: No, Admiral Felt?

Adm. M.: Yes. Admiral Felt's policy was to help the Vietnamese get organized, get trained, given the military equipment to fight their own war, but to keep U. S. troops out of that country. He felt that they could do the job if we gave them the tools and the training to do it.

Q: Admiral, at that period, was it apparent that supplies for North Vietnam were coming into the port of Haiphong and others? And, if it was apparent, what did we propose to do about that?

Adm. M.: No, it wasn't apparent that there was a lot of infiltration of supplies and equipment by the Viet Cong. The intelligence that we had didn't indicate that there was a great deal of infiltration of people and equipment from the North, and we were looking for that right along.

Q: I was thinking specifically of merchantmen from abroad bringing supplies into the harbor there, sea traffic.

Adm. M.: You mean into Saigon?

Q: No, Haiphong.

Adm. M.: Oh, certainly normal trade was going on at that time with all countries of the world. So, you might say, Hanoi and Haiphong and the government of North Vietnam was buying from everybody in the world. They had every right to have merchant shipping in there.

Q: This didn't enter into the discussions at the CinCPac conference?

Adm. M.: No, Sir. What we were concerned primarily was the military assistance program that the government of Vietnam had to have. The administration was pretty optimistic from the October conference when General Harkins and the Secretary of Defense laid out this strategy that they thought would win...

Q: You imply that others there were not?

Adm. M.: Well, we at CinCPac were cautious because we wanted to see the materials come, the equipment, and the guns and bullets and the aid, before we made statements that were too optimistic. And with a lot of the speculation that was going on at that time, some said it's going to be a long war, others favored the strategy that we held at the time. As I mentioned before, in 1962, the first six months, there were 188 attacks by the Viet Cong. The last six months of 1962, there were only 92 attacks. So it looked as though we were doing pretty well in getting the Vietnamese to do their own fighting and leave us as the advisers.

Q: Then, what went wrong?

Adm. M.: As I said, in 1962 we agreed on the build-up, we got people in-country as advisers, we got good equipment, we got them more airplanes, A1-HS, the Navy's Sky Raider plane, and agreed to give them about 25 more by the middle of 1963.

Q: Where were we training their pilots? In South Vietnam or were we then training them in this country?

Adm. M.: We were training their pilots in this country, and they turned out to be some pretty good pilots. As a matter of fact, as you recall, the present General Ky was the head of the Vietnamese

H. L. Miller # 5 - 330

Air Force, and he was a pretty hot-shot pilot. We even let him ride in the front seat coming aboard the carrier - the right front seat - coming aboard the carrier. He didn't fly it, but he saw. Also, you see, we were pretty optimistic too in a sense in 1962 because we had built 5,000 strategic hamlets, and this was quite an undertaking and it was very successful. So we thought it looked pretty good. Then, here came 1963, and right at the start of 1963, 2 January, to be exact, Commander, U. S. Military Assistance Command, Vietnam, came up with his three-year plan that Mr. McNamara ordered to conclude the war in Vietnam. It was approved and there were some people who were very optimistic about it.

Then, in May of 1963, there was another Secretary of Defense Conference at either CinCPac or Saigon, I forget which, and they agreed to accelerate the training of the Vietnamese Air Force. This had been pretty slow.

Q: And you and Admiral Felt were both present at that conference?

Adm. M.: Yes. What we wanted to do was build up their in-country capability and release U. S. units, turn the planes over to them and release our people. Also in May, President Kennedy said - I guess he was optimistic - he said the U. S. would withdraw our advisers any time the government of Vietnam would suggest it or request it. Then, also about that time, the Buddhists became very unhappy with Diem and the government of South Vietnam. There were demonstrations against President Diem...

Q: Was this the time of the self-immolation?

Adm. M.: Yes, those followed right along. That was in May. Then, in June, there was a tentative agreement between Diem and the Buddhists on their participation in the government and other activities. So it looked as though things were coming along pretty well. But the latter part of June, Henry Cabot Lodge came to Saigon and replaced Ambassador Nolting. Of course, at CinCPac, we liked Ambassador Nolting very much and thought he had done a magnificent job.

Q: Why did he step down?

Adm. M.: Evidently, President Kennedy and the administration weren't happy with the way Ambassador Nolting was running the show, or, you might say, influencing President Diem. I believe they felt he should have done more to get President Diem to unbend towards the Buddhists, and to run his country more like the American way. They felt there should be a better rapport there.

Q: Was it possible also that bringing Henry Cabot Lodge in was an attempt on the part of the administration to have a broader based support for their efforts? I mean this was a Republican being brought in to make a bi-partisan thing.

Adm. M.: No, I think they wanted Fritz Nolting out of there even though, in my opinion, Fritz Nolting did a wonderful job. But Henry Cabot Lodge didn't do anything overnight to influence the situation. In the latter part of August martial law was declared in the Republic of Vietnam because of the various groups who were creating trouble for the government of Vietnam. Also in the latter part of August, Cambodia broke relations with South Vietnam, but they kept the trade going. Sihanouk didn't want to let the money stop. Things really flared up there between the Buddhists and the Catholics and other groups to the extent that fires were started and attacks were made on various Americans and on government leaders. So, in the latter part of August 1963, the Joint Chiefs of Staff told the commander-in-chief, Pacific, to prepare to evacuate U.S. noncombatants from Vietnam. We thought this was a good idea because if you're going to go all-out to help a government and to train them and to get the Vietnamese to do their own fighting, then the best thing to do is to get our own women and children out of that particular country, since they really cost you a great deal of effort in housing, PX and other services that one should be devoting to the defense of that country.

They were talking at that time, too, that if Diem didn't do such and such for the Buddhists, maybe we should cut down on the aid for the Republic of Vietnam. But in September, President Kennedy said it would not be helpful at this time to reduce U. S. aid to South Vietnam. He was comparing it to the collapse of Chiang Kai-chek in China right after World War II. Kennedy said we want the war won, the Communists contained, and Americans to come home. Well, about the middle of September, Diem figured he had the situation well in hand, so he called an end to martial law, and the latter part of September President Kennedy sent the Secretary of Defense and General Taylor to Vietnam again to talk to Diem and look the situation over. I don't know what decisions resulted from that particular trip, but there was a lot of hocus-pocus going on that people didn't know about, because in October - remember the Secretary of Defense and General Taylor made their trip on the 21st of September - and on the 7th of October, Mr. Nhu, who was Diem's brother, accused the CIA of trying to stage a coup against the Diem government right there in Saigon.

On the 1st of November 1963, Admiral Felt was in Saigon and had just taken off from Ton Son Nhut airport. They waited till he got in the air, then the coup took place.

Q: He had no inkling of an impending coup?

Adm. M.: No. He'd had dinner and talks with Diem and everybody else. And on the 2nd of November Diem and Nhu were both killed. So you might say there was a period of time in there when the U. S. was very involved in taking measures to oust Diem. General Minh took over as the head of the military revolutionary council - that's "Big Minh," and Big Minh is still prominently involved to this day. And just to sort of bolster the morale of a lot of people in a very confused situation, the 13th of November General Harkins said that the overthrow of the Diem government had little over-all effect on the military campaign. Well, that was a bunch of hog wash! You just can't keep a country fighting when you don't have a government that is effective and active.

On the 20th of November we had another Secretary of Defense conference at CinCPac. The Secretary of Defense was there and the Secretary of State, Dean Rusk and others. After that the Secretary of State took off with other cabinet members of the U. S. government who were making a trip to Japan. They wanted to talk with the Japanese on future relations, and they were in the air when we received word on the 22nd of November that President Kennedy was killed.

Q: At that November conference at CinCPac, was the coup discussed - the overthrow of Diem?

Adm. M.: Yes. Not the series of events but the over-all effect, and of course support to Big Minh and the revolutionary council. On the 24th of November, following the assassination of President Kennedy, President Johnson re-affirmed U. S. intentions to provide military and economic aid to South Vietnam. The U. S. was not too happy with the turn of events as a result of that coup, because in December, Mr. McNamara and Mr. McCone, who was the head of the CIA, went to Saigon to evaluate the over-all effects of the coup. I guess they figured that they'd have to take other actions to help that three-man military command of General Minh, General Van Don and General Van Kim.

At that time the government was in a real state of confusion, so a little over a month later, on the 30th of January another coup took place...

Q: January 30?

Adm. M.: January 30th, 1964, when Major General Khanh took over and things didn't calm down a bit. In the first part of February there were about a thousand students who demonstrated in Saigon. They wanted Big Minh back in power. He was popular with a lot of the students.

H. L. Miller # 5 - 336

Q: He'd gone into exile at that point, hadn't he?

Adm. M.: I think at that point he went to Thailand, but on the 8th of February, Major General Khanh declared himself premier. He was trying to get the country straightened out. Then other events transpired, because on the 13th of January a deputy commander was appointed to the MACV staff, Lieutenant General Westmoreland. Also, the Air Force appointed Lieutenant General Moore to head up the U. S. Air Force effort there. So you could see this build-up taking place.

Then on the 10th of March the Secretary of Defense made the decision that the chief of staff to the U. S. Military Advisory Group in Saigon would be a ground officer, an Army officer, Major General Stillwell - Dick Stillwell. Well, Major General Khanh who was the premier in March, re-established relations with Laos, so that helped a little bit, but not too much. Then in April of 1964, at the SEATO meeting in Manila - and I was present at that meeting since the SEATO conferences used to come under my shop - the statement was made by the SEATO council, that the defeat of the Viet Cong in South Vietnam was essential to the security of Southeast Asia. SEATO would remain prepared to take further corrective steps. Well, that didn't mean anything because at that time the SEATO planning and the SEATO meetings were get togethers with those various nations, but there wasn't much business done.

Q: You mean it had lost some of its status, the status it had under Admiral Stump?

Adm. M.: No, it hadn't lost the status, but they really didn't do too much in the way of economic or military planning to help Vietnam. Later on, the Australians and the New Zealanders and the Philippines sent detachments in to help the Vietnamese, but not this particular time.

Q: At this particular meeting of SEATO, who spearheaded the resolutions to see that the Viet Cong was defeated?

Adm. M.: Oh, I think that was probably spearheaded by Dean Rusk. He's the head of the council. Admiral Felt was the U.S. military representative, adviser. He was the MilAd - military adviser - to Secretary Rusk at the SEATO council.

Q: Admiral, as you relate these events and the stepping up of the effort in Vietnam, it would appear that additional decisions must have been made by the administration as to our involvement. Were these reflected in any way in the meetings you attended?

Adm. M.: Yes. There were additional decisions made that headed towards more involvement. For instance, on the 25th of April 1964 General Westmoreland replaced General Harkins and right afterward there joint planning started on cross-border operations between

Vietnam, Thailand, and Laos, because now infiltration was building up and the North Vietnamese were coming in with more supplies and more people, more help for the Viet Cong. Then they got a greater consolidation of effort in May of 1964 when the Military Assistance Advisory Group in Vietnam was disestablished and the Commander, U. S. Military Assistance Command, General Westmoreland, assumed all of its missions and functions. This was approved by the Joint Chiefs of Staff, but CinCPac didn't concur, but we lost that battle.

Q: What was your opposition basically?

Adm. M.: We wanted to have Commander, U. S. Military Assistance Command in Vietnam to devote one hundred percent of his time to helping get the armed forces of Vietnam in fighting trim, and not to put up with all the details of military aid programs and guns and bullets and all that.

Q: In other words, you were advocating still the program which had been outlined several years before, the Vietnamization?

Adm. M.: Yes. So this was one thing we didn't like, and then the latter part of May Vietnam began getting some help and getting some attention from New Zealand, West Germany, Austria, and the Philippines sent observers to Vietnam, and others asked them if

H. L. Miller # 5 - 339

they needed some economic aid and help. This was very helpful. Then the 1st and 2nd of June, we had another Secretary of Defense conference at CinCPac. I wasn't there at that one, I went to see my son graduate from Auburn.

In the latter part of June 1964 another turn. General Taylor who was Chairman of the Joint Chiefs of Staff was then appointed as ambassador to the Republic of Vietnam, replacing Henry Cabot Lodge, and Alexis Johnson was named as the deputy to General Taylor in Saigon. I remember meeting Alex Johnson and briefing him on the general set-up as he came through CinCPac. Of course, General Taylor had to make some statements, so on 7 July he said a more vigorous prosecution of the war must be made against the Viet Cong.

Q: In the meantime, your own boss had retired, had he not?

Adm. M.: That's right. On the 1st of July, Admiral Felt retired and Admiral Sharp took over, and on the 20th of July, Lieutenant General Throckmorton was named as the deputy to Westmoreland in Vietnam. The latter part of July, the United States put 5,000 additional troops in Vietnam, so the effort was building up on all sides to really get after the Viet Cong and the North Vietnamese who were infiltrating.

Q: Admiral, with the advent of Sharp at CinCPac, replacing Admiral Felt, was there any noticeable change in philosophy?

Adm. M.: No, Sir. The same policies were supported by Admiral Sharp and he wanted the same clear-cut lines of communication and command. He wanted a military and advisory program and not involve a lot of U. S. troops there. But the build-up of troops continued and the build-up of U. S. involvement, because we laid out a very comprehensive construction program, a very comprehensive military aid program for Army, Navy, and Air Force units of the government of Vietnam, including training, economic aid, roads, airfields, hundreds of boats, tanks, and a build-up of port facilities - a tremendous program. And, as you recall, on the 1st of August there were mines found in the Saigon River - on the 2nd of August the USS Maddox was making a patrol in the Gulf of Tonkin, thirty miles off the coast of North Vietnam, and they were attacked by three North Vietnamese patrol boats. In an exchange of fire, the three North Vietnamese patrol boats disappeared from the scene. On the 2nd of August, President Johnson instructed the Navy that for any of those patrols they would have two destroyers plus combat air patrol over them, and they would attack any forces which attacked them with the intention of destroying those forces.

On the 4th of August the North Vietnamese attacked - patrol boats - attacked two U. S. destroyers in the Gulf and after a three-hour battle, two of the North Vietnamese boats were sunk and the other fled. On the 4th and 5th of August, U. S. aircraft made retaliatory attacks on four North Vietnamese patrol boat bases and the POL storage at Vinh. They damaged or destroyed twenty-five North Vietnamese patrol boats and they destroyed that oil depot at Vinh. Two of our planes were shot down.

Then, as you recall, on the 7th of August, the U. S. Congress passed a joint resolution assuring President Johnson of support for all necessary measures that he would have to take...

Q: The famous Gulf of Tonkin Resolution!

Adm. M.: Yes...and then, here we come again with trouble with the government in Vietnam. On the 12th of August, Ambassador Taylor said that the Republic of Vietnam needed continuity of government, and the beginning of unity in the government could already be seen, but to all of us it appeared that there was still a great deal of tug of war between various factions of the government. In August, too, the students in Saigon demonstrated against Khanh worse than they ever had before. Then on the 9th of September, Ambassador Taylor said the military situation was essentially normal, there's a general upward trend! Following that, on the 14th of September, they had another coup but it failed to overthrow Khanh. Then on the 18th of September, as you recall, there were the two destroyers, the Morton and the Edwards, that were attacked in the Gulf of Tonkin. Air cover was provided, but on a further investigation they didn't have sufficient evidence to find out the extent of those attacks. To further complicate things, on the 11th of September, Khanh fired Brigadier General Thieu, the man who is now in power.

There was one crisis after another throughout the last three or four months of 1964, and it continued right straight through into 1965 because Khanh replaced people who he felt were disloyal to him, and then on the 21st of February, there was another coup when he was thrown out and Big Minh took over.

Q: This was in 1965?

Adm. M.: This was in 1965. Also there was a continuing series of crises until June 1965, when there was another coup and General Thieu and General Ky took over, Thieu as premier and Ky as his deputy. You might say from November 1963, when Diem was ousted, to late 1965 - because it took an awful long time for Thieu and Ky to get some stability going - the government of Vietnam was in a continuous state of chaos. Nobody knew who had the ball, and it was particularly serious in that when they did have a coup and they put tanks on the runways, none of their planes could take off, none of our USAF planes could take off, and nobody knew who was running the show. And no one can say that our own military assistance and advice was effective during that time because we didn't know what the policy was there and who we were talking to. It was a very difficult period of time.

Q: May I ask a question or two? You cited several statements of General Taylor, our General Taylor, as ambassador, his statements being quite optimistic and, seemingly, quite contrary to the facts. What is the purpose, what is the advantage, of making statements like that which can be disproven so readily?

Adm. M.: I really don't know why he made them, because to any observer who was close to the scene, and there were thousands in Vietnam, who knew that it was a very precarious situation in that whole country and it was a very serious one. We weren't doing too well, and the government had to have some sort of stability or we'd never get anywhere. When Diem was living, we knew the one guy who was running that country. We knew who we were dealing with. But after that it was very confusing.

Q: I have another question. You stated that after the initial attack on the Maddox in the Gulf, President Johnson said that henceforth destroyers would go in pairs. This is my understanding. Is this correct?

Adm. M.: That is correct.

Q: Was this the beginning of the minute direction from the White House to the Department of Defense in naval matters in that area?

Adm. M.: Perhaps it was because we received many directives out in that area after we became involved in making attacks, on what bombs to use, what ammunition to use, what fuses to use. There were many, many detailed instructions that confused everybody and caused a great deal of unnecessary work and unnecessary involvement.

Q: What I was trying to develop was that prior to that time, in naval matters, it was pretty much a command.

Adm. M.: That's correct. In naval matters, whenever one was running a task force or a ship he was told to do a particular job, he normally had the necessary munitions to attach to the airplanes or to put into the guns and do that particular job, without being told by somebody in the White House or in the Secretary of Defense's office, or even the Joint Chiefs of Staff. I don't think anybody told General Patton what to use over in Europe.

Q: Well, now, to conclude this chapter properly, you were detached from CinCPac staff when?

Adm. M.: I was detached from CinCPac staff in August of 1964. I took my family to Alameda, California, I put them in an apartment there, flew out to the South China Sea, and took over as commander of Carrier Division Three and commander of Task Force 77, which included all the carriers of the Seventh Fleet.

Q: Thank you.

H. L. Miller # 6 - 346

Interview No. 6 with Rear Admiral Henry L. Miller, U. S. Navy

Place: U. S. Naval Institute, Annapolis, Maryland

Date: Thursday morning, 22 July 1971

Subject: Biography

By: John T. Mason, Jr.

Q: Good to see you, as usual, this morning, Admiral. The chapter today had to do with your command of the carrier division No. 3 and Task Force 77 of the Seventh Fleet in Vietnam covering the period from September 1964 to February 1966. Would you begin, Sir, by telling me about the assignment, what carriers were under your command?

Adm. M.: At that time my flagship was the USS Ranger. However, I relieved Admiral Gannon aboard the USS Bon Homme Richard on the 24th of September 1964, because the Ranger had boiler trouble and had to proceed to Yokosuka to get extensive work done on the boilers.

Q: She could be completely refurbished at Yokosuka?

Adm. M.: Oh, yes. There were very good ship repair facilities at Yokosuka. But I had an additional job besides my carrier division task. I was commander of Task Force 77 which included all the carriers in the United States Seventh Fleet. They consisted at that time of the USS Bon Homme Richard, the Ranger, the Constellation, and the Ticonderoga. However, there were several shifts of carriers during a two- to three-month period of time. After running some of the Yankee Team Missions from the Bon Homme Richard, we turned over the task to Admiral White aboard the USS Ticonderoga and proceeded to Yokosuka, Japan, via Sasebo to get back to the flagship, the USS Ranger. There really wasn't enough business on Yankee Station for those carriers. One carrier could do the photo missions from Yankee Station.

Q: Those photo missions began for the first time when you went out there?

Adm. M.: Photo missions over Laos were code-named Yankee Team. They started in September 1964, prior to my arrival. Remember I took over September the 24th, and the approximate position in the Gulf of Tonkin from which those Yankee Team missions were launched from the carriers was called Yankee Station. That was the origin of the name Yankee Station. The instructions and procedures that we carried out in running those missions, we put into a publication called Yankee Team Instructions.

Q: How soon after did you do that?

Adm. M.: When I reported aboard and took over the command, we had probably a hundred or two dispatches sent by CinCPac and CinCPacFlt and the Joint Chiefs of Staff that outlined the procedures that we were supposed to follow. So we put those all into a set of instructions, a book, and this took about two months because it was a very comprehensive job and there was a great deal of research to do.

Q: I was wondering if, after a period of time, you had incorporated into this book some of the experiences gained from actual sorties?

Adm. M.: Yes. In modifications to procedures that we found were more efficient, these were recommended to CinCPacFlt and were approved on a higher level.

Q: Because naturally such operations depend upon the terrain, don't they? I mean they're different in every locale.

Adm. M.: Yes, we found any mission situation changes with the weather, the terrain, and all the things that you run into in a wartime atmosphere.

Q: What was the real objective in these photo reconnaissance flights? What did you hope to gain?

Adm. M.: Those photo reconnaissance flights over Laos were set up primarily to find out how many Viet Minh from North Vietnam and war materials, trucks, guns, ammunition, were coming in over the Ho Chi Minh Trail through the regular routes in Laos.

Q: And did you succeed in that?

Adm. M.: We were not able to get finite numbers of troops coming in and/or the exact number of trucks and other materials. However, we did get a general idea of an approximate number of troops and materials coming in to Vietnam.

Q: Why did you fail with the specifics? Because of the dense jungle?

Adm. M.: At night, it's very difficult to get any good photography.

Q: Is this when they moved, at night?

Adm. M.: Oh, yes. They were very smart and moved at night or during the day under the jungle foilage. Later on we had some night recce missions that were armed, but in the main, at that time, we were not sufficiently geared up in our photographic ability to get good night photography. We did some experimentation out there with flares etc., but we didn't have good strong night photographic capabilities.

Q: Were the enemy aware of our efforts in this area?

Adm. M.: Yes. They saw our planes over there and they knew that we were out to find how many trucks and people and troops were coming in.

Q: Did they fire on our planes?

Adm. M.: Oh, yes, they fired at our airplanes.

Q: With some positive results?

Adm. M.: We lost only one RA-5C. However, that was due, not to small-arms fire, it was just a crash. The pilots were going too low.

Q: What was the normal altitude at which they operated?

Adm. M.: Normally, the RA-5C - and we had other photographic planes, too - would get up to, say, an altitude of 10,000 feet. They could get good photographic coverage. And, depending on the terrain, they could go to 20,000 feet and still get very good coverage, and at 30,000.

Q: How many planes in a sortie?

Adm. M.: Normally, in our Yankee Team photo missions we would send out a photo plane for that one mission plus an escort of three airplanes plus an electronics countermeasure airplane or one airplane that was configured to find out what frequency the North Vietnamese were transmitting on or using in their radar or gun laying operations. But normally, one photographic plane went out on each mission. It would either be a North American RA-5C or an LTV RF-8A or a Douglas RA-3B photographic plane. We used, on an experimental basis, the Douglas RA-3B for night photography. We didn't have the procedures down pat. We really didn't know if we could get good night photography, but we tried it. This should have been done a long time before at some shore establishment, but unfortunately the Navy hadn't done it. They were still not impressed with Test and Evaluation before combat.

Q: At that period of time, what was the destination of all these supplies the enemy was bringing down the Trail? Had they developed these underground depots?

Adm. M.: The destination for those supplies and for the troops were certain supply areas established in Laos and areas in South Vietnam.

Q: But at that stage of the game, we weren't thinking in terms of actual attacks on these places, were we?

Adm. M.: What do you mean? Our making attacks on them?

Q: Yes.

Adm. M.: At that time we were trying to determine how much material was coming in and where it was going. In September and in October, when I was there with the aircraft carriers, we did not have armed reconnaissance missions. However, as the enemy built up those supplies and their troops in these areas, we did start what they called Barrel Roll missions. These were armed reconnaissance missions and the object was to bomb and strafe supply areas, strategic bridges and military installations that we could find. Also to drop bombs with delayed fuses on roads that we knew they had to use.

Q: But this development did not begin until December of that year?

Adm. M.: That didn't begin until December of 1964. We launched the first Navy Barrel Roll mission on the 17th of December 1964 from the USS Ranger.

Q: In this developing picture, Admiral, did, in the interim between September when these photo reconnaissance missions began and December when the Barrel Roll missions began, did we as a government make any diplomatic overtures? I mean Laos was to be a neutral country, wasn't it?

Adm. M.: Yes, Laos was a neutral country, in accordance with the Geneva Accords of 1962. The flights were set up to gather information on the infiltration of North Vietnamese troops and material into Laos, in violation of the Geneva Accords. And these Yankee Team flights were conducted with the concurrence of the Laotian government. They wanted to know, just like we wanted to know. Those missions were flown by aircraft of the U. S. Air Force and the U. S. Navy, and the attack carriers assigned to these special operations in the South China Sea was called the Yankee Team carrier.

Q: In this small segment of time, a few months, this effort was largely, then, information-gathering, wasn't it? It wasn't used for any overt purpose?

Adm. M.: That's correct. We wanted to find out to what extent the North Vietnamese were building up their war potential in Laos and also in South Vietnam. And all during this period of time there were great tensions being built up as a result of the Gulf of Tonkin incident in August of 1964.

Q: Tensions where? In our government in Washington?

Adm. M.: Tensions built up in our government in Washington and throughout South Vietnam and Laos by the North Vietnamese infiltration.

H. L. Miller # 6 - 354

Q: And one other question. Did the infiltration gain in magnitude in those few months?

Adm. M.: Yes, it did, and the U. S. government came to the realization that perhaps we should do something about it, so that's when it was decided to fly armed reconnaissance missions over Laos to bomb and strafe these military supply areas and any trucks loaded with material that were coming into Laos from North Vietnam.

Q: Did you sit in on a conference when such a decision was made?

Adm. M.: No. I was sent the dispatch to do certain things, and I just carried out the orders.

Q: Admiral, with these reconnaissance flights over Laos, could you say something about our personnel? How they responded to this new effort?

Adm. M.: Oh, our pilots were delighted to have an opportunity to try out our new photographic systems and to take a look at strange territory. They were most anxious to get into the swim of it. They were very enthusiastic.

Q: Did you go on any one of these missions yourself?

Adm. M.: No, I didn't. I had previously flown over Laos in June of 1964 when I was attached to the staff of the commander-in-chief, Pacific. I was on a trip from Pearl Harbor to Bangkok and we went via Laos - we flew over Laos.

Q: At that time there wasn't a great deal of activity, was there?

Adm. M.: That's correct. In June of 1964 there wasn't very much activity in Laos. It looked like one great big jungle with very few roads.

Q: You said earlier today that shortly after September when the reconnaissance missions began, it was discovered that there wasn't enough work for more than one carrier, the Ticonderoga, and so you gave over this task to another Admiral and moved elsewhere. What did you do?

Adm. M.: There was a need for only one carrier there at Yankee Station to run the reconnaissance flights. We sent the other carriers to recreation areas. One went to Hong Kong. The Constellation stood by to run the last of the CinCPac weapons demonstrations for East Asian leaders from the latter part of November to the 3rd of December. I turned the job over to Rear Admiral Marshall White in the Ticonderoga and proceeded in the Bon Homme Richard to Sasebo for a couple of days prior to going to Yokosuka and transferring to my flagship, the Ranger, which was getting its boilers fixed up. The Bon Homme Richard was supposed to go back to the States after a long-term deployment.

We had a very enjoyable stay in Sasebo. The Japanese were very nice to us. Practically everywhere we went Japanese TVs were on, day and night, pointing at the Olympic Games that were then being held in Japan, and the Japanese had done a marvelous job of holding those games.

I transferred to the Ranger and was aboard for about ten days when we proceeded back via Okinawa and the Philippines to Yankee Station. We left Yokosuka on the 13th of November and on the 28th of November 1964, we arrived in the vicinity of Yankee Station. We continued to run photographic missions over Laos, but then with the build-up of the infiltration we received orders to run the Barrel Roll missions.

Q: As you describe this development, would it indicate that we had an over-all plan in effect from September on? It was a flexible, fluid situation.

Adm. M.: It was a very fluid situation, because we had many incidents of mortar attacks and/or bombings in South Vietnam by the Viet Cong or North Vietnamese. So, it was a period of growing unrest and tension, up and down the line. This was reflected in many stand-bys to bomb and strafe that we received in that period. We armed and de-armed. Stood by for retaliatory strikes, but this did not happen. We continued the Barrel Roll missions from December right up to the time I left in March.

Q: But actually you were under fairly heavy wraps from Washington during that time and not permitted to...

Adm. M.: That's true. We were under a great many restrictions from Washington on the ordnance to use, the number of airplanes that we were to send. There were really too many confusing directives.

Q: Were they as specific as they later became?

Adm. M.: Oh, yes. Every one of those missions was absolutely specific as to the bombs to carry and the rockets and ammo, etc.

Q: How did you commanding officers in the field react to this relatively new procedure?

Adm. M.: It was very frustrating, but you get used to anything I expect, and of course what you're supposed to do is obey the directives and that's what we did.

Q: You might, perhaps, want to say something about the weapons demonstrations in the Pacific, the last one which was held just about this time. I think it began on the 29th of November.

Adm. M.: That's correct. The <u>Constellation</u> ran that particular weapons demonstration. Admiral Guest was the carrier division commander, and the <u>Constellation</u> was his flagship. They picked up the Asian leaders in Subic Bay and on the way up to Okinawa ran carrier strikes and combings, strafings, rocketing, air-to-air refueling, carrier landings and catapult take-offs, and even took some of the Asian leaders up in the COD passenger planes to watch some of the demonstrations.

Q: Was this more of a diplomatic exercise than an actual one with ordnance, or were we actually testing our ordnance?

Adm. M.: It was, in the main, a diplomatic exercise, showing our Asian military leaders some of our capabilities in the way of conventional weapons that we had and our weapons systems, our airplanes, and our aircraft carriers. But following that, those leaders were deposited in Okinawa where the Army, the Air Force, and the Marine Corps put on demonstrations for them. So this was, you might say, a combined United States show for all of our allies over there, including our friends from Indonesia who weren't very friendly at that time. Sukarno, as you remember, was in power at that particular time period.

Q: Was there any noticeable boost to the morale of these Asian nations as a result of this demonstration?

Adm. M.: Oh, absolutely. These weapons demonstrations had a very good effect. First of all, it brought a lot of those Asian leaders together to meet each other for the first time.

Q: Well, the effort increased, then, in impetus, and you went on from the Barrel Roll to what's called the Flaming Dart Missions?

Adm. M.: Yes, Sir. You see, as I mentioned, with the tensions building up in South Vietnam and in Laos, our government was trying to make up its mind what to do in some of these areas and it didn't take long for the Viet Cong to call our hand, because on the 6th of February the Viet Cong launched a mortar attack against Pleiku Air Base, killing eight U. S. Army men and wounding 126, and with that, President Johnson ordered retaliatory strikes against the North Vietnamese barracks and staging area near Don Hoy. I had Task Force 77 at that time at Yankee Station and I launched 49 airplanes from the Coral Sea, the Hancock, and the Ranger. The U. S. Air Force was ordered to coordinate these strikes between the United States Air Force, the Vietnamese Air Force, and the Navy carrier planes.

The weather was very poor. We sent off a recce plane to pass the word to us on what the conditions were, and, as it turned out, the Navy planes were the only ones that did the bombing in the retaliatory strike that day. The U. S. Air Force and the Vietnamese Air Force didn't get off the ground because their weather man said that this wasn't good enough. Our Ranger planes could not bomb their areas because the weather was really too low, and they dropped their bombs in the water because, at that time, the orders were out if you couldn't hit your primary target, you're given a secondary target and if that was out, you couldn't hit anything, you had to drop your bombs in the water. There was no indiscriminate bombing. The Coral Sea and Hancock hit their targets which were open.

That retaliatory strike mission was labeled Flaming Dart 1. A few days later, on the 10th of February 1965, the Viet Cong exploded a bomb in the U. S. enlisted barracks at Qui Nhon, killing 21 and wounding 22. At that time, the President ordered another retaliatory strike on the North Vietnamese barracks and staging areas at Chan Hoa. I launched 100 airplanes from the Ranger, the Coral Sea, and the Hancock on that particular day.

It was a very successful strike.

Q: Did this type of strike take the enemy by surprise?

Adm. M.: Yes, it did. Of course, there was small-arms fire. We lost three planes from the Coral Sea, but only one pilot, and some of the other planes had holes from the small-arms fire, but in the main it was a very successful strike.

Q: One pilot, I read, was captured by the enemy on that occasion. Was he the first of the pilots to...?

Adm. M.: That's correct, and I think he's listed as still a prisoner of war, probably. The only prisoner of war in history that has had that long a stay in an enemy country.

Q: That strike, I believe, and some of the subsequent ones took our planes within 40 or 50 miles of the Chinese border. Were there any repercussions from China?

Adm. M.: No. We, of course, were told to keep away from the Chinese border and we did. I think there were a couple of planes on one strike several months later that got lost in bad weather and were shot down over China, but we were very cautious. We kept away from the Chinese borders. At that time, we continued with the Barrel Roll missions in Laos and with the Yankee Team missions, and after each one of our strikes on the 7th and 11th of February, we ran photo missions to find out bomb damage that we had made on the previous day. We called that BDA, bomb-damage assessment.

We continued to run the photo missions and the photo recce missions and, as more subsequent strikes and incidents built up in South Vietnam, President Johnson okayed 3,500 Marines to be landed at Da Nang for the security of the base. That amphibious landing of the 3,500 Marines was made on the 8th of March 1965, and my Task Force covered them with A-1H airplanes and photo coverage.

Q: As this effort increased and the number of sorties for photo reconnaissance increased, were the planes from a single carrier any longer sufficient, or was another one involved?

Adm. M.: Normally, when the tensions built up we had three aircraft carriers, but after the 7th and the 11th of February strikes we kept only two aircraft carriers there on station ready for any contingency that may occur. However, in the middle of February we had at one time four aircraft carriers on Yankee Station for the Yankee Team area. They were the Coral Sea, the Hancock, the

Ranger - those were the heavy attack carriers, and the anti-submarine warfare carrier, the USS *Bennington*. So, at that time, it was the greatest concentration of aircraft carriers and service force ships, plus destroyers and cruisers that they had had in the Western Pacific for many years.

Therefore, on the 17th of February 1965, I had an operation called Candid Camera, getting pictures of all those ships in formation, making turns. I got those with my photographic planes, with still cameras, and motion picture cameras. We used everything but surprisingly enough we did not get an outstanding group of pictures. I think that I have the only two big color photos of that operation.

Q: With the developing techniques of reconnaissance photos, were the ordnance people from Washington on the scene? Were they out there observing all the equipment?

Adm. M.: We had some visitors from Washington and we had some from Commander-in-Chief, Pacific Fleet, and Air Force, Pacific Fleet, but not a great influx at that time. This all came later as the war built up, and activity did build up because on the 12th of March 1965 Commander, Seventh Fleet, initiated surveillance patrols which he later nicknamed Market Time. This was initiated off the coast of South Vietnam to counter enemy infiltration by sea, and in the following months the efficient performance of our own sailors and the South Vietnamese sailors forced the North Vietnamese to seek other avenues of infiltration, because we put a pretty tight rope around the sea coast area.

And in the latter part of April 1965, the U. S. Coast Guard joined the U. S. Navy and the South Vietnamese Navy by assigning 17 82-foot Coast Guard cutters to the Market Time operation.

Q: Would you say something about the strictures that were placed upon you and the naval units in terms of supply ships from Russia and Britain and other countries which came in to the North Vietnamese harbors?

Adm. M.: At that time, we weren't concerned with the British or Russian ships that were there at that particular period, because we weren't bombing up in the Hanoi and Haiphong area. That all came later. However, we did have some trouble with the Russian spy ships, these small jobs that were in our Yankee Team area and probably collecting all the information they possibly could on our operations, and cutting across our bow, trying to embarrass us, and all that sort of thing.

Q: And passing that information on to the enemy, of course.

Adm. M.: Oh, yes. Passed it on to the enemy and then stored it in their locker for possible future use, too.

Q: These Russian spy ships, did they have any concern for possible collisions? Or was that entirely up to the U. S. Navy to prevent?

Adm. M.: That was up to the U. S. Navy to prevent because I feel sure that the Russians knew that we wouldn't cut them in two. We would always give way and not come close to them, so that it wouldn't provoke an international incident.

Q: You say the last raid under your aegis before you departed for the States occurred in March and it was termed Rolling Thunder. This became the designation for these air attacks in future. Was this the first one to be so labeled?

Adm. M.: No, we had Rolling Thunder missions planned earlier than that, actually during the latter part of February. However, Rolling Thunder missions 1, 2, 3, and 4 proved to be planning drills only.

Q: What do you mean by "planning drills"?

Adm. M.: Well, we loaded our airplanes but for some reason those strikes were called off, or there might have been at that time bad weather to prevent one or two of them. The first actual Rolling Thunder strike was Rolling Thunder No. 5. That was done on 2 March by a combined U. S. Air Force and Vietnamese Air Force effort against the Quang Khe naval base, and a U. S. Air Force effort against the ammunition dump. Navy missions at that time were confined to search and rescue only. On the 15th of March, Task Force 77, the Navy, participated in Rolling Thunder No. 6. It was a combined Navy-Air Force strike on the Phu Qui ammunition depot. Execution date for Rolling Thunder No. 6 had originally been established for 11 March with the following day, 12 March, as a weather alternate, but weather on both days proved to be unsuitable and the strike was canceled. It was finally accomplished on the 15th of March. We had just a few Air Force planes participating, and this strike was carried out with planes from the Ranger and the Hancock. We had a modified stand-down from three carriers to two carriers on the 22nd of February, and that stand-down was still in effect. The Coral Sea was in Subic Bay, and at the time of this strike they had just got under way. It was a very successful strike. We lost one AH-1 airplane from the Ranger. It was an apparent engine failure, the pilot ditched, and it was a very normal ditching but he didn't get out of the plane. We lost him.

Q: You have mentioned weather factors several times. Was weather a difficult problem to surmount in these raids?

Adm. M.: Yes, Sir. At that time of the year, we had low ceilings along the coast of North Vietnam, so the established procedure that I instituted was to launch weather recce airplanes with an experienced pilot to go up the coast close to the target area and radio back to the ship a "go" or "no go" for the particular strike that was planned. This proved to be a very good procedure.

Q: You had to supply your own weather reports, then?

Adm. M.: That's correct. We, of course, always received weather reports, but they didn't pan out to be too accurate.

Q: Did you notice in this short time an increase in the enemy defenses, ground defenses, for these aerial attacks?

Adm. M.: They improved slightly but not to any great extent, and that brings up a point in regard to the very sophisticated North American RA-5C airplane that had electronic countermeasures equipment, side-looking radar, and a tremendous photo capability. In our evaluation of the plane after these months of operation, we said it was a good airplane, it did a good job in photo reconnaissance, in using side-looking radar, but we could not really give it a good evaluation because the radars and the communications in North Vietnam at that time weren't sophisticated enough to match what we had in the RA-5C. In other words, we couldn't give the RA-5C electronic intelligence-gathering equipment a real good workout.

Q: Because you had no equal competitor?

Adm. M.: That's right.

Q: The equipment used by the North Vietnamese was Russian, wasn't it?

Adm. M.: Russian, and some Chinese. Later on, of course, Russia brought in very sophisticated equipment, better than we were geared up to take, and we had a rough time when the war expanded.

Q: Would you talk about the enemy radar in this early stage of the war?

Adm. M.: The enemy had radar that could pick up, just like we had radar, but their other equipment like surface-to-air missiles that the Russians brought in later on, none of those were there. They had light small-arms fire, they had light antiaircraft fire, and then they built up - they had some medium antiaircraft fire, but really they didn't yet have many antiaircraft firing installations around the country to be very effective. Later on, they did. They got hundreds of medium and heavy antiaircraft guns to many important areas of Vietnam, so it really created a tremendous problem for our pilots as that war progressed.

Q: Are the North Vietnamese adept at handling sophisticated instruments and so forth, or are they somewhat in the category of the Egyptians?

Adm. M.: No. They were very good. If they didn't know at the start, they learned in a hurry, because they had mobile installations that they dis-assembled, shifted, and set up in other places almost overnight. So they were very adept in running this game.

Q: From our intelligence-gathering, are they trained on the scene, or are they taken to Russia or wherever and trained?

Adm. M.: There's no doubt that some of them were taken to Russia and trained in some of the sophisticated equipment to be brought back and used as instructors for the Vietnamese. There were Russian instructors also in Vietnam, and the North Vietnamese caught on in a hurry and did a very fine job in using that equipment.

Q: After the March raid, you gave over your command and returned to the States for a brief spell.

Adm. M.: Yes, Sir. I turned over the command to Admiral Outlaw on the 17th of March and proceeded with the Ranger to Subic Bay after sixty-six continuous days at sea.

Q: What effect had this long period had on your nervous system?

Adm. M.: Well, surprisingly enough, not too bad. You know, like the old boxer, you sort of bend with the punch and you pace yourself to continue at any of those types of operations. We were a pretty happy group when we came in to Subic Bay, probably because we knew that we were on our way back to the good old continental U. S.

We came on back to our home plate at Alameda via Guam and a de-briefing session that we had at CinCPacFlt headquarters at Pearl Harbor.

Q: At that point, Admiral Johnson was CinCPacFlt wasn't he?

Adm. M.: He was CinCPacFlt. Admiral Sharp was CinCPac.

From the 4th of April until the 19th of October my staff was temporarily based ashore at the Naval Air Station, Alameda, California. We had a couple of inspections of the Hancock and the Ranger, and we participated in one exercise with the Second Fleet. This was exercise coded Hot Stove. It was conducted from 27 August to 3 September in Southern California waters, and my staff was embarked in the USS Ticonderoga. It was conducted without the benefit of a detailed operational order or a letter of instructions, in order to more closely simulate the operational conditions in the South China Sea that all those people were going to be concerned with from then on.

About that time I intercepted a dispatch that said that Commander-in-Chief, Pacific Fleet, wanted an experienced staff to proceed to Norfolk, Virginia, and bring the Enterprise and the nuclear-powered frigate Bainbridge around to the Vietnam war. It just so happened that Admiral Johnson, the Commander-in-Chief of the Pacific Fleet, was in San Diego on a trip and I flew in the last day of the Hot Stove exercise and told him that I had the most experienced staff in the Pacific at that time, and we volunteered to take the Enterprise around, also to give it an operational readiness inspection on the East Coast. And I think that sold it, so on the 18th or 19th of October my staff was airlifted to Norfolk, Virginia, and embarked in the Enterprise in preparation for the operational readiness inspection and the

H. L. Miller # 6 - 372

exercise that we would put that task group through in the Roosevelt Roads area.

Q: May I interject a question? I was wondering whether the CNO, Admiral MacDonald, or the Secretary of Defense showed any personal interest in talking with you as a result of your experience in Vietnam?

Adm. M.: Yes. In April, shortly after getting back from Vietnam, I was asked to come back with a couple of members of my staff and brief the officers in the office of the Chief of Naval Operations on the story, the strikes, and the operations that we encountered there in the South China Sea. So I did that. I held two sessions, one in the morning and one in the afternoon, telling the flag officers and the leading captains in the CNO organization just what transpired there in the South China Sea. Admiral MacDonald attended the morning session. Then I was held over a day to brief the Secretary of the Navy and some of the assistant secretaries...

Q: Was that Paul Nitze?

Adm. M.: Mr. Nitze, yes...at lunchtime. So we took about two hours to brief them. At that time, Captain Zumwalt was his

H. L. Miller # 6 - 373

aide, and we had a very fine two-hour session.

Q: What were they particularly interested in learning?

Adm. M.: They were interested in how we ran the operation, what difficulties we had, how the various weapon systems were holding up, what deficiencies we had, what they could do to help out. Well, of course, at that time, I don't believe that anybody realized that the effort out there was going to expand to what it came to later, but everybody seemed to be interested in helping out.

Q: Was there any concern at that point with our prisoners?

Adm. M.: No, not too much because we really didn't have but one or two prisoners at that time. All that came later and I'll talk to it in a subsequent period when we did have quite a few prisoners of war, and I don't think we did enough about it. But I'll talk about it later on.

Q: Fine. Did the Secretary of Defense show any personal interest?

Adm. M.: No, they didn't have me talk to the Secretary of Defense. Evidently, Mr. McNamara figured he had a pretty good handle on what was going on out there, and I think he was primarily concerned with the effort in-country, not from the aircraft carriers. I really don't think that he had a good feel on what we could do from the air picture, the air part of the show from the Navy point of view from aircraft carriers, and also from the amphibious. He was land-oriented and he didn't seem to be too interested in what the Navy and Marine Corps could do from ships. Certainly, he knew, or had a pretty good feel, I guess, for what the Army and the Air Force and the Marines could do from land bases, but not from the ship angle.

Q: General Krulak was out there, wasn't he?

Adm. M.: General Krulak was then Commander, Fleet Marine Force, Pacific, with headquarters in Pearl Harbor. I had dealt with him when I was on the CinCPac staff. His offices were right above ours in that building.

Q: Well, we got back to Norfolk!

Adm. M.: Yes, and we were very fortunate in that I got my Air Wing 9 that I had on the Ranger on the Enterprise. Sure, we had a lot of new pilots that had to be indoctrinated, but I had a very good Air Wing Commander and good squadron commanders, so we had a nucleus to really teach the Enterprise all about war.

As you can probably guess, the Enterprise had been a show boat. They did a wonderful job on their world cruise, but they were primarily geared to show the flag, and, of course, Admiral Rickover was very proud of that ship. I saw him before I left and told him that I knew the Enterprise would perform and I would send him operational data that he could use in selling nuclear power.

Q: That was precisely the sort of thing he appreciated!

Adm. M.: That's right. So we left Norfolk the 26th of October and proceeded to the Atlantic Fleet weapons range, which was down at Roosevelt Roads, and we gave the Air Wing and the ship an operational readiness inspection, and it was a tough one. We made up the whole exercise. We patterned it after the Vietnam situation, and after the completion of what we call the ORI on 2 November, the Enterprise and Bainbridge departed the Roosevelt Roads area for Subic Bay in the Philippines, via the South Atlantic, the Cape of Good Hope, around the southern tip of Africa, the Indian Ocean, the Straits of Malacca, the South China Sea, and in to Subic Bay.

Q: At this point, Admiral, it might be well to include a paragraph on the capabilities of the Enterprise, as she was demonstrated, the capabilities over and above those of the more traditional type ships like the Ranger.

Adm. M.: There are many, many advantages of having nuclear power on a ship, and I'll just go through several of them.

The planes that you fly, that you have aboard that carrier, are much easier to maintain and keep clean because you don't have any corrosive stack gas and soot. The same applies to the ship, to antennas, to other surfaces. You save hundreds of thousands of hours of cleaning, just manpower, and not only topside but throughout the ship, and you eliminate the soot problem.

Q: An interesting point. I hadn't thought of that.

Adm. M.: And then, in the groove, when the pilots are coming aboard, on the conventional carriers you always at some time or other have big columns of black smoke coming right down your lungs as you're coming aboard, and it's hard to see. It's a real nuisance. You don't have that smoke in the groove from a nuclear-powered carrier. Then, you have long-sustained speed without refueling. You can go from now for fifteen years without having to put in a new core, without having to refuel a nuclear-powered carrier, and that's a long period of time. You can steam, you might say, for ever.

Q: It outlasts the machinery, doesn't it?

Adm. M.: Yes. You can fly more missions because you have more space for jet fuel and you don't have to carry all that fuel oil, except to refuel some of the conventional destroyers. Or you carry more bombs and more ammunition, because you have about 25 percent more area that is available for bomb stowage and fuel stowage. You can accelerate and decelerate the ship on the order of a car, in comparison with a conventional ship. You pull that throttle and she stops. You give it the gun, and it surges ahead. Now, of course, you can't do that on a conventional ship because it takes a long time to build up your acceleration, a long time to decelerate.

With the absence of all the boiler uptakes, it has allowed better arrangement of communications and radar systems that are much superior to any other conventional ship. The radar, as you look at the Enterprise, you have a great big, tremendous, radar built into that square structure that is the island. With that immediate sustained speed that you can crank into the Enterprise, she makes a harder target to get at for a nuclear sub because she can outrace them and take evasive action almost instantly.

Nuclear power plants are also more reliable and rugged. Hence, there are fewer engineering casualties.

Q: Why is this a factor?

Adm. M.: It's probably because of the standards that Admiral Rickover and Company set up for the rugged machinery that you need in a nuclear power plant. They have fewer casualties than conventional plants.

Another very important item. Because the <u>Enterprise</u> does not have to refuel with black oil, she had fewer replenishments from our service force ships. She also has rapid maneuverability and, because of the absence of boiler air intakes, it enables the ship to close up tight for atomic, biological, and chemical warfare.

You might be interested - the total lifetime cost of a nuclear-powered carrier, with its aircraft, is only about three percent more than conventional aircraft carriers with their aircraft.

Q: That's the lifetime cost?

Adm. M.: Yes.

Q: But the initial expenditure is much larger?

Adm. M.: The initial expenditure is much larger, but the lifetime cost is only about three percent, and I'd gladly give that three percent for the tremendous advantages of nuclear power over conventional power...

Q: This implies that the life of the nuclear carrier is how much longer than that of the conventional?

Adm. M.: I think they consider it the same, really. Yes. And, then, you can add up a lot of this, speed and unlimited endurance of the Enterprise or a nuclear-powered carrier multiplies into increased tactical flexibility and freedom for independent action. It enhances opportunity to use evasive transit tracks. It gives improved capability to operate in bad weather, or to take circuitous routes to avoid storms. It has the ability to extend the track, approaching track or retiring track, along a greater perimeter because of the speed and endurance. It has reduced vulnerability to submarine and guided-missile attacks.

Q: Why?

Adm. M.: Because it can maneuver faster. It can accelerate and decelerate faster. It has reduced dependence on mobile logistic support. It can operate under severe threat conditions from remote distant bases, completely free of logistics support, except for, say, rapid supplying of ammo and aviation fuel in case you run short.

Another thing that you get from it is increased electrical power. This is a little-known fact that conventional ships cannot steam as far if you use large blocks of electrical power. The nuclear-powered ships are not effected. And when you take a look at new radars and sonars and other systems that have to have more and more and more electrical power, this gets to be quite a problem on ships. Another advantage, the immediate steam that you have available with nuclear power enables planes to be launched in less time than the conventional ships. You have immediate steam to the catapult. You have to build up steam with the conventional carriers. And whenever you go anywhere, nuclear power arrives completely ready to go into action.

And, remember this, too, from right alongside the dock you can release the lines and go from the dock to the open sea at full power. Maybe a good example of the advantages; you could have sent me with that nuclear-powered task force to any ocean area in the world, and from the time I got there, I could have launched planes carrying 200 tons of bombs per day and other ordnance, dropping it around the clock, day and night, for forty-four days and nights before I had to get more ammunition and aviation fuel. That's a tremendous capability.

Q: Then your factor would become a human one.

Adm. M.: That's right.

Q: I don't believe you said anything about damage control on such a carrier. Does that differ in any way from the conventional ones?

Adm. M.: Damage control, as far as the <u>Enterprise</u> is concerned, is much easier, for any nuclear-powered ship, because you don't have the smoke and stack gases that can get around the ship into other channels if something goes wrong. A pipe ruptures, or something like that. Now, just recently, in one of our new destroyers, with the air-conditioning system, they had an explosion in the fire room and the stack gases got into the air-conditioning system. The smoke got in there, and they were lucky that it didn't asphyxiate the whole crew. This is one of the tremendous advantages. Damage control is made much easier in nuclear-powered ships.

Q: The core of the power, on such a ship - is that terribly vulnerable to torpedo attack?

Adm. M.: No, because your core is so well protected by other voids on either side and other storage areas. It's almost impossible for a torpedo to get through the other protective areas to that core.

Q: So, you arrived out in the Far East.

Adm. M.: My Task Group reported to the operational command of Commander, Seventh Fleet, and Commander-in-Chief, Pacific Fleet, on 21 November, and we arrived in Subic Bay on 27 November. Prior to that, as we passed through the Straits of Malacca, I flew with the air wing commander in an F-4 aircraft to Saigon and checked in with the Army and the Air Force commands there, received briefings on the operations that were taking place. Then I flew to Da Nang and checked in with the Marines at Da Nang. At that time, it was Major General McKutchen, who just recently died from cancer.

Following that, we took off and I intercepted the Enterprise before it got into Subic Bay. At Subic we hurriedly took aboard extra gas tanks and other equipment that ships had left there for us, and we sailed. We got under way on the 30th of November and proceeded to Dixie Station, off the southeast coast of South Vietnam, arriving on 2 December. Dixie Station was about due east of Saigon, out on the water. The carrier was set up there to provide close air support and other support for the in-country effort in South Vietnam, around the Delta area and around the Saigon area. As you can well imagine, by that time, 27 November

1965, just about six or seven months from the time I left previously, the war effort had certainly expanded tremendously.

And on the 2nd of December, nuclear power went into combat for the first time. We had five plane-loads of newsmen who came aboard that day to get the word on nuclear power. It was difficult on the first day for the air wing to get in the swing of everything with five loads of newpaper people aboard, but they did a fine job. They didn't break any records. They left that for about two days later, at which time they established the record of 165 sorties - combat sorties - which is about 34 more than any previous carrier had done. Additionally, they flew other sorties, which totaled about 200 for the day. This was a pretty good indicator of what the Enterprise could do over and above the conventional carrier.

Well, the Enterprise stayed on Dixie Station till the 17th of December at which time we moved north to Yankee Station again and supported the effort up there. Probably the two biggest strikes of the Enterprise were in conjunction with the Ticonderoga and the Kitty Hawk on the Hong Bi thermal power plant. That was struck on the 22nd of December. It was a big strike, using aircraft from the Enterprise, Ticonderoga, and the Kitty Hawk.

Additionally, on that day, we had cameras installed on the airplanes, so that we got pictures of the power plant before the strike, during the strike, and at the end of the strike. Following that, the next day, we hit the Hi Duong railroad-highway bridge. The Ticonderoga and the Enterprise combined on that strike. The Kitty Hawk provided flak-suppression and anti-missile missions. Additionally, we had one of the RA-5C photo planes from the Enterprise get pictures of bomb damage on the highway bridge and also on the Hong Bi thermal power plant that had been hit the previous day.

We sent pictures of all of that over to the Kitty Hawk, where General Wheeler, Chairman of the Joint Chiefs of Staff, was spending the night. He saw where the Navy planes had really done an effective job.

On 24 December, a stand-down in operation against North Vietnam was ordered. However, increased emphasis was given to supporting the in-country effort. The in-country effort was in South Vietnam and in continued recce and armed recce missions in Laos. These operations continued - or began again on the 26th of December and continued day after day until we left Yankee Station...

We continued operations in South Vietnam and in Laos, and then the Enterprise was relieved and went off line at Yankee Station

on the 15th of January, at which time we proceeded to Subic
Bay, had a short stay there and quite a number of the officers
and enlisted personnel went to Baguio, the resort center in
the Philippines, about 5,000 feet in the air, a very wonderful
spot. And from Subic we headed for a delightful stay in Hong
Kong.

Q: R and R?

Adm. M.: This was for some good R and R. We arrived in Hong
Kong on the 26th of January 1966 and on the following day we
had about 125 visitors that we entertained aboard, including
the American consul general. As you recall, I said that previously the Enterprise had been a show boat?

Q: Yes.

Adm. M.: Well, from combat operations and a greasy hangar deck
and airplanes that were pretty battle-worn, you might say,
overnight the Enterprise got its show boat back in appearance with palm trees on the hangar deck, beautifully cleaned
up, a red carpet on the quarter deck, all the way across the
hangar deck to a reception area, beautiful exhibits, and a
wonderful show by the Marine guard in the exercise drills that
they put on. The Enterprise was just a champion ship. They
never did forget all the fine lessons that they learned.

We had a delightful stay in Hong Kong. From there, we went back on the line, continued our operations, and finally on the 16th of February, Admiral Tom Walker relieved me...

Q: Tom Walker?

Adm. M.: Thomas J. Walker...and I flew back to the continental U. S. via Pearl Harbor, where I de-briefed the Commander-in-Chief, Pacific Fleet, on the operations to date (copy attached), and then I picked up my family in Alameda and proceeded to Washington, D. C. via Corpus Christi, Texas, where I pinned golden Navy wings on my oldest boy who had just graduated as a naval aviator from advanced training at Corpus Christi.

So that was the end of my story for two tours in the South China Sea.

Q: Fascinating.

H. L. Miller # 7- 387

Interview No. 7 with Rear Admiral Henry L. Miller, U. S. Navy

Place: On board his barge in the Chesapeake Bay on Tuesday

morning, 29 June 1971

Subject: Biography

By: John T. Mason, Jr.

Q: This chapter is going to deal with the Admiral's period of service as Chief of Information, Navy Department, Chinfo. This began in April of 1966 and his tour of duty extended through October 1968. This was an exceedingly interesting period of time, Sir, and from what you've said a tremendous number of things happened, which is to be expected with you in command. Would you begin the story.

Adm. M.: My period at Chinfo was in very trying times with the Vietnam war going on. It was also a period during the McNamara regime where the office of information in the Secretary of Defense's office was pretty much a time for covering up of certain things that happened during the McNamara era.

Q: The military, as a whole, wasn't in as bad odor as it is currently, was it?

Adm. M.: No, that's correct, but of course Mr. McNamara had absolute control. Right or wrong, if he picked up the phone and didn't like something that the services were doing, the Secretaries of the respective services would just raise Cain with all of us, so that we didn't have the means or authority to do the job that we were supposed to do. The Secretaries were loyal and afraid of McNamara, and this carried over even after he became President of the World Bank, and I'll talk more about this later. But between tours in the Gulf of Tonkin, I came back to Washington and de-briefed what was happening out there to the CNO and other flag officers in the Washington area, plus Mr. Nitze, who was then Secretary of the Navy. Captain Zumwalt, at that time, was Mr. Nitze's aide.

Later I came back to Washington to be interviewed by the Secretary of the Navy for the Chinfo job. I didn't want it, but I was tagged for it.

Q: How did this happen? Because of your previous experience and the manual you had helped prepare?

Adm. M.: Perhaps some of the public affairs duty I had on Admiral Blandy's staff at CinCLanFlt, and perhaps also from de-briefings of the Vietnam war, when I told Mr. Nitze what was happening out there.

Q: Had you known Nitze beforehand?

Adm. M.: No, I had never known Mr. Nitze. I had met him on a couple of his trips out to Hawaii, but that was about all.

After this interview, I went back to Vietnam with the nuclear-powered task force, and sent a great deal of operational data on the uses of nuclear power to Admiral Rickover, and I talked to him about it.

So, when I took over Chinfo, I was most enthusiastic about improving the Navy's image and in selling nuclear power.

Q: What was your initial reluctance to the job?

Adm. M.: I liked an operational job better than a Chinfo job. Additionally, I knew that Mr. Sylvester, who was then Assistant Secretary of Defense for Public Affairs, kept a very tight rein on anything that the services wanted to put out, as far as information to the public. So I knew before I walked in to the job that my hands were tied. Also, I wanted to sell nuclear power and so did Admiral Rickover. Unfortunately, Mr. McNamara and his assistants, namely Dr. Enthoven, analyzed the dollars involved for nuclear power and said it was too expensive, and he ordered the Navy to cut it to the bone.

The Chief of Naval Operations didn't tell me to cut my advertising or selling of nuclear power, but the Secretary of the

Navy sent a Rear Admiral around to tell me not to become such a super-salesman for nuclear power, that we had to be careful because there were other sources of energy that might surpass nuclear power. Well, this Admiral didn't know that I had written a research paper when I was at the Industrial College of the Armed Forces on present and future sources of energy, and what he was telling me was a bunch of hogwash. But that was the power that McNamara had. I never did quit selling nuclear power. It was good for the Navy. However, this did not sit well with Nitze.

Q: Does this imply that Rickover was under a blanket in that time?

Adm. M.: Rickover has always had people over him who wanted to cut the nuclear power program.. The Navy wouldn't have the present nuclear power program, if it hadn't been for Admiral Rickover years ago, and at the present time. He has the Congress behind him. He doesn't have Secretaries of Defense and the Secretaries of the Navy for him, but he has the Congress behind him. And then he has another job on the Atomic Energy Commission, so through these contacts and this support, Rickover has been able to keep the Navy's nuclear power program going better than anybody else could.

Q: What did you do, what were you able to accomplish in this two-year period in the realm of nuclear power?

Adm. M.: Well, first of all, I sent Admiral Rickover an awful lot of information on the advantages of nuclear power in a combat environment, and he used this information in his testimony on the Hill, so it went into the Congressional Record. We sent literally hundreds of those prints of his testimony to all the flag officers around the Navy. We also gave it to organizations such as the Navy League and Naval Reserve officers, etc. I also gave many speeches around the country on the advantages of nuclear power.

Q: Did you get any reaction on any of this from the Secretary of Defense?

Adm. M.: Not from the Secretary of Defense, but I later learned that Mr. Nitze didn't like this selling of nuclear power.

Q: You did a great deal in the realm of combat art. Tell me about that.

Adm. M.: When I took over the job at Chinfo, I remembered that the Navy had a great many combat art originals dating back from World War II. I had seen those in a couple of big rooms in the old Navy Department building just before going to the Atlantic Fleet staff as the Public Information Officer in 1948.

Q: They weren't on display, they were simply stored?

Adm. M.: That's correct. Originally, they did have a curator. It was a woman, and I think she just about drank herself to death over the years, so they made the handyman around the place, Charlie Lawrence, who is a colored man - a very enthusiastic man - the curator of the Navy combat art collection. So I wanted to see. I went over to the old Navy Department building. Fortunately, the two rooms where they had all this art were air-conditioned. Charlie Lawrence and another man were the only two working on Navy combat art i.e., framing the art, sending exhibits out to various sections of the country, and really keeping tabs on the Navy combat art.

Q: Was it on display in some of the naval museums?

Adm. M.: The Navy didn't have an inventory at that time. There were about 3,500 pieces, some of which were really outstanding, and over a period of time various Chinfo's had let pieces of it go to friends to hang in their offices and what not. As a matter of interest, I was at the Brooklyn Navy Yard Officers' club and I saw these beautiful originals of Admiral Radford and Admiral Mitscher, plus a few others, over the bar. I asked them what these were doing there and they said, well, they'd been there for quite some time. So I told the club to get them back to Chinfo, and later on I ran into Admiral Radford and told him that I got his portrait back from over the bar in the Brooklyn Navy Yard officers' club and put it back in the E ring of the Pentagon where he'd get more of a place of honor. I think he appreciated that.

Q: Some of America's best artists were represented in this World War II material?

Adm. M.: Absolutely, and one of the best was Mr. Murray. He had quite a number in the Navy combat art collection. Well I saw this enormous file of combat art, some were in frames, some were just stacked up on the deck like cordwood. It sort of made me mad because there hadn't been enough interest paid to that. I asked Charlie Lawrence for the history of how everything happened, and he had a pretty good handle on it.

So, from there, I went back to the office and, in about an hour's time, I got $20,000 and an old building in the Washington Navy Yard that I would have to rehabilitate if I wanted to do something about a home for the Navy's combat art collection.

Q: How did you latch onto the money? From what account?

Adm. M.: Well, I think there was some extra money in the office of the Secretary. I called up the Comptroller, and it was very easy to get it. I'm still surprised I did get it. However, I think it cost more than that. I think the Navy Yard helped in the rehabilitation of that building, because they did a beautiful job and we commissioned a Navy Combat Art Museum there. We air-conditioned it, de-humidified it, and gave the people working on the art plenty of room. We also enlisted the services of the Salmagundi Art Club in New York City to advise us. The Salmagundi Club has a group of artists who have donated their services every year in going to various places around the country and overseas to paint originals for the Navy.

Q: Oils and water colors?

Adm. M.: Oils and water colors, sketches. And each year there's an annual banquet where this art is presented to the Navy. This is on the East Coast. In Los Angeles, the art club has a similar setup on the West Coast.

Q: What motivates these groups to do this?

Adm. M.: They like the Navy. We pay their expenses going to an assignment, their per diem, but we really don't pay for the paintings.

It's a very fine program, and on the East Coast it's the Salmagundi Club and the LA Art Club on the West Coast, and they're very proud that they're in that program.

Q: So yearly there are additions to the combat art?

Adm. M.: Oh, yes. I got a big kick out of the art program of the Navy. I sent some of the artists to Vietnam, some down to Cape Kennedy to get sketches and paintings of the space shots. I sent them all over the country, and we had some outstanding paintings and sketches from these assignments. They're very proud of the annual dinner and presentation that is made at the Salmagundi Club each year. The same applies to the LA group on the West Coast.

Q: And is it the task for the Chinfo to speak at this annual dinner?

Adm. M.: To speak and also to talk to the artists. It's a fascinating program, and they have a very fine bunch of professionals in it.

Q: How large did the collection grow to be in your regime?

Adm. M.: Normally each year we'd get about a hundred additional originals from the East Coast and the West Coast, so I imagine now there are over 4,000 combat art originals in the Navy's collection.

Q: And they're not all on display at any one given time, are they?

Adm. M.: Oh, no. They do have a mobile unit that takes a certain number of the collection to various cities in the United States who want to put on an art show, say, for a period of a week or ten days. We do send those mobile units out on those assignments. Then we have special groups of originals that we send to various art museums that have requested them.

Q: Do you still send them out to decorate offices and that type of thing?

Adm. M.: I didn't. I recalled a lot of them because they were around in cubbyholes in the Pentagon, lieutenants and lieutenant commanders had them on their walls, and civilians had them and didn't want to let them go. It was really disgraceful. And a lot of Admirals got violently upset when I said I was putting the Navy's combat art where it belonged, in museums, in other places around the country. This art belonged to the American people, not to a bunch of naval officers.

Q: So you created another public relations job within the framework of public relations!

H. L. Miller # 7 - 397

Adm. M.: Well, now I see there's a lot of it going back on the walls around the Pentagon, but not during my regime.

Q: Tell me about the reproductions in your program then.

Adm. M.: The Navy had a reproduction program. Really, it was done by the Naval Air Systems Command. Each year, the Naval Air Systems Command would allocate a certain amount of money for reproductions of naval subjects. They'd put out, say, 100,000 of them, and any ship or station in the Navy could write in and request a certain amount of those reproductions. The reproductions were very poor because nobody really looked over the shoulders of the lithograph people. So I asked NavAir if they would supply the money and let me run the program. They were very happy to do that, and I got a committee of art specialists, including the art shop at the Naval Institute, first, to recommend the best reproduction companies that they knew and, secondly, to look at the first runs and mark defects that had to be corrected in the overall lot. This improved the reproductions, I'd say, at least 90-some percent.

We got wonderful cooperation from the Naval Air Systems Command and also from the lithograph company. We must have put out about 250,000 reproductions which were free to the Navy. Then we put the reproductions into the Navy Publications and Printing System such that if you wanted a set - a certain set - of these reproductions, you could send a dollar or more to Navy Printing and Publications and get a set of these reproductions.

Q: How popular did this prove to be with the general public?

Adm. M.: I haven't followed it, but in the Navy it got to be very, very popular, because I see those reproductions all over the world, and in every Navy office that I go into. I think they did a wonderful job in the reproduction program.

Q: It's appropriate to ask you, do you personally have some interest in art, some understanding of art?

Adm. M.: Not especially. I like art, I like good art, I like all types of art, but I have absolutely no background in the art business. It's a fascinating profession. I admire the artists and what they can do with a subject that looks so inanimate but they make it so real. And they're a very interesting crowd, a very intelligent crowd, and a very nice bunch of people.

Q: I daresay this personal interest was a motivating factor in getting this tremendous program under way.

Adm. M.: I certainly was interested in it. I saw the potential that was lying there for the Navy because it shows a very nice side of the Navy and it shows it to all the people who go through the art museums and various conventions and annual shows around the country.

Q: Would you say that the sale of these reproductions has, on balance, now financed this aspect of the program?

Adm. M.: I don't think so. I don't think they make enough money. I don't think they push it hard enough. It could finance the program and keep it going, but I believe the Naval Air Systems Command is still subsidizing it, although I haven't seen any new reproductions come out lately.

Through the reproduction program the great American public buys reproductions for a dollar or so. It also helps to establish a better Navy image and do more of a selling job for the Navy. It really does show Navy subjects, ships, airplanes, people, and gives the public an insight, you might say, to the artistic side of the Navy.

Q: This is terribly important because our people, as a whole, have not been really Navy-conscious. We're a land-oriented nation.

Adm. M.: That's correct. Now I think they're getting more conscious of the Navy, certainly not through the combat art program or the reproduction program, but through a combination of

H. L. Miller # 7 - 400

all of this.

Q: Now you want to tell me about the development of the movies program under the aegis of Chinfo?

Adm. M.: We felt at Chinfo that one of the best ways to sell the Navy was to get it on TV, and one way to get it on TV was to have either a good fourteen-minute color movie on a Navy subject, or a twenty-eight-and-a-half-minute movie on a Navy subject.

Q: Had this been done at all prior to your coming there?

Adm. M.: Yes, Sir, but it was a program that was sort of dragging its feet, so I did get over a million dollars from the Naval Air Systems Command and we programmed a series of twenty-six movies to be made over the next couple of years on various Navy subjects, like the Navy in Vietnam, the Military Sea Transportation Service to Vietnam, the drug-abuse program, the amphibious Navy, destroyers, the carrier Navy, and we did a very beautiful job on the battleship New Jersey.

Q: How did you arrive at this agenda, these various subjects?

Adm. M.: We arrived at it from people who made suggestions on what we should be showing the great American public and other interesting facets of the Navy. One of our best was Spirit of Freedom, and that evolved from a presentation that was made at the annual Navy League dinner in Washington, D. C. The Navy band had a series of slides showing the Navy and the Army from Revolutionary War days through to the Vietnam War, and the trials and tribulations that this country experienced in all of those wars, and the music that was part of our country during that particular period. The Navy band played the music, the conductor showed the slides, and Rock Hudson did the narration. Rock Hudson was in the Navy as a truck driver in WW II! Secretary of the Navy Ignatius was tremendously impressed with it, and the next day he asked me why we couldn't get it into a movie and get Rock Hudson back to narrate it. I told him that we had discussed it in my office that morning because we also were impressed with the presentation the night before, and we were going to ask Senator Dirksen to do the narration. He allowed as how maybe that was a better suggestion...

Q: How did you arrive at Dirksen as the narrator?

Adm. M.: Dirksen was a born actor and he had the voice that could sell anybody, and he was the Number One guy who you'd think of for selling patriotism. Really, Rock Hudson doesn't have the voice to sell like the other two that we got; the one to do most of the narration was Glenn Ford. Glenn Ford is an ex-Marine and Navy. He's in the Naval Reserve at the present time and he certainly does an awful lot of work for the Navy.

So, as it turned out, we had Senator Dirksen introduce the movie, we had Glenn Ford do the narration, and we had Senator Dirksen end the movie and send everybody home happy that they had seen it. He did a magnificent job, so did Glenn Ford. It's a great twenty-eight-and-a-half-minute patriotic movie.

Q: Where was it made?

Adm. M.: It was made in various parts of the country. They got some of the scenes in Boston, some in other places, the rolling countryside, historical scenes that you'd associate with patriotism and what evolved at that time. It was a well-put-together movie.

Q: How much would a movie like that cost to produce?

Adm. M.: Well, Senator Dirksen and Glenn Ford donated their services free. This one was, I think, one of the cheapest that we did - probably around twenty thousand dollars. Most of the movies cost (twenty-eight-and-a-half-minute movies) seventy to eighty thousand. Some more than that. Others where we had loaned people putting them together would be a much smaller bill. Actually, when Senator Dirksen donated his services he wanted to see the completed product, so when it was put together I got it over to the old Senate Office Building and put it on a projector. He had some of his staff and a few other friends in, and when it was over, he turned to me and said, "Admiral, that's a great movie." There wasn't a dry eye in the house. It is very emotional - Doggone good and well put together.

Q: Did it go over equally as well on television?

Adm. M.: Yes, everybody that saw it liked it. We also put together thirty-second and one-minute TV spots. This, for recruiting, retention and morale. We used a professor from the University of South Dakota, Professor Book, who had been on Madison Avenue. I think at one time he had the Dupont account and turned the ugly image of Dupont from a bunch of warmakers into a great institution that did everything for mankind through chemicals. Professor Book got tired of that and went back to the University. However, Madison Avenue was still in his blood and he wanted to get back into some of it, so we enlisted his services from time to time for the thirty-second and one-minute TV spots. If they're done right and they're good, the TV spots probably sell more Navy than the fourteen-minute or the twenty-eight-and-a-half-minute movies. There was quite a bit of controversy over that because I can see the spots could do a lot more because you can get them on TV more frequently than the movies.

Q: They would be on local stations, would they?

Adm. M.: All over the country. The way we got the movies and the TV spots on television was through our branch offices in New York, Chicago, and Los Angeles. We established those branch offices to contact as many media people in the country as we possibly could. The TV stations, the radio stations, the weekly magazines, the weekly newspapers, the daily newspapers - everybody who had to do with public information, and the officers we had in those branch offices were continuously on the road taking our films and TV spots and any other features that we had to talk to TV or radio stations and put them on the air.

We also had a "Dial Navy" news service. You could call this number in various parts of the country and you could get current Navy news for the morning, or the current Navy news for the afternoon, free of charge, except for what it took to dial that number.

Q: You mean naval operations in various parts of the world?

Adm. M.: That's right, in various parts of the world, Vietnam, or any catastrophe or anything else, we put in on "Dial Navy" news. Our branch offices in New York, Chicago, and Los Angeles informed media reps and agencies around the country that we had "Dial Navy" news, we had movies, we had these TV spots and we showed them, and we had other one-minute to five-minute silent, color movies with a script that we made for TV stations, showing a particular item of Navy news. We put out many of those over the years and we are continuing to do that. It's a very good program. It's timeless because the Navy subject you can put on any time, you don't have to worry about getting it out on the road right this morning.

So, we did the movies, the selling, the TV spots, and then the regular Navy one to three and five-minute movie spots with a script to all these stations, along with "Dial Navy" news.

Q: And this was really done through your branch offices in various areas?

Adm. M.: That's right.

Q: This was quite an innovation, wasn't it, in terms of public relations Navywise?

Adm. M.: Art Sylvester and Company in the office of the Secretary of Defense didn't like that because he thought we were getting a jump on the other services.

Q: They didn't have anything similar?

Adm. M.: No. They didn't have a "Dial Navy" news and this is what he was really mad about, because we were ahead of him.

Q: Once you had it in operation, was there any inclination on the part of the other services to do anything?

Adm. M.: Oh, yes, they started their outlets, too.

Q: And now they have them?

Adm. M.: I don't know if they have now, but they started at that time to get them.

Q: Did you have any problem with any of the media in using these films and so on?

Adm. M.: Normally, a station will give a certain amount of its time to the armed services for their recruiting program, which, of course, this was aimed at including retention and morale.

Q: What percentage would you say they did give?

Adm. M.: There is a certain percentage, I think, that they're supposed to give. I believe it's 15 percent, but I'm not sure.

Q: Is this under the terms of their license?

Adm. M.: This, I think, is under the terms of their license. They're supposed to give not only the armed services but other government activities free TV and radio time. But, additionally, as you might surmise, it's the individual who goes to those TV stations and if he does a good selling job your film gets on the tube in a hurry. If he doesn't do a good selling job, he has to come back and repeat and repeat. As you well know, there are a great many former Navy people, retired or who have been in the Navy, in TV and radio stations around the country, so they help out tremendously in getting the Navy story on the air.

Q: In other words, the Navy has friends in various places.

Adm. M.: Yes, and you can say the same for Army and Air Force, but contacting those particular Navy people at those radio and TV stations or at the newspaper or the magazine certainly helped the cause tremendously.

Q: Since the individual officer employed in these branch offices was very important in his personal characteristics, did you have a hand in the selection of these men? Did you see to that?

Adm. M.: Yes. We were very careful with the ones that we sent to the branch offices, because we knew we had to have good representatives who were interested and would do a good selling job. This was very important.

Q: How did you go about selecting the right men?

Adm. M.: We knew who the good ones were. The public affairs community is a very small community, so you know everybody very intimately.

Q: But the men involved in public affairs in the Navy are likewise subject to rotation, are they not?

Adm. M.: Oh, yes, but it's good at some of those places because a new face and a lot of enthusiasm certainly help out.

Q: Did you have any special facilities for training these men in salesmanship, or anything of that sort?

Adm. M.: No. You might say a good public affairs officer is a salesman. That's what he's supposed to do. If he isn't, he shouldn't be in the business.

Q: You said previously that you established a program for public speaking, and it seems to me it would feed right into this.

Adm. M.: The public speaking program got started on one individual's idea. Before a CNO's meeting one day, this officer came up to me and said that if we got a very small amount of money, say, on the order of about $10,000, he could build a speech laboratory there in the Chinfo spaces at the Pentagon, with a play-back tape, a video tape, the loudspeakers, the TV, so that the individual who wanted to practice a speech could go to this room, turn it on, talk, hear himself, see himself, and get a pretty good handle on what was wrong with his speech technique. He could see himself and hear himself, and he didn't have to have anybody there to kibitz.

Well, I went to the CNO meeting and when it came my time to talk I mentioned this and said that if we could get the money we could probably have that equipment in and have the speech lab going in three weeks. Surprisingly enough, when I got back to the office, I had calls from the Bureau of Naval Personnel and from the CNO organization. They gave me the money immediately to get that project started.

Q: Obviously, this met a need, then?

Adm. M.: There certainly was a need for it and it was used and it has been used right along by a great many officers in the Navy Department who either have to make presentations on the Hill or speeches in various parts of the country.

Q: Why was it so long delayed in being set up?

Adm. M.: I don't know. The Pentagon sort of stays in confusion and it takes, you might say, some small suggestion like that to get them started and keep them going. This was a very good idea and it certainly took hold in a hurry. And from that, this same officer, who is now my deputy here, Captain George Watkins, started a public speaking seminar. We held the first public speaking seminar at Andrews Air Force Base, in the Navy section there - a one-week affair - and we invited Navy captains and admirals, both active duty and Reserves, and at the end of the week, we had a regular contest to see who was the best. It was very enlightening.

During the week we had continuous sessions of speaking, research, putting speeches together, we had luncheons, barbecues, and a final banquet dinner.

Q: Features at all these occasions!

Adm. M.: Oh, yes.

Q: Did you have a staff of experts to advise them and help them in learning these techniques?

Adm. M.: Yes, we had speech experts who were there to advise and to coach. That first seminar was a resounding success.

Q: How large a student body would you have at a seminar like that?

Adm. M.: We had about thirty. They've continued that annual seminar ever since.

We also had an annual public affairs seminar of about three or four days, getting as many public affairs officers from all the commands around the world - the Navy public affairs officers - to this annual meeting in Washington, D. C. There we went over history, you might say, what had happened the previous year, we told them what was coming up, we enunciated new procedures, we brought them up to date, and we tried to predict what was coming up in the future. So everybody from Washington and the farthest command around the world would know what was going on in the public affairs business, not only from the Navy viewpoint, but also from the Department of Defense.

Q: Were there certain phases of the public affairs office which were peculiar to the Navy in contrast with the Army and the Air Force?

Adm. M.: We have a little different set up in the Navy because of the public affairs problems constantly coming up aboard ship way out on the briny deep and not subject to immediate advice. The Army and the Air Force are pretty much shore-based and have access to all the communications that they need to get the story out to the great American public. The Navy has a little more of a difficult time to do this. It takes more work, it takes more imagination.

Q: These on-board-ship programs are largely educational for the crew, are they not?

Adm. M.: Yes, but then if anything happens we want to get that story out to the public. Additionally, aboard ship we have an internal relations program. That is, telling home town newspapers some of the things that are happening to their particular boys who are in the Navy, from that ship or from any other ship. The Fleet home town news program has been going now for about twenty-three or twenty-four years.

H. L. Miller # 7 - 413

Q: That's something you initiated in the Atlantic, isn't it?

Adm. M.: No, it originated about 1947, the Fleet Home Town News program. The office is at the Great Lakes Naval Training Center in Illinois, and this is how it works. Each ship or station sends in information concerning a particular officer or man on a special form to the Fleet home town news center at Great Lakes. They, in turn, send those out to that individual's newspaper, and it almost always gets printed. The weekly newspaper always prints the information regarding the boys in the armed services, so do the dailies, as you can see in every newspaper. This is a program that has been pushed by all the services, to give the recognition that that boy deserves for being in the armed services. Most of the time they send a picture of the boy, too. It helps morale on board ship or any station. There's not an individual I know who doesn't like to see his name in print or his picture in the paper. I think it's a very good program.

Q: Admiral, I would think that the on-board public affairs program - the success of it - would depend largely on the skipper himself. Did you have any program to aid skippers in appreciating the program and using it?

Adm. M.: We sent, periodically, information to various ships and stations around the country and a monthly magazine that was pointed for the commanding officer and anybody that he had assigned to public affairs. It gave all the necessary information to keep his public affairs program going, a vigorous, aggressive public affairs program, and that little magazine still goes out every month to all Navy ships and stations, and if the commanding officer or the individual assigned to public affairs follows the guidance in there, he's going to have a pretty good public affairs program. Of course, you have to have the interest in it, too, and that must come from the commanding officer, but most of our commanding officers today are public-affairs-conscious.

Q: Is there any attempt in the Naval Academy and elsewhere to indoctrinate future naval officers in this area?

Adm. M.: No, Sir. There is, as far as I know, no public affairs course at the Naval Academy. I think they certainly need one.

Q: Didn't this tempt you as a possibility when you were in Chinfo?

Adm. M.: I had many things to do at Chinfo. I did think of getting something into the syllabus at the Naval Academy, but at that time there were so many changes going into the curriculum at Annapolis that they were having a most difficult time just trying to keep up with the changes, and they weren't too happy about including another change for public affairs. They felt that could come later.

Q: Was there any correlation between Navy recruitment and the effect of your branch offices?

Adm. M.: Yes. Our branch officers were instructed to check with Navy recruiting officers around the country in their particular areas. Additionally, our branch officers were instructed to also contact presidents of the Navy League councils in their particular areas and the Naval Reserve Association chapters in their areas, or anybody who was vitally concerned, or interested, in the Navy. And this is how it worked.

If we had a thirty-second or one-minute spot that we wanted to put on television, our officer from the branch office would contact the Navy recruiter in that particular town or city. Now, if the Navy recruiter was new, our branch office man introduced him to the particular television or radio station. If the Navy recruiter was an old hand, he did us the tremendous job of introducing our people to local radio, television, newspaper, and daily

H. L. Miller # 7 - 416

newspaper media. It worked very nicely. Essentially what we were trying to do in the Office of Information was to project a good image of the Navy to the great American public and tell the American public what we were doing with the monies that they had allocated to us in the Navy. This was in addition to the over-all program of helping recruiting, retention, and morale in the Navy. So, this was, I thought, a very well-coordinated program. In addition every Friday, in my Office of Information, I had a meeting of my department heads, and in addition, I invited - and they came 98 percent of the time - the officer in charge of Navy recruiting from the Bureau of Naval Personnel, the Public Affairs Officer in the Bureau of Naval Personnel, and others who were interested in the over-all program of recruiting, retention and morale.

Let me say this, when the invitees came to that meeting, I told them what we had done the previous week in Chinfo and what we had projected - what was coming up in the future. I asked if that helped their recruiting program and their retention program? If it didn't, what changes could we make to aid recruiting and retention? I thought we had a very well-coordinated program. We helped each other and I think we knew what was going on.

Q: Was there any particular problem with recruitment in 1966-68?

Adm. M.: No, there wasn't any particular problem. Because of the draft, the Navy had a very good selection of recruits. However, the problem of retention was still there. We weren't getting the numbers that we wanted in the retention program.

Q: What percentage of re-enlistments was there?

Adm. M.: To tell the truth, I forget, but it was too low and it kept getting lower. I guess one of the reasons was because the Navy and I say the Bureau of Naval Personnel did not go all out in the people program. As a matter of fact, to one high ranking officer in the Bureau of Naval Personnel, I said, "You know, I've talked to your people many times and you should have, when you look at your title, 'The Bureau of Naval Personnel," the biggest public relations factory in the Navy. The people that you have in BuPers should be coming in every morning and saying, 'What can I do for the people in the Navy today.' You know, the thing that's wrong with a great many of your people in BuPers, they don't like people, and as long as you have some of those people in the Bureau of Naval Personnel, they're not helping the Navy, they're damaging it, and giving the Navy a bad image."

Q: You, in fact, share Admiral Zumwalt's point of view?

Adm. M.: Absolutely. They can talk about the hair-dos and the side-burns, that's incidental. But you've got to worry about people and you have to continue to worry about people every day of your life in the Navy, or you're not going to have a good outfit.

Q: In that time, would you say that the percentage of re-enlistments was equal to the present rate? Admiral Zumwalt said earlier this year that it's about thirty percent.

Adm. M.: I think it's going up. Now, of course, people may say because of the economy it's tougher to get a job on the outside. Yes, that's some of the influence, but when you take the programs that are going on today and are continuing it should go up. Admiral Zumwalt has the ideas coming in and he's implementing these ideas. He's a do-it guy, and this is the way that it should be done. I'll give you a couple of examples.

At the annual test pilot school reunion, he was our guest speaker at the luncheon. He gave a wonderful talk, and afterwards the commanding officer of the Naval Air Station at Patuxent said, "Admiral, I was out there with you on the China Station right after World War II." So they started talking and the subject of housing came up. The commanding officer of the Naval Air Station, Patuxent, said they had a very difficult housing problem and to alleviate this they would like to get one of those Navy exchange motels, but BuPers gave it to areas - population centers like San Diego and Norfolk where they had great numbers of motels for people coming in - but here at Patuxent they had very few hotels and they extended all the way out to twenty-five miles and were very expensive. With that, Admiral Zumwalt asked the commanding officer, "Have you ever requested one?" Oh, yes, he said, "but BuPers said that we weren't on the list because we weren't a critical area, whereas in housing we were a critical area." And with more facts laid on the line, Admiral Zumwalt said, "You call Admiral So-and-So and you tell him to get off his rear end and get a Navy exchange motel down here right now."

Well, the commanding officer called the Admiral's captain assistant, whom he knew, and he told him that story, and in about two days' time the motel man from the Brooklyn PX organization was down at Patuxent. He ordered the furniture, and by 15 June, one month's time, we had twenty-seven units of the old BOQ rehabed into a motel.

H. L. Miller # 7 - 420

Q: A man of action, indeed!

Adm. M.: That's a man of action. The other day at the Naval Institute meeting, I told Admiral Zumwalt of my report from the publisher of the weekly newspaper in my area, the Enterprise. The publisher had been invited to the global strategy session at the Naval War College, an annual event. He took his wife. He's an Army captain, retired, with a World War II disability. He's a dedicated Army man but he does everything in the world for us in the Navy. Mr. Moliter is his name. He said that the global strategy course was one of the finest incidents in his life. He thoroughly enjoyed it. It was well organized. The wives were taken on tours, to luncheons. All the participants were taken care of, morning, noon, and night, and no matter how many social events the night before, the next day you had to be on deck at the appointed time. He raved about it, then he said, "And here's what I'm doing. Our committee was 25-strong, students, faculty, and civilians. I suggested to them that we'd had such a good time and we learned so much, why not during the year, if we see anything of international or national importance that we feel the other 25 should see, write off a quick memo to the 25 and send this particular piece of information along? I'm sending the first one today."

Then he said, "You know, I have the Enterprise newspaper, it's a weekly newspaper, and everybody reads it down there in St. Mary's County from cover to cover." And I backed that up because I read it from cover to cover, too, every week. Mr. Molitor said that he did not believe that the Navy was doing enough in selling the Navy story, projecting the Navy image, to the weekly newspapers, and, with that, I said, "I go along with that 100 percent because I took about 252 weekly newspaper editors on Atlantic command exercises when I was on the staff of Admiral Blandy as public information officer. We had a series of articles in those newspapers for weeks. They talked about the sailors from their particular area, the exercise in general, Navy philosophy, Navy tactics, Navy strategy." And he said, "You know, out in the countryside they don't get The New York Times or the Wall Street Journal, but they sure do get that weekly newspaper and they read it, every bit of it. It's a good place to put the information."

Well, another Admiral allowed as how the statistics didn't back that up, but television was the thing and this was the way to go. I told him, "sure, people looked at TV but people still read newspapers when they wanted to know what's going on." TV was certainly important, but a lot of people today aren't looking at

TV as much as they used to. With that Admiral Zumwalt turned and said, "I agree with you, and you call Bill Thompson who is now the Chief of Information and you tell Bill to get off his rear end and get the Navy into weekly newspapers."

This is the way Admiral Zumwalt works. He listens to both sides of it, but you know he's interested in people, and this is one thing that the whole Navy has to worry about that they haven't been worrying about, chiefly the Bureau of Naval Personnel. You'd think that at this stage of the game with the word out that Admiral Zumwalt is going to be worrying about people and wanted the Navy to worry about people twenty-four hours a day, that the Bureau of Naval Personnel was going to be coming out with all these things. But, today, over a year later, the ideas are still coming from a young bunch of bloodhounds right under Admiral Zumwalt's thumb. They're producing the ideas and the Bureau of Naval Personnel is implementing them. BuPers should be doing the originating and the implementation, but the direction is still coming from Admiral Zumwalt and he's staying right on BuPers' back.

Q: Admiral, is this not in part due to the Navy system of rotation, the fact that the CNO has a term of four years, then he disappears from the scene, and BuPers goes on for ever? The ideas generated by CNO percolating down and being implemented is a very difficult one to achieve?

Adm. M.: No. The way I look at it, if you're appointed as the Chief of Naval Personnel, you should be just about the Number One or Two guy in the Navy that is absolutely personnel-conscious. But it hasn't worked out that way. It's worked to appoint people who get there by a gradual increase in their status in the Navy, whether or not they're going on to three or four stars, regardless of their real-people experience. Most of the people who have been chief of Naval Personnel have been in that spot from their previous experience in BuPers, and that's wrong because they've never forgotten the old methods and the old ways of doing business in BuPers and so they've perpetuated all the wrong things that we've been doing. Regardless of who's in there, Admiral Zumwalt is cleaning out all that old way of doing business, and they know it, so does he.

Q: You talked about using the Navy League and the Reserve chapters for one aspect of your program, did you use them in other areas? What was your relationship with these two organizations?

Adm. M.: I worked with the Navy League...

Q: As Chinfo, I mean.

Adm. M.: As Chinfo - it goes back farther than that. I started working with the Navy League and the Naval Reserve Association back in 1957 when I was the director of the Progress Analysis Group and selling sea power. So I used every chapter or council of the Naval Reserve Association and the Navy League councils all over the country. These I continued to use, and they used me too, in selling the Navy. I'd been in touch with many chapters of these national organizations ever since 1957.

Q: How effective are they in implementing the ideas of Chinfo?

Adm. M.: It all depends on who the president is at that particular time. If he's a charger, he really does a wonderful job of getting his organization projecting a good image of the Navy and telling the Navy story. If he's a so-and-so sort of an average guy, the story doesn't get told until an aggressive relief comes in. That's the way it goes.

Q: So it gets right down to personalities once again!

Adm. M.: Absolutely.

Q: As Chinfo, what relationship did you have as a direct relationship with Congress?

Adm. M.: I had some relationship with Congress due to my previous contacts on the Hill, and the only other way is inquiries that came from congressional members on certain things that their constituents asked them about the Navy. And then my defense of the public information budget on the Hill. It was very interesting when I went up one time to get the money to save Chinfo's life. The senior member of the Armed Services Committee, Appropriations Committee, on that particular day, was Congressman Sykes from Florida, and he said to me, "Well, what do you need this money for," and I told him. When I mentioned the combat art program, he said, "What good is that?" I said, "Well, it tells part of the Navy story in another light through art." And he said, "Do you have any good art?" I said, "Yes, we have some really outstanding pieces." He said, "I bet you have a bunch of junk." I said, "Well, there are some pieces that aren't too good, but..."

Q: I notice something esoteric in his...

Adm. M.: No, he was leading me on, and I said, "Just like everything else, you have some good and you have some bad, but this is a very progressive program and a very fine program." I learned later that he was interested in it because he had taken up painting! But he wanted to know and I told him. I got my money. That money was hard to come by because they said via the grape vine that I wasn't going to get a dime of that $200,000 that I was requesting, but I got it back.

Q: I know at one point when Navy witnesses were to testify before congressional committees, the JAG office got involved in preliminary training and rehearsal and the like. Did Chinfo get involved in that?

Adm. M.: No, Sir. The only time that I got involved when I was at Chinfo and testifying on the Hill was going up and talking nuclear power. That was the only instance, except for defense of my budget. But no real what you call lobbying up on the Hill.

Q: What about other aspects of the Navy program in their presentations? Who prepared the witnesses?

Adm. M.: Well, at the present time the Office of Legislative Liaison helps to prepare the witnesses. By now the Navy has finally progressed to the stage where every naval officer who goes up on that Hill knows that he's supposed to be good. Unfortunately, there are still too many who go up there and do not know the answers to the questions that they're supposed to know. As an instance, when I went up to reclamer my $200,000, there were about twelve officers up there, including a couple of admirals who were to testify in regard to specific Navy programs, and I was absolutely amazed that they did not have the answers to many questions that were asked. So I don't think the program is working out too well.

Q: This is a very definite technique, isn't it, being a witness - you may have all the information in your briefcase...?

Adm. M.: You have to have it in your head, and if you don't you're in trouble.

Q: And you have to anticipate the fact, perhaps, that some of the members of these committees are pretty well informed and they know the answers to the questions they ask.

Adm. M.: Absolutely. A lot of them are seeking information and you should have it there and give it to them. If you don't have it right there at hand, then they'll always allow you to send them a letter or memo filling in the blanks on the information that you didn't have. It's hard to believe, but when they say they want this, some of the witnesses go back and send them the wrong information, and that just kills you.

Q: You have to be on the ball!

Adm. M.: In other words, we still have some people who don't give a damn. And that's where Chinfo got in trouble because the civilians who testified on the Hill for us from the administrative office in Sec Nav gave the wrong information, and then gave wrong information in the paper that he submitted afterwards. He didn't let me know

H. L. Miller # 7 - 428

anything about it until I saw it in the Congressional Record.

Q: This had a tendency, then, to discredit all other information?

Adm. M.: That's right.

Q: Tell me about the minority group program that you developed under Chinfo?

Adm. M.: The minority group program was a very interesting program in our Office of Information. Normally, you'd say it should be under the Bureau of Naval Personnel or under, say, the Assistant Secretary for Manpower and Reserve, or something like that. But nobody had done anything about it until the Bureau of Naval Personnel said that they were very disturbed. The first Naval ROTC at a black college was at Prairie View College in Texas, which is a predominantly Negro college - I think there was one white student. Prairie View is about fifty miles from Houston. Well, the Under Secretary of the Navy was going to commission that NROTC unit on a Sunday afternoon, and on a Sunday afternoon in Texas, fifty miles from Houston you're not going to get many reporters to come and report the commissioning of a Negro NROTC.

Q: It was a bad time to select.

Adm. M.: And, of course, when you asked them they said, "Well, what's so new about that - is the Navy just finding out about Negroes?" And they had a very good point. The Under Secretary didn't think about it that way. He was mad as hell because he didn't have his picture in the paper and headlines saying that the Navy had commissioned an ROTC unit at a predominantly Negro university, or college. So he was really furious about it and no matter what we said about no interest by the media, it didn't satisfy him. He said he wanted a minority group program for the Navy, and he said we're vitally interested, and all that sort of thing. I said, well, if you're vitally interested - and everybody is - then we should have some high-powered Negroes in the E ring of the Pentagon, which is the Navy ring of all the Navy high moguls. Then when the Office of Civilian Manpower and Management, which is a civilian organization in the Navy, said the same thing, I asked them where were the Negroes in their establishment, other than those that empty the wastepaper baskets and swab the decks. They didn't like it, but I can assure you, today, there are some Negroes around some of those front offices in the Navy.

Q: It wasn't, then, that they couldn't find personnel who qualified?

Adm. M.: That's right. And from there, we whipped up this minority group program, it was bought by the Bureau of Naval

Personnel, the Under Secretary of the Navy, and the Office of Civilian Manpower and Management...

Q: On what basis?

Adm. M.: Because it was a good program that had been whipped up for them.

In addition, I got a Negro lieutenant commander in the Office of Information to bird dog that whole program, and to keep on everybody's back to ensure that it was implemented. But, you know, from there I came down to Patuxent and I asked them about their minority group program and the civilian personnel department outlined to me the measures they had gone to in many areas to get the Negroes into the Patuxent Naval Air Test Center. Of course, it was the biggest whitewash job that I had listened to in all my life. They didn't want the Negro. They were doing a beautiful job of keeping him out. But, today, we have Negroes in every level of the Naval Air Test Center, and today we also have Negroes in some of the high offices in the Navy Department, including the Office of Civilian Manpower and Reserves, who is a Negro.

Q: Well, Admiral, has this, in your estimation, resulted in a lessening of tensions?

Adm. M.: It's bound to. You've got to have the ethnic groups.

Don't limit it to the Negroes. You've got to consider the Indians, the Negro, the Italians, the Poles, the Asiatics. Look at the Filipinos in the Navy. There are tons of them. You've got to consider the ethnic groups and give them a voice, otherwise you're going to have trouble. So, at least this was a start. The minority group program that we whipped up in Chinfo was a darned good thing for the Navy.

Q: Tell me about setting up the global strategy course at the Naval War College.

Adm. M.: Actually, the Naval War College sets up their own global strategy course, but they asked Chinfo for nominations...

Q: Was this a new procedure on their part? How long has this program been in operation?

Adm. M.: This has been in operation for several years, but they always ask Chinfo and my former office, Op-09 Dog, the Director of the Progress Analysis Group, for important people from around the country to attend the global strategy course. And we always sent in hundreds of names every year, new ones and old ones. It's a doggone fine public relations effort on the part of the Naval War College to acquaint leaders of this country with Navy policy, Navy philosophy, Navy strategy, and Navy thinking.

Q: Is there any feed-back from these individual conferences?

Adm. M.: Oh, yes, Sir. As an example, the publisher of the Enterprise, our weekly newspaper in the Patuxent River area, Mr. Molitar, thought it was one of the finest events he's ever attended.

Q: And this is reflected in his publication?

Adm. M.: That's right.

Q: Tell me how Chinfo goes about setting up a list.

Adm. M.: Well, Chinfo has actually worked on this list for years. In our contacts around the country, congressmen, senators, the media representatives - we like to see heavy media representation because we deal with them in Chinfo - presidents and vice presidents of corporations. Anybody that has an influence on the nation anywhere in this country.

Q: Do members of congress actually attend?

Adm. M.: Oh, yes. We have congressmen attending and they enjoy it. I'd say in the main, 99 percent of all the attendees certainly enjoy that global strategy course. You're always going to have one percent who say, well, so what. You find them anywhere.

Following that, as far as the Naval War College is concerned, each year we have a public affairs seminar for the War College, too. It is about a three-day affair.

Q: Where?

Adm. M.: Conducted at the War College for all the students in various groups. We had teams, and a team consisted of individuals from all departments of Chinfo. We invited prominent media representatives from around the country. For instance, one was at that time Number Two Man in Associated Press, Stan Swinton, from New York. We had Glenn Ford from Hollywood. Glenn is a former Marine and now a Naval Reserve officer. You can send Glenn anywhere in the world and he'll do it free for the Navy. He's a real dedicated guy, and he's so proud of that Navy uniform that he'd wear it 365 days of the year if he could. He's that kind of a guy.

We had others, Frank Blair of the Today Show, on that panel. We'd give and take between the students and the performers at the seminar. We visited various classrooms and talked about all aspects of public relations - a very, very fine three day affair. The students got a lot out of it, so did we, and so did our participants.

Q: May I ask, Admiral, why wouldn't this work on the undergraduate level as well? Why couldn't it be installed as a permanent feature at the Naval Academy?

Adm. M.: That's a good question. We thought about it and we asked them about it, and I said it should be started, and I believe when I get back tomorrow I will call Chinfo and ask them about setting it up, see if we can't get it started.

Q: Is Admiral Calvert receptive to that sort of thing?

Adm. M.: I don't know, but the Naval Academy should get into the public affairs business more because the naval officer is concerned with it all his life.

Q: It impresses me as something not necessarily for graduate level, but equally important for the undergraduate.

Adm. M.: Oh, absolutely. From the time a midshipman graduates from the Naval Academy until he's through with the Navy or through with life, he's going to be concerned with public affairs, and certainly he should know about it and get in the swing of it from the time he starts his career in the Navy.

Q: Now tell me about the cruises.

Adm. M.: About every time that a carrier went to WesPac and cruised through Hawaii, we used the potential of the aircraft carrier and the operations in which it would participate to educate a certain number of media representatives and VIPs from various parts of the country in naval operations. So, we could send about fifteen to twenty of these people aboard the carrier from the West Coast to Hawaii. They would see operations en route, be briefed in all our naval philosophy and the way we do business. When they arrived in Honolulu they would be briefed by the commander-in-chief, Pacific, Pacific Fleet staff, and the commander of the Hawaiian Sea Frontier, and the other commands that we have in that area.

It was a very informative cruise. They enjoyed it and they certainly did an awful lot in carrying the Navy story wherever they went after that.

Q: Chinfo certainly had, does have, a natural set-up for the proliferation of news about the Navy, doesn't it?

Adm. M.: Oh, yes.

Q: But it takes a man with imagination and direction. And there must be feed-back from other Navy brass, so to speak, who see opportunities.

Adm. M.: Definitely. We have a great many commands in the Navy who send in ideas on how to sell the Navy story. We also have many suggestions submitted by junior officers and others in the Navy, enlisted, civilians, to new tricks of the trade in telling the Navy story to the great American public and getting our ideas across.

Q: Is there any correlation, perhaps, between the standing of the Navy in the estimate of the American public and the number of ideas which are fed in to Chinfo?

Adm. M.: Yes. The Navy image is reflected, at the present time, through a different source. Admiral Zumwalt and his idea crew. They've been pushing these ideas through every week. He signs them out, they're implemented, and aside from the haircuts and the sideburns, it's a great program. The haircuts and the sideburns are okay, except some of the commands let them go until they're falling off their backs. Admiral Zumwalt is the "people" guy and "idea" guy, and this is what you have to have.

Q: Incidentally, and this would only be a footnote, but the Zumwalt z-grams have been a consummate kind of public relations thing. Did they originate with Chinfo, or did they originate with the Admiral himself?

Adm. M.: They originated with Admiral Zumwalt. It was a doggone smart idea. He's Mr. Z and it's a great trademark.

Q: It certainly reached the headlines.

Adm. M.: It's reached the Navy, all parts of the Navy. A lot of the Navy don't agree with some of those things. They just can't stand the haircuts and the sideburns, but that's incidental to the 101 other items that have been implemented through z-grams.

Q: Tell me about the commissioning of the John F. Kennedy carrier.

Adm. M.: First, the commissioning of the John F. Kennedy at Newport News, Virginia, was an out-of-the-ordinary commissioning because of the whole Kennedy family.

Q: This was in the year 1968.

Adm. M.: It was a very unusual commissioning because all the Kennedys were involved. The captain of the John F. Kennedy, the carrier, was Captain Buddy Yates. Buddy is now a rear admiral, but at that commissioning he almost turned out to be Seaman, Second. It just so happened that there really wasn't much interest in the commissioning of the John F. Kennedy, as far as the Navy high command was concerned, because it had been launched and it had been a big event the previous year. Everybody was there. But at this time, of course, there was Jackie and her family plus the Ted Kennedy family. Bobby had been killed. It was going to be a very routine affair until they said McNamara was going to be the principal speaker. Now, at this time, McNamara was President of the World Bank, but Secretary Ignatius had been one of his former pupils in the Department of Defense, so when he learned Bob was coming back and being the principal speaker, he called for an immediate presentation from the captain of the carrier, all details, on how much it was going to cost, etc.

So, Captain Yates came up from Norfolk with his executive officer, and Captain Yates is a very precise guy. He has everything worked out to the smallest detail. He presented the whole program on a time schedule to the Secretary of the Navy, and then, at the end, he added up the commissioning bill of about $130,000, at which time Secretary Ignatius hit the overhead. He was very cost-conscious from the McNamara regime and he asked Captain Yates why it took $130,000 to commission a Navy ship. Captain Yates said the Navy had been in the commissioning business for about a hundred years and when they did it, they did it right, and a big ship cost an awful lot of money. Well, the Secretary didn't like that. He told Captain Yates to go back, study his lesson again, and come up with a new set of figures, because he could not go for $130,000. He was thinking in terms of about $30,000.

Captain Yates went home, he went over his procedures, he cut down expenses, he came back for a second presentation, and he got the bill down to about $110,000. There were many more questions and answers during this presentation. The commissioning ceremony

H. L. Miller # 7 - 439

took about an hour and a half to satisfy Mr. Ignatius.

Q: Was Chinfo involved in this presentation?

Adm. M.: Oh, yes, Sir, because we had contacts, we had to supply transportation, we had to do a lot of things, get the media there, and quite a few other people to ensure that the whole thing was smoothed out. Certainly, we were involved every step of the way. Captain Yates had to come back a third time and make a presentation, and that's when Mr. Ignatius bought the program for about $100,000. Well, when the big day arrived the commissioning ceremony was perfect.

Q: Would you more or less in a general way break down that $100,000?

Adm. M.: The $100,000 was involved in transportation for people, additional resources and facilities that were needed at the commissioning ceremony, such as microphones, platforms, food for ten thousand people, special cables, special services that were required in a hurry, a reception at one of the big hotels right close aboard to Newport News, all of this added up to $100,000, and when you consider over ten thousand people at a full-day ceremony, including lots of press and other media, it was a very reasonable price for a one-day affair.

Q: Did the media advance any funds for their reproduction of the scene?

Adm. M.: The media never pay a dime. They expect everything free and they get it free.

Q: They expect to be there, too!

Adm. M.: Oh, yes. Wherever the media go they know they're free, and maybe that's a good point for a second career!

Anyway, the big day arrived and all the Kennedys were there. They were all vying for different seats up front, although they knew where they were supposed to sit. The Secretary of the Navy, Mr. Ignatius was in his chair and he fidgeted and sweated until the last two minutes of the whole commissioning, even though it was going 100 percent perfect.

Q: Where was Chinfo?

Adm. M.: Oh, don't worry! Chinfo was sitting out there in the audience just watching. Jackie and the kids were there, and finally Mr. McNamara got up at the appointed time to give his speech. He was so emotionally torn apart that he broke down almost every other sentence, almost cried throughout the whole speech. It was really an exhausting few minutes to hear him up on the platform. Nobody knows what he had to say and nobody seemed to care because all they wanted to do was see him get off that platform.

Following the ceremony, almost like waving a magic wand, the hangar deck of that enormous carrier - they had the ceremony on the hangar deck - cleared. Sailors put up tables, food, soft drinks taking care of thousands of families and friends of the officers and men of that ship. The flight deck also had soft-drink stands set up for people who watched the Blue Angels putting on their show right after the ceremony. Following that, a great many of the VIPs went to the hotel where a very lavish cocktail party and reception was held for quite a number. When Mr. Ignatius saw that, he was convinced that the Navy knew how to commission a ship. It was well worth the $100,000. But, I'll tell you, Captain Buddy Yates had a hell of a time trying to sell that program, and he's lucky at this date that he's an admiral.

Q: Tell me a little about Mr. Ignatius.

Adm. M.: Mr. Ignatius was put in the job as Secretary of the Navy by McNamara. He was a loyal, devoted slave of Mr. McNamara, and he worked for Mr. McNamara, not for the Navy. Maybe that's the way it should be, but whenever you have a leader you look to him as the man looking after your Navy interests, and if he doesn't have them, then you look askance at his capability to lead you.

Q: Did he have a Navy background?

Adm. M.: He was a lieutenant on a jeep carrier in World War II. I think he was ordnance-handling officer. But that really didn't give him much of a Navy background, and I really don't think he contributed anything to the Navy during his tenure. Right now, he is the President of The Washington Post. Mrs. Graham, of course, is the chairman of the board. But it's interesting right now when you consider the controversy that's going on over the publishing of top secret papers of the Department of Defense. Mr. Ignatius is the president and what has he said about breaking security. As the former Secretary of the Navy, I should think that he is bound by principle and former rules and regulations, that he should have honored these rules and not published those top secret documents from the Pentagon. So, again, I question his judgment in the performance of his duty when he was Secretary of the Navy and subsequent to that.

There's an awful lot of questions that I would like to ask him about his conduct after leaving the Navy Department and taking over that job. What does he consider security? I know doggone well when he was Secretary of the Navy working for McNamara that anything like the Pentagon Papers and he probably would have had a conniption fit if that release would have happened on his watch. If an admiral had done this he would probably have busted him to Seaman, 2nd.

H. L. Miller # 7 - 443

Q: Tell me about Mr. McNamara as Secretary of Defense. He's such a controversial figure and there are so many points of view about him. You, as Chinfo, had some direct dealings and enough to form an opinion.

Adm. M.: To my mind, Mr. McNamara was a dictator. He didn't want to have anybody telling him what to do or anybody disagreeing with him. He had his immediate group of advisers whom he relied upon, and anybody who disagreed with those advisers just wasn't on McNamara's team. And, looking back and talking to people since that era, I just haven't been able to find many supporters of McNamara.

Q: Within Navy circles?

Adm. M.: Within any military circles. He is probably one of the most disliked men that was ever in the Defense Department.

Q: He's generally credited with not really liking military figures, men in uniform?

Adm. M.: That's correct, and when he came out to CincPac at a Secretary of Defense conference, Maxwell Taylor introduced me to McNamara. Well, I'd met him before, but he said, "Well, how are you? It's nice to meet you," and with that he turned right around with his back to me and started making penciled notations of what was going on.

Q: Were you then a captain or a rear admiral?

Adm. M.: I was a rear admiral. He's a very cold individual. He doesn't have any of the milk of human kindness or warmth in him. And I've never heard of anybody saying that he was congenial or warm or a likeable guy. He was just cold.

Q: What were his assets, then, in terms of the Kennedy administration or the Johnson administration?

Adm. M.: Well, of course, Kennedy hired him as being a recommended analyst, a cost-effective guy who wanted the facts and the figures, and with a computer mind. But, you know, Johnson inherited him from the Kennedy administration, and it came to pass that President Johnson fired him. So, somebody found out that McNamara wasn't infallible. He had a team around him who just disliked the military, and you know that's not the way to go. If you want to get a job done, there has to be mutual confidence. If there isn't, you have a pretty messed-up department

Q: This team comprised the so-called Whizz Kids?

Adm. M.: That's right. The Whizz Kids could do no wrong. They could smack you in the face and that was it. Enthoven was one of them. He's with Lytton Industries now. I guess he's doing all right. But that was quite a crowd. They were insolent. They were just the antithesis of anything that you'd consider a going business firm.

Q: Were they nonmilitary in their orientation?

Adm. M.: They were non-nothing. You take just a business, you still have to get along with people in business to progress and what-not. I don't think they would have done well in business because they were against everything. In business you've got to get along with people and with other companies. These people couldn't get along and didn't want to get along with any of the military. Maybe that's the way McNamara wanted it.

Q: One factor in their inability was their age. They were quite young, were they not, as a group?

Adm. M.: That's right. But still, good, smart young people - Good Lord, look at my son, he's a graduate of high school now, and he looks at both sides of a question and I think does a remarkable job of getting along with all elements, the conventional and the revolutionists. He does a darned good job, and he's 17, will be 18 next month. But the gang that McNamara had was just an inner circle and they just walked the military out. It was a bad thing.

Q: Admiral, I know perfectly well that in World War II days, the Navy high command was very much opposed to publicizing any Navy activity. The Navy had for generations been known as the silent service, and public relations, disseminating to the general populace was not thought necessary. When you were at Chinfo, things had changed somewhat. Would you comment on this general area, and has it been to the advantage of the Navy as a service?

Adm. M.: There was a big change. Certainly during World War II nobody wanted to talk. Admiral Lovett was Chinfo, at that time, or the Office of Information, or whatever they called it. Then Admiral Nimitz, I believe, had Captain Min Miller - Captain H. V. Miller - who was his public affairs officer, and Min did a tremendous job. I heard from Min the other day.

Q: This was when Nimitz was CNO?

Adm. M.: This was when Nimitz was CinCPac and CinCPacFlt. Then Min came back to the Office of Information and did a very fine job trying to get the Navy to respond to publicity and getting an image going. Through the years we've progressed, but we've really progressed very slowly. Today, certainly there are many officers in the Navy who realize the potential of good public relations throughout the world. Some of them do just a marvelous job of projecting the Navy image. Others do a pretty lousy job.

When I was at Chinfo we had supporters in all elements of the naval establishment, but we also had people who disliked public affairs and would not support us. This was the tough part of the whole ball game during the time that I was Chief of Information. In that job everybody is picking at you and you need all the support you can get, so when your own Navy doesn't give it to you its pretty tough.

Q: You said at the outset of your conversation about Chinfo that you demurred at taking the job because you knew that you would be restrained somewhat. Was this actually realized? Did you feel restrained?

Adm. M.: I knew there were people who were against the business of publicizing the Navy and trying to improve the Navy image and some of them almost came out and told me that, others were violently opposed to really pushing the Navy story or the Navy image. But I didn't fall back. I just charged ahead and told those individuals that if they didn't like it the way I was doing it, tell it to the judge.

Q: Were you handicapped somewhat by SecNav and by the Secretary of Defense?

H. L. Miller # 7 - 448

Adm. M.: Definitely, because SecNav didn't want to sell nuclear power, and of course I went out there to prove that nuclear power was the way to go for the Navy. So there were two opposing heads there, and he was the boss.

Q: But you did it, nevertheless!

Adm. M.: I kept selling nuclear power and I kept feeding the information to Rickover to do the same - sell nuclear power.

Q: What about the comparison of the Navy's public relations set-up with that of the other services?

Adm. M.: The other services had more money assigned to their public affairs set-up. They had more people. But I don't know, I think we did just as good a job as they did, or better. We had a lot of kids in there who had many ideas and we put these ideas to work.

Q: You imply that in a broader sense the other services were more sold on the idea of public relations.

Adm. M.: That's right. I think there's a greater realization in the other services of the value of public affairs in the over-all business of selling their services to the great American public.

Q: Have they reaped advantage from this understanding of the need for public relations?

Adm. M.: I think so. All of them have. They realize that you've got to keep selling as long as you live, and this is in any business, in any of the armed services. You just have to do it, if you want to survive. You've got to tell the American public what you're doing with their dollars and why you think you're spending them in the right way. They want to know. They want to know if you're dumping the dollars down the drain. They want to know what good those dollars are doing, and unless you tell them, they don't know and they aren't going to be studying books to find out.

Q: In an over-all sense, then, in a total sense has the Navy's reticence in public relations worked to the detriment of our whole national defense picture?

Adm. M.: I certainly think so. We've got to do a better job of selling, and over the years it's been tough. We've improved gradually, but we've still got to do a better job.

Q: Why is this reticence built in to the Navy like that, in terms of public relations?

Adm. M.: I think probably because it hasn't been instilled into their over-all knowledge at the Naval Academy or in the ROTCs from whence they come around the country, or at the officer candidate schools. You've got to plant the seed right at the beginning.

Q: You fell into my hands there, Admiral. I think that you should do now what you can to implement the indoctrination of Naval Academy midshipmen in this area, and the value of it for the Navy as a service.

Adm. M.: Every man in our ROTCs, too, because we get the big chunk there, and in officer candidate schools.

I just want to add that during the time I was Chief of Information, I was President of the Industrial College for the Armed Forces Alumni Association from June of 1967 to June 1968. We had a wonderful year. We had luncheons once every quarter. We always got a prominent speaker, and we always had a sell-out at the luncheons. Our No. 1 alumnus, who was always there, was General Aurand, who is the father of our Admiral Pete Aurand in the Navy. General Aurand was a classmade of General Eisenhower from West Point. The last luncheon - and I know most of you recall that in June of 1968, there was a great deal of racial strife throughout the country, we got Mr. Puryear, who was the head of the Urban League, as our luncheon speaker. Now, this was a very touch-and-go situation because we didn't know what the reaction would be, but the big day arrived, there was a sell-out crowd for that last luncheon. Mr. Puryear did a great job.

It was interesting, several months before, he had been a man weighing about 220 or 230 pounds. He had a heart attack and he came down to about 160 or 170 pounds. He was in great shape. He was on a speaking tour that would almost kill any man, but he was watching his diet and pushing his whole program. It was a great success and I was delighted that he was the principal speaker at my last official function as President of the Alumni Association. Also, prior to that, in May of - April or May of 1966 - I was appointed to the Board of Control of the Naval Institute, a position that I have cherished ever since.

Q: What has that contributed to your knowledge and what has it contributed through you to the Navy service as a whole?

Adm. M.: As far as the Naval Institute contributing to my knowledge and intelligence, it's been a great relationship because I've read a few hundred articles submitted...

Q: Do you find that burdensome, the task of reading all these?

Adm. M.: Oh, no. It's really a great, stimulating experience all the way. There are articles on many, many different subjects, by many authors, all with different styles. It's really a treat to read these articles and render an opinion on whether or not they should be accepted or rejected or revised by the Naval Institute Proceedings. This has been quite an experience. And, of course, from my operational and other experiences in the Navy, I think I've been able to contribute to the Board of Control in various subject matters and various articles that came up during the time that I've been on the Board. It's been very enjoyable and very rewarding to me. I hope I've contributed somewhat to the Board of Control.

H. L. Miller # 8 - 453

Interview No. 8 with Rear Admiral Henry L. Miller, U. S. Navy

Place: U. S. Naval Institute, Annapolis, Maryland

Date: June 24, 1971

Subject: Biography

By: John T. Mason, Jr.

Q: You're going to talk about the Naval Air Test Center. You came there as commander in October of 1968 after your tour of duty as Chinfo.

Adm. M.: Yes, Sir, as a matter of interest there, at the Naval Air Test Center I have three jobs.

Q: This must have been an exhilarating command that you were approaching. Were you enthusiastic?

Adm. M.: Oh, yes, because I knew I was going to be dealing with a young crowd of test pilots and fleet pilots.

Q: Had you sought this command?

Adm. M.: No, it was given to me and I was very thankful that I got it. I'm in command of the Naval Air Test Center. I'm also commander, Fleet Air, Patuxent, and I'm the coordinator of test and evaluation of the Naval Air Systems Command.

The Naval Air Test Center is the largest and busiest air test center in the world. Normally, we have about six hundred projects that we're pursuing and we complete just about that number every year. We have a plant value of about two hundred and fifty million dollars. We employ twenty-two hundred and fifty civilians, three thousand Navy personnel in the test center, and there are about another three thousand in the fleet establishment. We do about a hundred million dollars worth of business a year, that includes fleet activities. Since October of 1968 when I reported aboard to the present time, I've flown in about fifteen to twenty types, jets, propeller driven planes, helicopters, and gliders.

Q: Would you perhaps tell me about some of these projects. You say you have over six hundred projects in a year. Give me an indication of what a project is.

Adm. M.: Here's an example of one of the projects. We took the British Harrier airplane, we put it through its paces, checking it for flying qualities and performance, suitability aboard our carriers and also our amphibious type carriers. We also checked the avionics of that airplane, and its stall characteristics. We fired all the ordnance that's supposed to be carried by that airplane, all the bombs. We do a complete and thorough testing of everything that's in that airplane.

Q: With the idea that if it passes the test we might be willing to purchase some of them from the British?

Adm. M.: That's correct. We've already contracted for eighteen Harriers and we have put four of those Harriers through their paces. It has performed very well. One crashed the other day in a rocket run. We do not know at this time what caused it. However, yesterday we did recover a couple of the wings and we're still searching for the engine and the rest of the airplane.

Q: With a project of that sort involving a plane from abroad, does the manufacturer have a representative there as a consultant?

Adm. M.: Yes. For any one of these airplanes the manufacturer has several representatives there to help us in the testing of that particular airplane or any changes that are made to that particular airplane. They help us in the over-all business of testing.

Q: Since you cite the Harrier, a British plane, as an illustration, does this imply that you search the world for new types and test them at Patuxent?

Adm. M.: No, we don't do the searching. We do the testing and evaluating of the airplanes or support equipment that is used in naval aviation. In the ground support equipment, it's a tremendous job because there are so many pieces of equipment that you use on the ground to support airplanes.

Q: Would you give me a second illustration of one of these six hundred projects?

Adm. M.: Yes, a simple one. Take the generator that we use in airplanes and other equipment. We have an electrical evaluation laboratory, probably one of the finest in the world. I think there's only one in the United States that's as good and Boeing Aircraft has it. We check that generator under all types of conditions, overloads, salt spray, sand, heat, cold, altitude. We give it a very thorough test and evaluation and report back to the particular company whether or not it has held up in accordance with specifications.

Q: Then, your staff there includes scientific minds. Are they all under Civil Service?

Adm. M.: Yes, they're all under Civil Service. They're very competent. They know their business. We have civilians, enlisted and officers in five test divisions. The first is the flight test division that checks the airplane for flying qualities and performance and for suitability aboard an aircraft carrier - that's for landings, catapulting off a carrier, and landings aboard a carrier.

Then we have a service test division which checks that airplane for reliability, for maintainability. Can the sailors maintain that airplane or do you have to take a whole bunch of factory representatives aboard to keep the planes flying? The service test division also checks for endurance. They'll keep the plane flying around the clock. The same for engines. They do a thorough job on aircraft engine testing.

I forgot to add for the flight test division that they have an automatic carrier landing system. In other words, the plane lands aboard automatically, without the pilot touching any of the controls, and it works. We have that system at Patuxent. We also have a catapult and arresting gear there.

Our other active service test division is weapons systems tests.

Q: May I ask one more question about the planes? How many on an average - how many types of planes - do you have under consideration at a given time?

Adm. M.: The biggest bag of different types of airplanes of any place in the world is at Patuxent. It numbers over one hundred different types and modifications of airplanes. So we really have quite a number to play with.

Q: And this is an average? This persists year after year?

Adm. M.: Yes, we have around a hundred planes all the time. In the weapons systems test, just as the name implies, we test the whole airplane - its avionics, its ordnance - the whole kit and caboodle. In that division we drop the bombs, we shoot the guns, we test out the electronics, the countermeasures, everything concerned with the total system in that airplane. It's very comprehensive and very complex.

To help out we have a computer services division that's really big business. They reduce the data that we obtain from tests and try to give it back to the pilot in real time. Another division to aid computer services and also the test pilot and testing in general is the technical support division.

The technical support division puts all the instrumentation into that airplane so that we will have accurate data when that plane is flying, performing its test. Additionally to get that data to the pilot in real time, so that he can make corrections in the air and complete the test in a shorter period of time. In order to do this and save money, we have certain points that we have to check in all of these tests. Perhaps on one flight we'll have five or ten points checked out. Now, if we can keep that plane in the air and complete another nine or ten points, you can see that it will save a lot of time and money. So we do have tankers that refuel planes in the air.

Q: How new is that technique?

Adm. M.: We've been tanking airplanes in the Navy for a long, long time. The Air Force has been doing the same thing. But in aviation testing we just started the tanker business last year. It's a real plus in the test and evaluation business. This saves Thousands and thousands of dollars and time.

Q: Admiral, after a given test flight with various pieces of ordnance to be checked out, how soon thereafter is a comprehensive report made on that flight?

Adm. M.: Depending on the amount of data that has been recorded and the complexity of that particular series of tests, we try to get as much of a read-out as we possibly can that day, the day of the test, or, at the latest, the next day. However, there are complex tests wherein data has to be analyzed and that may take a couple of weeks. All the tests of a new airplane or changes to the airplane are performed under the auspices of the Board of Inspection and Survey. The Board of Inspection and Survey is based in Washington, D. C. They have a unit at Patuxent for what we call Bis trials -

Board of Inspection and Survey trials - and this is the official test for any new airplane. The report is sent from the Board of Inspection and Survey at Patuxent to the Secretary of the Navy. I provide the directors of my test divisions as additional duty to the Head of the Board of Inspection and Survey at Patuxent. This is to provide him with all the technical knowledge he needs to complete his reports and submit them.

Q: Is it not a matter of policy to re-test the same things over and over again?

Adm. M.: Whenever a major change is made to an airplane wherein the flying qualities and performance may be affected, we have to check that to ensure that the plane will do the job with those changes in it.

Q: What sort of a factor is weather in conducting your tests?

Adm. M.: Remember that we like to have airspace that is guarded so that we don't have commercial airlines going through during the time of testing, and we like to have different kinds of weather. If you test under ideal conditions, you're not really putting the plane or the equipment through the maximum environment that you may encounter in any area of the world.

Q: This means you'd welcome hurricanes and that sort of thing?

Adm. M.: Just as a matter of interest, we have a weather plane, a big four-engined plane that was supposed to gather data in a hurricane. We tested three different types of airplanes in a hurricane - this was two years ago. That was a one time test. No, we don't march into a hurricane with these airplanes, but we do test in cloud formations, at altitude, cold, heat, all that. And if we're to do the complete job we'll normally put the airplane through the environmental hangar that the Air Force has at Eglin Field. That puts the airplane and engine through various degrees of cold, ice formations, rain, the whole works, and we pay the Air Force for the use of that facility.

Q: You must have a highly sophisticated unit of the Weather Bureau there?

Adm. M.: We have a unit of the Weather Bureau at Pax River. We also have the radar at Patuxent that provides the information to Washington National and all the broadcasting agencies in the Washington, D. C. area telling then what the weather is within two hundred miles of Washington.

Q: Since you've mentioned twice a relationship with the Air Force, do you want to talk about that phase of the operation?

Adm. M.: Since the Navy has more types of airplanes than the Air Force, we have a bigger test program. Let me give you just a short rundown on the Navy test facilities because that is part of my job as coordinator of test and evaluation for the Naval Air Systems Command.

At Patuxent we test the airplanes, we drop bombs, we shoot guns, we check out the electronics. At the Navy Missile Center at Point Mugu, California, they check out the missile firings from those airplanes. At the Navy Weapons Lab at China Lake, California, they do a lot of the research and development in weapons that are fired or dropped from a naval airplane. At Albuquerque, New Mexico, the Navy test facility checks the airplane for atomic bomb, or marries the A-bomb to the airplane, checks loading procedures, and bomb drops with dummy atomic bombs. At Indianapolis, Indiana, the avionics facility there does work in the Polaris and the Poseidon field. They are strictly in the avionics research and development business. The testing of their products normally comes to Patuxent. Trenton, New Jersey, is the Navy engine test facility. They take the engine when it comes from the contractor and put it through accelerated service tests on the ground, also altitude tests on the ground, humidity, sand, salt water, and other environmental tests. When that engine is ready to be put into an airplane, it's done by the manufacturer of the airplane and we test that engine at Patuxent in the air. Lakehurst, New Jersey, the Navy Test facility there checks out, tests, and evaluates catapults, changes to catapults, arresting gear and changes to arresting, and the barriers that we have aboard aircraft carriers to catch a plane that's lost its hook or is in trouble and any changes that were made to the barriers. The test facility at Lakehurst is a very unique arrangement.

Q: Is that the location of the lighter-than-air plant originally?

Adm. M.: Yes, the lighter-than-air was at Lakehurst and they're using those hangars now for helicopter squadrons that are based there.

Q: May I ask you one question in this area. You say that at Albuquerque they use dummy A-bombs, but at Patuxent when you test with bombs and ammunition, is it live?

Adm. M.: No, Sir. We use the dummy bombs. They're configured just like real live bombs. We aim them at a target and measure with our instrumentation how far it misses or whether it's a direct hit.

Q: Is there ever a test made with live bombs in order to be absolutely certain that the bomb itself and the mechanism is perfect?

Adm. M.: Oh, yes, they do that at China Lake, California.

The next test facility that the Navy has is in Philadelphia, and Philadelphia does material testing. They also do a great deal of work in the organization and procedures for the testing of ground support equipment. We do most all of the specific testing of ground support equipment at the Naval Air Test Center, Patuxent. Philadelphia used to be in the catapult and arresting gear test business, but the area there now is so restricted that most of their business has shifted to Lakehurst. They also had the turbine engine testing for ships, but all of that is now being moved to the engine test center at Trenton, New Jersey.

Then, just north of Philadelphia, we have the Naval Air Development Center at Warminister, Pennsylvania. They are in the development business, as the name implies, for many antisubmarine warfare equipments and for other things that the Navy has in all weapon systems. Now we go down to Panama City, Florida, where the Navy Ships Systems Command has a laboratory. Naval air has a helicopter unit at Panama City, a test laboratory, which does a lot of test and evaluation in mine warfare, the sweeping of mines by helicopters, the towing of this minesweeping gear by helicopters, the location of mines by helicopters, and other ship system testing that would be related to mine warfare or mine countermeasures.

Our test and evaluation unit at El Centro, California, tests parachutes. They also test ejection seats. They have airplanes there that actually throw a dummy out of the back seat of this particular airplane. Also they have experimental work going on out there in coordination with the U. S. Air Force of snatching parachutes out of the air with a grappling device from helicopters. I watched that last year. It's a very successful operation, and they've been doing this for a couple of years.

Our last evaluation facility is the Naval Air Station, Brunswich, Maine. We have an operation going on up there that drops sonar buoys, a certain number out of each lot to determine, percentagewise, how many are duds and how many are good ones. That, in general, takes in the twelve test and evaluation agencies that the naval air establishment has around the United States.

Q: Admiral, how does your command relate to these various test stations? Are they subordinate to you? How do you achieve a proper coordination in the conducting of all these various types of things?

Adm. M.: As the coordinator of test and evaluation for the Naval Air Systems Command, I sort of look over the shoulders of these twelve agencies that I have just named. I handle about 350 of the RDT & E aircraft that are allocated to these test facilities and weigh the air projects that are stacked up against those RDT & E airplanes. If the Naval Air Test Center at Patuxent isn't doing enough with a particular airplane, I will take it away from them and either give it to some other agency that can utilize it more, or put it out in the desert in storage or send it to the fleet. Over the past three years we have taken 112 RDT & E aircraft out of the inventory. Some of them were dogs that were just hanging around for some gent to fly once in a while. We took some of those airplanes, gave them to museums, and the rest we put out in the desert. They can be used later on, but the cost of keeping those 112 airplanes is an awful lot of money for the Naval Air Systems Command.

Q: You maintain an operational fleet of 350?

Adm. M.: I think today we're doing more test and evaluation with 112 less airplanes in the inventory than we did when we had close to 450. We're more efficient.

Q: How frequently do you add to this number with new types?

Adm. M.: When any new type comes into the system, it is tested and we add that particular airplane to the inventory. We may give one or two of those types to Patuxent, one or two to China Lake, one to Mugu, depending on the number of tests that that particular airplane has to go through. The test matrix schedules each particular item that has to be tested for a brand-new airplane. It's tremendous the number of items. For instance, Grumman, for particularly complicated airplanes, like the EA-6B, puts it through 19,000 avionics tests. The test and evaluation business is complicated and it's big business.

Q: That's one phase, I take it, that you have to be very close to, to test planes as they're coming out?

Adm. M.: That's right. At the time a contract is signed with a manufacturer, as the coordinator of test and evaluation, I call a conference of all interested agencies, including the manufacturer, to set up a test plan for that particular airplane. Now, that plane is probably two years away and the test plan at that initial meeting is not going to be the master plan when that plane comes off the line. But, we firm up the outline of the test plan so that we'll see what additional facilities we're going to need two years hence for the completion of the test of that airplane. We may have to get some new military construction, some new instrumentation, better range facilities, all of this. We start right from the time the contract is signed and begin our planning. Now, for any airplane or any piece of equipment we take a look at the requirements that will be needed for the test and evaluation ofthat airplane, and, as the coordinator of test and evaluation, I weigh the resources that are sitting at the Naval Air Test Center, Mugu, China Lake, and all these facilities, against the requirements. Then, I make out a schedule of sending that airplane to those particular test centers, or test areas, to do the job in the shortest possible time and for the least amount of money. So, you might say, as the coordinator of test and evaluation, the big job is to bring people together to look at the problem, make up a test plan or a plan of action, and assign action items to the appropriate agencies. Also, a milestone schedule to ensure that this is going to be done at a particular time.

As an example of that, we are putting in a tactical support center in 1972 at Adak, Alaska. This is for antisubmarine warfare. Last week I sent a message to various agencies that we were going to have a meeting at Adak, the subject was the installation of the tactical support center in 1972, and I would like to have these representatives from the following commands there: ASW, Pacific; Naval Air Force, Pacific; Fairwings, Pacific; people who were going to be using this system at Adak; the Naval Communications Command; representatives from the Naval Electronics Systems Command; representatives from NavAir; my own NATC; and the antisubmarine warfare program manager's office in the Chief of Naval Material Command.

Also the people in the SOSUS system and the Naval Engineering Command Office that will be putting in this installation. They all congregated at Adak, and we briefed all of those representatives on what the tactical support system was. We showed them slides and we had a movie. We also described the concept - how every piece of equipment worked. Then we told them that this would be the first installation of a modular concept, ten aluminum modules that would be holding this equipment. When we put them all together, we have a tactical support center.

We also told them what their particular commands would be responsible for. Then we went to the site - the agreed-to site - at Adak and saw where the installation was going. We came away from that meeting knowing full well that the schedule was going to be met, and the people responsible would be sending a message every month giving us their percent completions for the particular items that they had. I think that it's the only way to do the job - getting these people together.

Q: Admiral, how long did it take to assemble a project like that?

Adm. M.: It took one small dispatch telling them the agenda and what we wanted, and the representatives that we had to have there at this meeting.

Q: The message had to originate with you and your advisers, and the total scope of the project you had in mind? And then it was implemented by whom?

Adm. M.: That's right. The message was implemented by the numbers of people who came from those various commands to listen to our concept and to our plan of action and agree to all these action items that their agencies would be responsible for. I thought it worked very smoothly.

Q: May I ask another question, which I think is of some interest? How long did it take you to get on top of a job like this? It's so complicated and it has all these component parts.

Adm. M.: The coordinator of test and evaluation for the Naval Air Systems Command is only three years old. It was started in February of 1968.

Q: So you created the job?

Adm. M.: No, I didn't create it. It was there waiting for me when I arrived in October of 1968 at Patuxent, and it was up to me and the staff that they gave me to get the commanding officers and whoever else they wanted to bring along from the twelve agencies that I listed, Naval Air Test Center, Mugu, etc., to come to the initial meeting in December of 1968 at Patuxent River, Maryland, and be briefed on the job that I was supposed to do as the coordinator of test and evaluation. And, as you can well imagine, when you call twelve independent agencies in and tell them that you have a job to coordinate them, a lot of fur is likely to fly. Everybody came to that first prayer meeting with their .45s cocked and aimed right at me. But we went over the twenty-one tasks that I had in the instructions from the Naval Air Systems Command and I told those twelve agencies that if they didn't like the wording, let's change it to get agreement and establish procedures that were acceptable to everyone.

Well, the first day was pretty rough. We didn't get through the twenty-one tasks that we had. We discussed, perhaps, the first fifteen. But, at the end of the day, everybody there was absolutely convinced that coordination had to be done, that we were remiss in never having done it before on a scale that NavAir wanted. So after we completed describing the twenty-one tasks the second day, we split into committees. They revised the twenty-one tasks. Everybody was happy with it. We went home and we set the coordinator of test and evaluation into action.

Q: Now you've been there for a few years. Have you been able to witness the positive results of this new effort at coordination?

Adm. M.: Oh, absolutely. We had subsequent meetings about every six months. The second meeting was at Albuquerque. The third meeting with all these agencies was at Point Mugu.

Q: It was a rotating kind of a thing?

Adm. M.: Yes. The sixth meeting was at China Lake. And it was very interesting because other agencies heard about this - other Navy agencies from Electronics Systems Command, Ships Systems Command, etc. So, I put them on as an information addressee, and said you are invited to attend. It's interesting to note that at every one of those meetings we had twenty-three agencies show up, and I'm responsible for only twelve.

Q: They were learning how it's done!

Adm. M.: They were learning and they were most enthusiastic, and they wanted to be cut in on what we were doing in the coordination business.

Q: How many of them have gone and done likewise?

Adm. M.: None. None of those others. I think some would like to but it had to start at the top and no one has started at the top yet in coordination of test and evaluation in the other systems commands. I believe they are now going to start a T & E coordinator in the Office of the Secretary of Defense.

Q: It was a great adventure and it requires a rather unique person, doesn't it? I mean you brought to the job a vast knowledge from your career, but you also brought the ability to work with people, which is the important thing, I would think, in coordinating.

Adm. M.: One part of it that was in my favor was that I knew quite a number of these commanding officers and quite a number of officers subordinate to them who worked for them and who came to that original meeting. But I believe that one of the reasons they accepted it was because they saw that it was needed and we didn't try to shove it down their throats. We said, here, you revise, you help us revise the instructions that will be acceptable to you. And we have just as strong - or maybe a stronger - set of instructions when they'd finished that we did originally.

Q: They saw it actually at that December meeting, didn't they, when they had to wrestle the twenty-one points?

Adm. M.: They did. We'll have another meeting on the 24th and the 25th of August of this year.

Q: They have continued on a six-month basis?

H. L. Miller # 8 - 474

Adm. M.: No, Sir, we haven't. The last meeting was almost a year ago - October of 1970. And one of the reasons that we didn't have it was because of travel and money.

Q: Has there been a fair degree of permanency in the command of these various test centers?

Adm. M.: No, you'll find that they'll be shifting commanding officers right along, so we have to stay in touch and keep up with who's in power at that particular time.

Q: Do you have any one of them in mind for training to succeed you?

Adm. M.: No. My relief will be coming from Commander-in-Chief, Pacific Fleet, staff, and he's never been in the business before, but that's the way the Navy does things.

Q: Tell me, Sir, why doesn't it make sense when you cooperate with the Air Force to just have a kind of reciprocal system, rather than to have to pay for using their facilities.

Adm. M.: Well, you see, at the present time the Naval Air Test Center is under Navy-industrial funding. In other words, you come to me and you have a piece of equipment you want tested. I'll say, great, I can test it, but where is the money because all this is costing me money and I have to account for every dollar that the

Naval Air Systems Command gives me today. The Air Force is going into the same kind of funding, industrial funding, so if you don't have the dollars you don't get the work done.

Q: Even though you're all under the Department of Defense and working toward the same end?

Adm. M.: We have to account for all the dollars given to us and we can't give them away.

Q: Do you have at Patuxent a wind-tunnel installation, or is that something...?

Adm. M.: We have a small wind tunnel for models, but not for any big airplane. We have some very unique facilities. We have, as I mentioned, catapults, arresting gear, the automatic carrier landing system, a very modern electrical evaluation laboratory, the only prototype tactical support center in the Navy, the only - at this writing - electro-optical range in the country, and other testing facilities for electronic countermeasures. We have just about everything to cover the field of testing.

Q: How do you tie in with the needs of the various fleet commands?

Adm. M.: We tie into fleet commands through two sources: directly talking to that fleet command when we have to check out that aircraft carrier that belongs to him or any of the airplanes that are going aboard that particular carrier. That's Number One - directly with him, and/or we do it through the Commander, Operational Test and Evaluation Force at Norfolk, Virginia. He does the operations evaluation for the tactics of a particular airplane. He does the tactics.

Q: That's the ComOpTevFor outfit, isn't it?

Adm. M.: Commander, Operational Test and Evaluation Force. He's supposed to work out the tactics for that particular airplane. Will it perform all these jobs in the tactical environment where it's supposed to be? We also certify the carrier deck, catapults, etc.

Let me give you an example of a carrier that's been in a Navy yard for a year. Take the Enterprise. The Enterprise was in the Newport News Shipbuilding and Dry Dock for about a year getting a new core for its nuclear reactor, many changes made, and new things into the ship. The Enterprise came out of the yard and they had a specific period of time that the ship, including all equipments, had to be checked out before they proceeded to the West Coast for deployment to Vietnam. This is this year, 1971.

The carrier came out of the yard. Their first exercise, a check-out period of all the equipments, was curtailed due to bad weather. It seemed as though nothing worked when they came out of Newport News yard. They did find hundreds of items that they had to correct right now back in the yard before the last and final check-out period before proceeding to the West Coast. Remember, they were on a definite schedule that they had to make. So the last period came when the Norfolk area was just solid overcast, miserable weather. They told the Enterprise to head for Bermuda. I had sent about a hundred officers and men and civilians to the Enterprise at Norfolk before she sailed - they got aboard. I also sent helicopters and other equipment to Norfolk, but I flew the airplanes from Patuxent to Bermuda. They didn't have any starting equipment at Bermuda for my fighters, so they intercepted the Enterprise 120 miles southwest of Bermuda and landed aboard. Nothing worked - the radios, the radars - there was one little port--able radio on the landing signal platform that worked to talk to the pilots. That was all.

That was on Friday. Sunday by four o-clock the Enterprise was supposed to put on 30 knots and head for the West Coast. So the electronics people and my people worked all day Friday. They started making passes. The automatic carrier landing system didn't work. They had to make adjustments, and this was pretty hairy, you know, when you're coming down that glide slope and there's a light staring you in the face and you've got to get out of there. But everybody turned to and worked around the clock. My people flew and helped them make adjustments. On Saturday afternoon, after many passes and landings, and whatnot, they got the automatic carrier landing system adjusted, radars were working, radios were working, but people still kept checking everything. Everybody got up early Sunday morning and the day began. They made fifteen passes in a row, hands off the controls, on the automatic carrier landing system. By Sunday afternoon, we had completed approximately 120 approaches, quite a few landings, and everything was checked out thoroughly. During that Sunday they were helicoptering and COD-ing my people over to Bermuda. At four o'clock they catapulted the rest of my fighters off for Patuxent and we had the transports bring my people back from Bermuda. And the Enterprise was thoroughly checked out before she left for the West Coast.

Q: I hope her skipper gave you a "well done!"

Adm. M.: He was selected for admiral. I think if he'd arrived on the West Coast without all that he'd have been a seaman, because he had a tough schedule to keep on the West Coast and AirPac told him to be darned sure to get that ship checked out before he sailed. This was an example of how we try to give them the best service in the quickest time possible. We did the same for the <u>Midway</u> when the Midway came out of the yard on the West Coast. I sent about ninety people out there, and all the types of planes that were supposed to fly off that deck. We checked out everything, the catapults, the arresting gear, radars, name it, and we did it. And we did it in about one-third less time than they anticipated.

Q: It's certainly a new concept, isn't it?

Adm. M.: Well, there's an awful lot to be done when a ship comes out of a Navy yard. That's a good spot for the Naval Ships Systems Command to start thinking about a test and evaluation coordinator, because there are hundreds and hundreds of items that have to be checked.

Q: Admiral, there's one area that you haven't touched on at all and I think it's intensely interesting. You told me once that test pilots were a very special breed and most of them, seemingly, were prima donnas. Do you want to talk about the test pilot?

Adm. M.: Actually, the key to all of this business is the test pilot. He is the key to the success of the Naval Air Test Center.

H. L. Miller # 8 - 480

The whole test and evaluation business depends on the Navy test pilot, the Navy flight officer who goes through the test pilot school, and the civilian engineer who gets the academic course at the test pilot school, plus quite a few rear-seat flights. Now, when you take the integrated team of the Navy flight officer, the Navy test pilot, and the civilian engineer in the test and evaluation of these airplanes, you've got the finest, the most talented group that you could ever get together. They know what they're doing.

Q: What is the average age of a test pilot?

Adm. M.: The average age is around, I'd say, thirty-one years. The test pilot school trains all the Navy and Marine Corps test pilots, they train all the Army test pilots, they train all the U. S. Air Force helicopter test pilots. We have the only helicopter test pilot course in the United States. And we train foreign test pilots. This last class had a Canadian, a Japanese, an Italian, a U.K. and a German, but the German test pilot flunked out but we have another one in the next class.

Q: In the case of these international fellows, their expenses are paid by their respective governments?

H. L. Miller # 8 - 481

Adm. M.: Their expenses are paid by the governments. In certain instances it may be that the U. S. pays through the military assistance program. We have more requests than we can honor from foreign governments and our own aircraft industry, who would like us to train more of their test pilots.

Q: You have certain basic requirements for the applicant, do you not?

Adm. M.: Oh, yes. He has to have a degree, he has to have so many hours in the air, and then we give them eight solid months of awfully hard work - about sixteen hours a day, six days a week. When that eight months are finished, that whole class has a great big bash. But it's interesting - let me tell you, the class that graduated in June, the 11th of June, they took off the next day on their field trip to the test centers in Italy, France, Germany, Sweden, and the test pilot school and test center at Boscombe Downs in the UK. So they really had a wonderful tour.

Q: How many men were involved in the class?

Adm. M.: About twenty-five. There are more than that if you include the engineers taking the academic course. We encourage all of our engineers at the Test Center to enroll in that academic course. It's very good.

Q: Who are the instructors?

Adm. M.: The instructors are former test pilots, Navy and Marine Corps, and we have an exchange instructor with the UK who have gone through the test pilot school and have had at least one tour, or part of a tour doing test pilot work in a flight test division, or a service test division, or weapons system test. Normally we pick the top ones as instructors in the test pilot school.

Our test pilot school, I believe, is the best in the world. It has a terrific reputation, and we now give an award for the Number One Navy test pilot of the year, the Number One Navy flight officer of the year and, reaching down to the civilian engineer, the Number One of his class for the particular year. It's presented to them at the Tail Hook Reunion in Las Vegas, Nevada. It's also presented at the annual test pilot school reunion, and I'm trying to get that also presented at the annual meeting of the Society of Engineering Test Pilots and also the Navy League of the United States, to give them the recognition that they deserve.

The annual reunion of the graduates of the test pilot school, is quite an affair at Patuxent. About 1,450 pilots have graduated from our test pilot school, and about 800 show up from all over the world to attend that annual reunion. It used to be two or three days of just raising hell and drinking, but now we have the golf tournament on Friday; Saturday, of all things, we have a symposium. This last one that we had in May, I thought that probably at 9:30 in the morning, fifty would show up for the start of the symposium, simply because the night before they all got together at various places and talked over old times and did an awful lot of drinking. But at 9:30 in the morning the Crow's Nest at the Officers' Club was standing room only when I opened up the meeting.

Our first presentation was a brief on the F-14 aircraft and movies of the first flight and then the subsequent flight where it crashed, including the pilot's punching out. Of course, the two pilots from Grumman gave that presentation. The next presentation was on the British Harrier. That was just before lunch, and following the brief of the Harrier, we said, now, if you'll step outside the Officers' Club it's waiting for you in midair. It was right there and went through its paces, did its dance, and everything else. They got a big kick out of that.

Then I had the Chief of Naval Operations, Admiral Zumwalt, as the luncheon speaker and it was standing room only in the Officers' Club, the big dining room. Following that, I had a former test pilot school graduate from NASA who gave a briefing on the super critical wing, and, to climax the whole business, I had Captain

Jim Lovell go through the story of Apollo 13. He had everybody sitting on the edge of their seats - one crisis after another on Apollo 13, it seemed almost to the point where people were almost ready to say, "Jim, did you ever get back alive?" It was terrific. That night was the big affair; the dinner and movies of aviation from years back. About sixty people wanted the F-14 brief and movie shown again after four o'clock because they'd missed it. So, it's a good example that if you have a darned good symposium people are going to come.

Q: What caused you to structure these sessions in contrast to just a general get-together?

Adm. M.: Well, the first year I was there in 1969, we had what I thought was an interesting program talking about the S-3 that we had contracted for with Lockheed, the F-14 airplane, and some other things. It wasn't very well prepared and we didn't get much of a turn-out. I started to think about it and I said, Good Lord, we have the most interesting projects in the world. You could take any number of them and put on a symposium that would be the most interesting one that you could ever put together.

So, the next year I said, first of all we've got to be able to take care of a crowd, so get a circus tent and let's attach it right on the Officers' Club to accomodate people. Next, let's get a symposium that will knock'em over dead and they're going to come listen. We had a pretty good one in 1970, including Pete Conrad and Al Bean - Captains Pete Conrad and Al Bean - from Apollo XII. They gave a beautiful rundown on Apollo 12.

This year we cranked up the symposium and everybody came. It was really standing room only all day. Next year, I've already got Al Shepherd for Apollo XIV, he's going to put that on.

Patuxent really is the home of the astronauts and this year we presented the astronauts with the test pilots school Hall of Fame plaque. And we are going to have a test pilot school Hall of Fame because we have some very famous test pilots. In industry Navy test pilots and some still in the Navy are terrific. My deputy, Captain George Watkins, has 10,000 hours in mostly single-engine planes. He's a former Navy test pilot. He's perhaps the Number One pilot in the world today. We have some very famous names in the whole space program who are graduates of the test pilot school. The first one was Captain Alan Shepherd. Al was recently selected for admiral. He was the first man in space and in command of the third team on the Moon in Apollo XIV. He was in class 5 of TPS (Test Pilot School).

Next, we had Colonel John Glenn, U. S. Marine Corps.

Q: Was he not the first man to be in orbit?

Adm. M.: Yes, he was the first man to be in orbit, that was in Mercury III. He was in class 12 of the test pilot school. Then we had Commander Scott Carpenter, Mercury IV. He was the class of 13 of TPS. We had Captain Dick Gordon, who was in Gemini XI and Apollo XII. He was in the class of 18 at TPS.

Another real old-timer in space is Captain Walter Schirra. He was in Mercury V, Gemini VI, Apollo VII. He was in class 20 of TPS.

Q: He's a son-in-law of Admiral Holloway.

Adm. M.: That's right. Then we had Captain Charles P. Conrad. Pete was in Gemini V and XI and Apollo XII. He was in the second team that landed on the Moon. He was also of the class of 20.

Then we had Captain Jim Lovell. Jim has more time in space than anybody. He was in Gemini VII and XII. He was in Apollo VIII and XIII. His Apollo XIII flight was really one crisis after another.

Q: The whole world was cognizant of that!

Adm. M.: He was also the class of '20. Then we had Captain John Young, who was in Gemini V and XI and Apollo X. He was the class of '23, and John Young was selected to command Apollo XV. No, it must be XVI because Apollo XV is the Air Force team.

Then we have Captain Allan Bean. He was in Apollo XII, class of '26 at TPS. Mr. Vance Brand. He's a Lockheed engineer. He was in our test pilot school, class of '33. He's a back-up pilot for Apollo XV. We had Lieutenant John Bull, who is the class of '36. He was in the astronaut program but was dropped for medical reasons. I think his eyes went bad.

We had one Captain Clifton Williams, U. S. Marine Corps, of the class of '38. He didn't get into space. He was killed in a T-38 crash.

But those are some of our famous grads of the test pilot school, and I might say very famous.

Also at Patuxent is the unique Squadron VXN-8. It's the oceanographic squadron. They fly laboratory equipment and other very precise equipment in measuring the thickness of the Arctic ice, photographing ice floes and open areas, and keeping track of what's going on in those ice floes. They also measure temperatures. I think you'll recall that when that tanker, the Manhattan, went through the straits there to get to Prudoe Bay, VXN-8 played a big part there in telling the Manhattan which areas were open and which were closed. VXN-8 also measures the temperature of various water layers in the Atlantic for ASW.

Q: Quite an accomplished crew I would think.

Adm. M.: Yes, and then they do magnetic surveys all over the world. This is very interesting because their airplanes are chock full of scientific gear. They do the geomagnetic surveys all over the world, they put these in a central computer system for use by our scientists and engineers in the United States, and they send that information that is peculiar to that country to them. They have never been refused landing rights or short stays at any one of these free countries around the world. And it's interesting because looking at the airplane you'd say, sure enough, that must be a spy plane, but everybody knows it's above board and they're doing a great job.

Q: Do they cooperate with the Iron Curtain countries at all?

Adm. M.: We have never done it for the Iron Curtain countries, always in the Free World. But I think it's probably a pretty good idea to mention that now since we've opened up a little, and technology is a good way to open up relations with anybody. That's why, as a result of this field trip of our test pilot graduates this year, we may propose to either invite the Russian test pilot school over next year or have them invite us.

Q: Well, we have as a precedent the international geophysical year, when there was this cooperation among scientists everywhere.

Adm. M.: Yes, and we still have the greatest cooperation in the world between the Russians and the United States in the Antarctic. We're still very close together down there and exchange information.

Finally, at Patuxent I have quite a number of patrol planes, the P-3 series of planes, the four-engined Lockheed Orion, and we do an awful lot of antisubmarine warfare flying out of Patuxent every day of the year. We also have the training squadron for the VP pilots transitioning to the P-3s. So, it's a pretty going concern and a very busy place. And I believe that probably in another year, because of the tactical support center there and because of the expertise that we have in antisubmarine warfare in command and control procedures, that perhaps before too long you'll find the Test Center at Patuxent River being a center for command and control in certain aspects of antisubmarine warfare. Why? The people. We've got a gang of young engineers, enlisted men, and officers who, you might say, have taken the ball away from industry and other

Navy facilities in antisubmarine warfare. And nobody can get it back. It's right there now. And next year they'll put in four tactical support centers at various places. That's fourteen million dollars. So if you get the tigers and put them to work you get the business. They will eventually put together about 14 Tactical Support Centers for the Navy around the world.

Q: Thank you very much for a fascinating chapter.

Interview No. 9 with Rear Admiral Henry L. Miller, U. S. Navy

Place: U. S. Naval Institute, Annapolis, Maryland

Date: Tuesday morning, 27 April 1971

Subject: The White House Youth Conference, Estes Park, Colorado

By: John T. Mason, Jr.

Q: It's wonderful to see you this morning, Admiral.

Adm. M.: Thank you.

Q: You're going to tell me, and I've been anticipating this since yesterday, about the White House Conference on Youth which you attended last week at Estes Park in Colorado. First, would you tell me about this conference, which is scheduled to be held every ten years. What is its objective and how was it set up?

Adm. M.: The White House Conference on Youth was started in the year 1909 and was set up then for every ten years, but I think this is going to change because ten years is too long a span on all the major issues of the day.

Q: As a matter of fact, the youth discussed that, did they not, and wanted it every four years?

Adm. M.: Some proposals were made for every year and every two years, but really the conference is called to examine the major issues of the day confronting youth. And also to find new approaches to the solution of these problem areas and to open up channels of communication between youth and adults. Youth also wants more of a say-so in the decision-making process of the government. The conference this year examined and made recommendations on the ten major issues or problem areas that they feel are confronting the youth of the nation today.

The first one is foreign relations. The next is environment. The third is race and minority-group relations. The fourth is drugs. The fifth is education. The sixth is the draft, national service, and its alternatives. The seventh is poverty. The eighth is legal rights and justice. The ninth is economy and employment, And the tenth is values, ethics, and culture.

Q: That certainly is all-inclusive, isn't it? Tell me how you happened to go, Sir. Were you representing the Navy or what were you representing?

Adm. M.: No, I was just representing H. L. Miller. I was invited principally because one of my former aides is the director of the staff of the White House Conference on Youth.

Q: Hess?

Adm. M.: No, that was Mr. Hanzlik. Mr. Hess is the over-all chairman of the White House Conference on Children and the White House Conference on Youth. Mr. Hanzlik is the director of the staff, and over the past year we've talked about various aspects of the Conference on Youth and I've helped them in several details. So, I was issued an invitation to attend as a delegate and I was very happy to participate in this conference.

Q: How many delegates were there, to get the picture of the conference?

Adm. M.: There were 1,500 participants, 1,000 youth and 500 adults. There were additionally, 100 invited from foreign countries to participate as delegates. Additionally, on top of all that, there were observers who were invited from the 50 states. Normally there were representatives from the governor of each state, and then there were some from various committees of the various states.

Q: How were these delegates selected?

Adm. M.: The delegates are selected in accordance with certain criteria set up: 1) the population of the country; 2) the geography, they had delegates from business, education, the ghetto, all ethnic groups were represented.

Q: Do they propose their own delegates? Do they elect their delegates? Or is it done differently in different areas?

Adm. M.: Certain delegates are invited by a special committee. Others are nominated by the individual states. Certain ones are selected from the armed forces, not on the upper-levels, but on the lower rates and ranks. Each delegate of a youth group is sponsored by a business or an institution that pays their travel costs. The board and room is paid for by the government. Adults pay their own way. They had a very fine cross section of the population, age groups, sex, work force, geography, and education, plus ethnic groups consisting of the blacks, the Chicanos, Cubans, Porto Ricans, Polish, Italian, Greek, Japanese, Hawaiian, and Asian. They had quite a cross section.

Q: What about the foreign representatives, did they come from the Western World, or were they worldwide?

Adm. M.: The foreign representatives were worldwide, representing most of the leading countries of the world.

Q: Did our government finance their transportation?

H. L. Miller # 9 - 495

Adm. M.: I really don't know, but I suspect that the governments paid their own way as far as transportation is concerned.

Q: Well, that's the delegate set-up. How were the speakers chosen? Some of them came from the administration. I know Richardson was there.

Adm. M.: As a matter of fact, Mr. Richardson opened the conference. However, there were no speakers that were chosen by the administration. The speakers who represented the task forces were nominated by the respective task forces, so the speakers were talking for the task force and made the recommendations that were accepted and submitted by each task force.

Q: One question, as kind of a footnote on the locale, Estes Park. I merely ask this because one of the carping critics whom I saw quoted said that the administration wanted it as far away as possible from Washington. What was the reason for Estes Park in the Colorado mountains?

Adm. M.: The idea was to get away from the telephones, get away from the night life, get away from the busy Washington area, where people have more free time to think and to do the job. As a matter of fact, I said that it was a God-send that we went up there because we worked long hours. There were no distractions. For instance, we normally worked till 10:30 every night, would go back to our respective cabins and probably work till 12 or one o'clock in the morning there, re-writing a certain recommendation, or preambles that we wanted to submit.

Q: It sounded like an ideal set-up to me, isolated.

Adm. M.: It was and although some people didn't like to walk, it was 7,700 feet of altitude, it snowed three feet in four and a half days, and actually it took quite a bit of walking to get around some of those slopes. However, even though it was a little bit strenuous, I didn't see any heart cases up there. There should have been. There was a lot of gasping for breath in some of those walks. However, I think I lost about two inches off my waistline, and I was very happy about that. But it was, I think, an ideal set-up even with the snow. We ate the same food, and people said the food wasn't so good, but I said it was OK, and we didn't go up there to eat. We had the exercise between sessions, we had to walk, and this was good for us. It sharpened us up a bit.

Q: I would think it would. Stimulate the mind to do that. Now, about the conference itself, the gutsy part of the conference: What task were you assigned to?

Adm. M.: I was assigned to the task group on drugs, and my particular subcommittee on drugs was concerned with drug abuse in the armed forces.

Q: Is this an assignment you sought, or were you simply arbitrarily assigned?

Adm. M.: No, I was assigned to it because I had taken quite an active interest in the drug problem in St. Mary's County and at the Naval Air Test Center at Patuxent, Maryland. We held workshops on the drug problem. We held seminars. I got people down from Washington to lecture and talk and present movies and slides on the drug problem, nationwide. Naturally, of course, in the armed forces we're watching it and I was particularly interested in this area.

Q: You were well qualified, then, to be a leading member of that task force.

Adm. M.: Well, prior to going, of course, I called the Navy and I wanted the latest information on what they were doing on the drug problem. I also asked the Navy to get me a paper from the Army, the Air Force, and the Marine Corps, which they did. Following that, I called Admiral Mack in the Department of Defense - the over-all drug business came directly under his office - and I was particularly fortunate in getting his latest testimony that he had made two days previously on the Hill. I also received a copy of the 27 recommendations made by the special task group of the Department of Defense. It was their report that was approved by the Department of Defense last October for implementation by the services. So, you might say, I arrived with all the latest information on what the armed services were doing in the drug abuse problem, and it was very interesting because when the whole session was over, the armed services were far ahead of the rest of the nation in dealing with the drug abuse problem.

Q: Far ahead of cities and what-have-you?

Adm. M.: Far ahead of everybody. So little is known, nationwide, on the drug problem that you might say we should have a national program on information and education regarding drugs.

Q: Tell me about the discussion within your task group on this whole area.

Adm. M.: In our task group, as far as the drug problem is concerned, there were several aspects of it. For instance, in the problems of drug abuse, the consequences of the use of drugs, the treatment and rehabilitation of people who have taken drugs, law enforcement, education and prevention, telling the world all the things that are bad about drugs, and some of the preventive measures, research in finding out about the effects of drugs, the nonchemical alternatives, that is, talk groups or people who apply psychology to the problem and get people doing other things besides taking drugs...

Q: You mean a counterpart to the alcoholics...?

Adm. M.: Yes, and the marijuana dilemma. And marijuana got a big play all the way through the conference. As a matter of fact, the conference recommended that marijuana be legalized in the country today.

Q: What was the thinking back of that recommendation?

Adm. M.: There were a great many arguments that were posed on both sides, for and against marijuana, and the black caucus told us that they were against the legalization of marijuana. Why? Because they said, they had enough problems in the ghetto today without introducing marijuana. However, on the other side of the fence, parallels were given from prohibition days, when alcohol was not legalized, or beer - the Mafia got a headstart during prohibition days. They made billions on crime and selling illegal whiskey, setting up quite an organization. Then we legalized beer, we legalized whiskey of all different brands. We had standards that were set up and controlled that we never did have before. There were no purity standards as far as whiskey was concerned. The same applies to marijuana. There are various brands of marijuana that are being smoked today. Believe it or not, in certain areas of the country, in middle class and rich people's habits, they are smoking marijuana just like taking a highball before dinner. It's standard practice in quite a few areas today.

The conference felt that if marijuana was legalized, number one, it would be controlled. There would be one standard of purity. It would be controlled like whiskey is today, as far as age groups drinking it or, as far as marijuana, smoking it. They could devote all the money and the people that are now directed toward arresting or punishing people who are smoking marijuana, to the effort necessary in the hard drugs, such as heroin. Very little heroin is intercepted in this country today, and one of the reasons is because they just do not have the money or the people to put on the job, and they feel that in our courts today there are thousands of cases of marijuana-users who are still being held in jail because there isn't sufficient time or judges to go ahead and prosecute these people, while the heroin-pushers, the sellers, the distributers are all getting away, scot-free. The task force felt that all this effort could be devoted to the hard drugs that have to be arrested in this country.

Q: Did you wrestle with the testimony of certain people who say that the use of marijuana leads to the use of hard drugs? That, inevitably, this is the development?

Adm. M.: Yes, and that argument was posed by a few, but the facts don't back that statement up. Nobody could prove that marijuana led to hard drugs. There were many papers submitted by knowledgeable people and research groups on that particular subject, but nobody could prove that the smoking of marijuana led to the use of harder drugs.

Q: That's interesting. Did you deal with the motivation for drug-taking as a whole?

Adm. M.: Yes, we did. There are many reasons for taking drugs that were presented at the conference. One was the pressures of the times, the pressures in given environments, like, say, graduating from high school and going to college, finding that it was much more difficult to get the marks and pass the test that they get in college than, say, in high school. It was an easier road in high school. Or the pressures that are suddenly confronted - or confront a young man entering the armed services. He's not used to that kind of life. Or the pressures that are met in shifting from a protected life in the home to doing a particularly difficult job on the outside. And the frustrations that youth is encountering in various areas, certain issues that are confronting them today, certain laws passed by the administration, all these. There are many reasons why people turn to drugs. Boredom is another one.

Q: Did they also consider the fact that we're blanketed by the media with all sorts of news about impending doom, and that kind of thing?

Adm. M.: Yes, that's part of the issues of the day plus the war in Vietnam. And, today one of the areas of major concern, as far as drug abuse, is South Vietnam because it's there for the asking, it's very cheap. It's easy to get on every street corner, and a great many of our armed services personnel are getting drugs and trying them out in South Vietnam, marijuana and others. So, this is a problem of major concern in the armed services today.

Q: What does that do to the discipline of the armed services? I mean the use of drugs?

Adm. M.: Well, the use of drugs slows up an individual's thinking and, depending on what the drug is, it's difficult to ascertain whether or not he will carry out his orders. However, there are just a few cases of individuals in South Vietnam who, you might say, were incapacitated to do their job, but no mission was ever unsuccessful because of drugs.

Q: That's an interesting point. It is possible to discern when a chap has taken drugs and is under the influence of drugs. Is he then culled out from the battalion or what-have-you if there's an operation under way?

Adm. M.: I don't know, to tell you the truth, what the Army does in South Vietnam when they find that one of the men has smoked pot or taken some other drug. In the armed forces, in general, of course, right now we're taking active measures to look at the drug problem and see what we can do to help those in the service who have taken drugs to divorce themselves from the habit and do some rehabilitation of the individual.

Q: Was this question of rehabilitation considered seriously by your task group?

Adm. M.: Absolutely.

Q: Are there any existing methods which they approve of?

Adm. M.: There are two I'd say large institutions in the country that are doing something about rehabilitation. The one in Lexington, Kentucky, and the other in New York City. They do have the Odyssey House in New York City and several other places, wherein the drug addict can come in and talk to other drug addicts there. He lives with them, he works in the house, he is asked to participate in various programs like art, decoration, things like that, and they have rehabilitated quite a number of drug addicts. I'm speaking there of the hard drugs, heroin people.

Q: And that, of course, is predicated on his willingness to cooperate, isn't it?

Adm. M.: Oh, yes. There really is no solution to the problem unless the particular individual is willing to cooperate and participate in this program. One of the very fine individuals that we had as an adviser on the task force was Mr. Jim Murphy from Odyssey House in New York City. Jim works at Odyssey House. He started taking drugs when he was 13 years of age, and he kept taking drugs until he was 24. He is rehabilitated now and is an active worker in the drug abuse program to save others. He's quite an individual.

Q: Is it considered a permanent cure, a permanent release from drugs, once one has been an addict, or is it always a possibility to fall over again?

Adm. M.: Oh, there is always a possibility of falling into it again, just like an alcoholic. However, once he has been rehabilitated and gets off the drug habit, it's pretty easy to stay off it as long as an individual keeps busy and has a good objective in life. But once he starts taking it again, he goes right back into the habit.

Q: I take it your task group considered the various possibilities now being explored as to rehabilitation, and the Odyssey House method was the one that you focused on as the most acceptable?

Adm. M.: No, we didn't focus on Odyssey House as the most acceptable. There has to be a lot more research done in this country on the methods of rehabilitation and the nonconventional approaches that could lead to easier ways to rehabilitate an individual. By that I mean groups like Alcoholics Anonymous, close groups that stay together, stick together, and talk it over, do things other than worry about the drug habit, or where they're going to get money to get the next shot of heroin. At the present time, there are too few agencies in this country that are doing what I think should be done as far as the drug abuse problem is concerned. Take, for instance, the armed services. The Army now has a group at Fort Bragg. You might say this is looking at the drug addicts, the hard drugs, the heroin-users and LSD, etc. They do not have enough data today to really have many answers as far as rehabilitation of the individual, his habits, the different approaches they use on various individuals, the successes on different individuals. All that is going to take time. The Army has an educational program, but mainly for their security people, the police, and how to deal with drug addicts. The Marines are also sending people to that Army school. The Navy does not have a rehabilitation center. The Navy started a school in San Diego, California, on the 1st of March of this year to educate sailors on the drug abuse program. The idea is to graduate about 20 sailors a month, and these are selected people who will go back to their respective commands and coordinate or help others start an education and information program regarding drug abuse, and then help coordinate the various commands, various units in a big major command, to have a progressive program going.

It's going to take some time before the Navy knows just how many of these specialists are required in the over-all Navy program.

The Air Force has a rehabilitation center for hard-drug users at Lowry Air Force Base at Denver, Colorado. This was started about 15 years ago as a rehabilitation center for enlisted men in the Air Force who had either dishonorable discharges or undesirable discharges. They could ask to be sent to Lowry to be rehabilitated, strictly on their own, and they were given all the help in the world. Today, the Air Force is starting another rehabilitation center at Lowry Air Force Base for all those enlisted men who have administrative discharges.

The Department of Defense has done considerable work in the last year in putting together a program for the armed services to implement. Twenty-seven recommendations were made, approved by the Secretary of Defense, and the services were directed to lay out a program to implement these 27 recommendations. I think when they put their programs together, there will be real, solid, progressive drug-abuse programs in the armed forces. In my opinion, today we are not progressing fast enough. There's much work to be done. We're too slow in attacking this problem. There's just an awful lot that has to be done in the armed services and in the country as a whole.

Q: Is the Navy, by virtue of its physical set-up, less vulnerable to the drug habit, drug abuses, the procurement of drugs, than the Army and the Air Force?

H. L. Miller # 9 - 508

Adm. M.: No, I wouldn't say that because the Navy goes all over the world. Take, for instance, the source of drugs, France, Turkey, Greece, Southeast Asia, the Far East - Navy ships are there the year round and they're always putting in to these ports. So it's very easy for sailors to get drugs of any description.

Q: But isn't it possible to exercise greater control over them aboard ship?

Adm. M.: I wouldn't say that it's easier, because they can hide small doses of drugs in their lockers or in any out-of-the-way place, in the overhead, and they can't be identified with anybody. So, I'd say that it's just as easy for a sailor to get drugs and use drugs as it is for a soldier or an airman or a Marine.

Q: Going back to your task group, did you have any special expert opinion on the chemical drugs, the LSD and things of that sort, as contrasted with heroin?

Adm. M.: As far as LSD is concerned, the information that is now available to the public is sort of sparse. I remember a young Navy surgeon who was put on camera for 47 minutes on the effects of LSD. This was done, I believe, about four years ago. He, of course, alerted everybody to the fact that after maybe one year of using LSD a flashback could occur and an individual didn't know what he was doing. However, today we still do not have all the information that is needed on what certain drugs will do, and LSD is one of them. Drugs affect an individual differently, of course. His make-up, his physique, his general health condition - the effects will be different with each individual.

Q: Now, with your task group, you met in sessions over a period of what, three days? And what did you come up with as your final set of recommendations for adoption by the conference, the plenary session?

Adm. M.: First of all, how did we work? We had 150 adults and youth in our task force. There were 100 youth and 50 adults. I mentioned the fact that we covered about eight areas in drugs. I was in the task force that considered the problem of drugs in the armed forces, because certain people were assigned to two task forces, we only had five individuals in the task force on drugs in the armed forces. They consisted of a civilian, an Air Force colonel who represented the Department of Defense Office on Drugs, an Army E-4 soldier whose normal duties are driving a car at Army headquarters in Washington, D. C. He'd had two years of college and was a very smart, capable man. Then we had a personnelman, third class, a wave from the Bureau of Naval Personnel, and myself.

Our modus operandi was to examine all facets of drug abuse in the armed forces. Well, we first reviewed what the Army, Navy, Air Force, and Marine Corps were presently doing in the over-all problem. Secondly, we looked, examined, and discussed the 27 recommendations that were made by the Department of Defense task force on drug abuse and further discussed other aspects of the problem and ideas for handling the drug problem in various installations of the armed forces. Everybody had his say-so, and this is one of the significant results of the entire conference. Anybody that had anything to say was allowed to get up, express himself, tell everybody within hearing distance what he believed and what he recommended. So it was a free exchange between ethnic groups and, of course, youth and adults. The five people in our task force talked as long and as hard as he could to get his ideas across, and we had unanimous agreement on the recommendations that were submitted.

Q: That gave them added strength, didn't it?

Adm. M.: Yes, Sir, and I know you'll be surprised at one of the recommendations that were made. First of all, we started out and said that we recommended that the armed services implement as a matter of priority the 27 recommendations that were made by the

Department of Defense. We feel that that was the most important recommendation, because if the services do that, they're going to have solid programs in the whole drug-abuse problem. They're going to do an awful lot. They will lead the way for this country, because this country isn't doing enough, either.

Well, that was our first recommendation. The second recommendation, we said "without impairing military efficiency, the armed forces to pioneer in the evaluation, under modern and enlightened controls, of marijuana in such a way as to recognize its relation to the real world of many young adults. In making this recommendation, the task force recognizes the unique situation of military service which makes such a program particularly applicable." This was quite a surprise to the over-all task forces that were examining the drug problem and some of the other task forces; i..e., education and racial, etc...

Q: Coming from the military, this was...!

Adm. M.: Well, there is so much to learn, we have to learn, about the effects of marijuana. Why people take it, what effect it has on different individuals, the purity that should go into a particular marijuana, a standardized brand, you might say, of marijuana? And we know that in the military if it was set up at some out-of-the-way place and you sent your marijuana users there, at least we could gather statistical data and find out what's going on. We could do an awful lot of research that isn't being done right now. If we found out that this so-called experiment, or pioneering effort, was getting us nowhere, except in trouble, we could cut it off tomorrow. But there's no place that you can do that in civilian life. So this is one of the things, we'd have control...

Q: You were very astute to see that, to utilize that.

Adm. M.: Well, we could put it into a small unit. We could put it ashore in some out-of-the-way place. We could put the men who abused it out there and were continuing to use it. We could possibly get volunteers who would like to be used in this experiment to find out more about marijuana. We could keep statistics and publish them all around the country. We'd have controlled conditions. We'd try to have an experiment with, say, a standard brand of marijuana. There are many, many things that you could do under controlled conditions in the armed forces. Now, we know that there would be a terrific reaction of certain mammas and papas if such a controlled unit were set up some place...

Q: Repercussions as far as recruitment goes?

Adm. M.: Yes, and what are the armed forces doing this for? Well, we proposed it and now we'll see what comes of it.

Q: Did this represent for you personally any reversal of opinion, this proposal?

Adm. M.: It wasn't my idea, but after we had a thorough discussion we thought it might be a pretty good thing to set up. We've got to find out more about the use of marijuana. How we go about that, I'm not the expert. But maybe this is a way that we could use under controlled conditions.

Q: The fact, Admiral, that your task force of five came up with this recommendation to your larger task force of 150, did this ultimately result in the adoption by the whole conference of the recommendation that marijuana be legalized?

Adm. M.: Well, we knew that prior to making this recommendation - or I should say we were pretty sure that the conference as a whole was going to come up with a recommendation to legalize marijuana.

Q: How did you know this? By soundings?

Adm. M.: Oh, yes. There were various groups there at the conference who were talking about the legalization of marijuana, and a paper was submitted in regard to legalization of marijuana. Various delegates really talked about the legalization of marijuana from the time we first got there on Sunday, the 18th. So we knew it was in the wind, and we were thinking about what the armed forces could contribute in the over-all knowledge concerning drugs. As a matter of fact, at the conference at one time it was proposed to legalize heroin and control it by the government, much like the way they did in Britain. I understand that Britain has sort of given that up now, but it was considered at the conference, to legalize heroin. I don't know if it would be good or bad. I don't know if it was handled well in Britain, but Britain doesn't have the drug-abuse problem that we have in this country. It's practically no problem in Britain in comparison with the U. S.

Q: Was there any thought that there might be a diminution of the drug problem in this country if we got out of the Vietnam War, if this were no longer an issue?

Adm. M.: The Vietnam War plus other pressures and frustrations were, of course, considered as contributing to the drug-abuse problem, but it isn't the only reason for drug abuse. The conference did recommend getting out of Vietnam now, not waiting, but now. That was a controversial issue for the entire conference. For instance, the day before the conference ended, getting out of Vietnam now was defeated in the task force, but there was quite a bit of lobbying done on the last day and that resolution was passed by a large majority - 450 yeas to 115 nays, as far as getting out of the Vietnam War was concerned.

Q: This was in the plenary session? Did the others just abstain, or what?

Adm. M.: Yes. Well, you see, in the open session of say 1,500 people were walking in and out. Perhaps only half of those individuals took ballots, marked them, and turned them in. We were given a ballot as we walked in to the closing session on the last day. This session lasted from one o'clock to about six thirty that night. So there were people easing in and out of the conference all during that time. They had an opportunity to vote on all issues that were presented, you might say lump-sum-wise, because they couldn't on each one - there were 150 to 200 recommendations, and naturally you couldn't cover all those and get a vote on them in a short afternoon like that.

But there were very many good suggestions that were made. Let me just tell you about other recommendations from my own armed forces task group.

Q: Yes, do.

Adm. M.: Well, the next one, we said, "recognizing the success of informal hotline arrangements geared to the special problems of certain communities, the task force recommends that the military should establish 24-hour hotlines and trouble centers, using telephones and establishing, at these trouble centers, psychiatrists or doctors who could help these people out that wanted help, and these people that would check in on the hotline their communications would be privileged, they couldn't be used against that individual in any court-martial or any other actions." We felt that this is needed because people on the drug habit want to talk to others. When they need help they've just got to talk to people, and they must be protected, otherwise they're just not going to turn themselves in unless they are protected.

The facilities we envision for these trouble centers would be - and the people - would be able to handle the frustrations and the stresses and strains of all these young people that are normal to them plus any special frictions or frustrations that are normal or indigenous to a military environment. Let them talk and let them get advice. We felt that this was needed and it would get the people who are experimenting with drugs, or regular users, into the channel to get rehabilitated. It's a starter. Some installations do have a hotline arrangement right now, but this should be universal in the armed forces. In other words, we've got to make an all-out

H. L. Miller # 9 - 517

effort to get at this problem.

Q: Was this adopted?

Adm. M.: Oh, yes. This was accepted by the whole conference, 1,500 people. All of our recommendations were accepted.

Q: And probably considered rather enlightened recommendations, too, were they not?

Adm. M.: Well, now, you see, all of these recommendations had to be approved and accepted by the 150 task force group, before being presented to the 1,500. It was most unusual. For some unexplained reason, the colonel representing the office of the Secretary of Defense was absent from the session wherein we had to present our recommendations to the 150 people of our task force, and answer the questions. I didn't want to be the chairman of the adult group presenting, because I was a rear admiral and people would think that it was a real planted effort. So the civilian on our task group and I talked it over, and we selected the Army E-4. Gary was a very fine representative. He did an outstanding job and handled some of the questions expertly. We told him that we wouldn't let him get stuck or get into trouble, that any of those questions that he couldn't handle we would pipe up. And many questions were asked and fortunately we had gone over all of the material that we had, each individually, and discussed it, so we were pretty well armed to answer the many questions of our task group.

As a matter of fact, I think that we did a better job in answering the questions to that task force of any group that was there. And I believe that everybody of those 150 were really impressed with the amount of effort that the Department of Defense had spent on the drug-abuse problem.

Another recommendation that we made, we said "we recommend the creation of a structured system of professional education in preventative drug abuse, utilizing the most recent material and its dissemination uniformly throughout the armed services." And when we say a structured system of professional education, we meant just that, at various levels. For instance, at West Point today there is an orientation lecture given to the incoming cadets on drugs and drug abuse. Then there is another follow-up course in drug education given to the upperclassmen. There is a continuing program of drug education, as they learn more about drugs at West Point. Additionally, their graduates at West Point are given a course to take with them to tell their own troops in the battalion they're reporting to. So, we adopted what we call a structured system of professional education that we knew was going on at West Point.

We feel that there are levels of drug education that should be given in the various commands of the military, to enlisted men and officers.

Then, another recommendation that was made: "We recommend the expansion throughout the Department of Defense of informal and confidential mental health care clinics, available on both a non-referral and referral basis, for therapeutic counseling of military personnel and their dependents." What we had in mind is setting up a care clinic that would answer questions for people who had been on drugs or were thinking of taking drugs or other things that came to their minds, other problems than drug problems. A place where they could come to visit, talk to psychiatrists or other people that were knowledgeable on the problems of youth, because the young man in the armed forces is considered in the youth group. I should say that youth is considered between the ages of 14 and 24 years of age, and I believe the average age in the armed services today is either 22 or 24.

Q: That was actually the span of the conference, wasn't it, 14 to 24?

Adm. M.: Yes. So, when you talk about the youth of this country, we're getting that youth right in the armed services today, and we have got to be concerned with all of these problems.

Q: Did you have evidence or statistics or something dealing with the problem of mental health and its relationship to drug-taking? Does it precede the taking of drugs, or is it a product of drug-taking?

Adm. M.: I'm not the professional, and you could probably put a footnote on this and say I don't know what I'm talking about, but the frustrations that come with military life or any change of status, change of work, a life-style change is going to bring on anxiety, may bring on boredom. There are many of these young men today who want somebody to talk to. Now, it may not affect his mental health, but it will certainly bring on many questions that he'd like to have the answers to. And you might say youth today wants to know how, when, where, what, why. They're a lot smarter than we were in our day - at that time of our development - and they want these answers. They should be getting them, but we haven't geared ourselves to changing our habits and our methods of dealing with these young men. So, we said, OK, maybe one of these care clinics would help these young men in getting their answers, or getting some of the answers. We also included dependents because if a young man is married and he has one or two children, maybe the wife would like to get some answers, too. So this is why we proposed it.

Q: This, of course, is parallel to Alcoholics Anonymous, too, in that they have sessions for the other partner to the union, or they have sessions for the children.

Adm. M.: Yes. Those were the most important recommendations that we made, and the last one "was to ensure that the research that has been made in the military on drug abuse, the statistics, the analyses that have come up, all of this be disseminated to the civilian community." I don't know to what extent it has been done, but this is one of the things that I should find out. I know that the Navy, in reflecting back on a couple of test units that I know of, I think the Navy has a research group in Egypt. They're looking at the environment there, and possibly drug abuse over there, and the same in Taiwan, but I'm not sure. I just mention that because we do have certain statistics that have been gathered, I guess, on drug cases. We may have some information that could be passed on and help the civilian community.

There isn't enough information that is circulated today on the drug problem. It seems as though the National Institute of Mental Health is the god-papa of all the information that goes out to the great American public, but very few people know that you can go to them and get all this information.

Q: Admiral, you say that the task group as a whole, your task group of 150, collectively were impressed with the recommendations and the amount of work that went into those recommendations as they came out of your small task group for the military. Was there any notice taken of the fact that perhaps intelligent discipline in the military had some relationship, some bearing on this?

Adm. M.: That's a good question. I believe the answer to that as far as our small group was concerned lies in the fact that we came properly armed with all the information regarding drugs that was currently available in the armed forces. We also came armed with the 27 recommendations that had been made by the Department of Defense task force on a program for drug abuse. Remember, in a period of about five months that Department of Defense task force, using many, many people, gathering information, and submitting ideas from the four services, thousands of hours were spent on those 27 recommendations. So you might say we had a leg up on most of the other people in the conference. We had studied our lesson and we came with the facts and with the recommendations. The additional recommendations that we made resulted from ideas that came from this small group and our discussion of them during the day and a half or two days that we spent together.

Q: On this same subject of discipline, I see and understand a certain discipline in a man's religious faith. Was that considered at all in connection with the drug problem in the plenary session?

Adm. M.: No, Sir, because drugs have hit every ethnic group and every religious group. You look at the various areas of the world where the basic stuff comes from, they're all religious, they're all nationalities. It's a worldwide problem.

Q: I was just curious to see whether the subject of religion per se came up in discussions of the drug problem.

I think we'll take a different tack at this point. Tell me, since you were a prominent representative of the military at this Youth Conference, about the general attitude of the youth there toward the military and how you coped.

Adm. M.: I went to the conference in my uniform, but as soon as I got there I shifted to civilian clothes. I left the conference on the last day in my uniform. The White House Conference staff was a little bit leary of inviting the military simply because, I think, they believed that some of the militant groups up there would probably tangle with any military personnel. There were some enlisted personnel who were invited from the Army, Navy, and Air Force. They were told to come in civilian clothes. I was the only admiral/general there. There were probably one or two officers and enlisted men from each of the armed services assigned to the original staff of the White House Conference on Youth. They were not there in uniform. They had been working on these problem areas since last August. They were in civilian clothes too. I had a name badge that was on my chest that said, "Rear Admiral Henry L. Miller," but the first day in talking to various groups and introducing yourself very few people looked at the badge. I talked to many of the youth groups from various areas, various ages, the Chicanos, blacks, Porto Ricans, etc. I listened to them to what they had to say and all the problems that were confronting the youth of our day. Every young man that I came in contact with, after they knew I was an admiral, called me Admiral Miller. I talked with them. I listened to them. They listened to me. I believe that they extended me more courtesies and more respect than any individual attending the White House Conference on Youth. So I don't think that the youth of this country is anti-military, because they certainly could have been anti-military to me and to the other enlisted men and officers who were present at the White House Conference on Youth.

H. L. Miller # 9 - 525

It was quite a revelation to me because I thought there were quite a few anti-military people that would be at that conference. If they were, they certainly weren't apparent because all the people, and I spoke to a great number of youth and adults, were very courteous to me.

Q: Does this indicate, perhaps, that there isn't enough contact between the military and the civilian youth of the country, I mean those outside of the services?

Adm. M.: Yes, Sir. I think that's a very good observation. As a matter of fact, I wish that the Army, Navy, and Air Force had sent officers and enlisted personnel from their, say, Bureaus of Personnel to the White House Conference on Youth in Colorado just to get a feel, because there was the youth of the country that they were going to draw from for the armed forces. Youth groups were right there. They could have listened to their problem. These were going to be the same problems that we would face in the armed forces with these youth groups. All ethnic groups, all ages, all geography. It was a golden opportunity to sit there and listen and observe what was going on in the minds of the youth of our country. We missed a golden opportunity to really cash in on this meeting.

Q: Will you try to implement that idea with the military for future conferences?

Adm. M.: If I have any power to do it or any influence, I certainly will ask the military to send a large group of observers just to sit and listen. They'll really profit from a few days' session like that.

Q: A specific question about one delegate. In one of the comprehensive news reports on Estes Park, a William Lavage was mentioned as one of the prime movers of the preamble that was ultimately adopted. Lavage was just discharged from the Navy about a week before. Did you get to talk with him?

Adm. M.: No, Sir. I didn't have an opportunity to talk to him. I spoke to a great number of youth and adults. One of the things I did find out there were some of the adults that really talked too much and didn't listen to the problems that our youth groups have. Other adults didn't seem to know how to mix with the youth and communicate with them. Some of them were wallflowers. They couldn't communicate with youth and they couldn't communicate with adults, either.

Q: Were they not as carefully selected then as delegates? Were they selected for their reputations, or what?

Adm. M.: Some, I guess, were selected for the positions that they held around the country, for instance, on a committee on drugs in their particular state. We had some delegates there who were very representative. They communicated well. They were experts in their own field and they certainly contributed immeasurably to the success of the conference. There were some very fine people.

Q: I would think that one of the prime requirements for an adult representative to a conference like this would be his personality, his "outgoingness", and his ability to relate.

Adm. M.: If an individual at the White House Conference on Youth couldn't relate, couldn't communicate, he had no business being there because we wanted to draw out all the issues, the frustrations, the problems that are facing the youth of this nation today and find out what we can do now to help solve some of these problems, now and in the future. This was one of the purposes of the WHCY. We had to really be able to talk to all the ethnic groups, sound them out, get their feelings and thoughts, and see if we could put this together in recommendations to the president to solve these problems that are presently facing the nation today and those that will be facing the nation in the years to come.

Q: Admiral, would you talk about the contribution made by the foreign delegates? Did they add a new dimension to some of the discussions?

H. L. Miller # 9 - 528

Adm. M.: Yes, Sir. There was a 16-year-old delegate from India, Matthew George Adgie. He was a brilliant boy. He contributed in all the sessions. Now, it was certainly revealing to me, the youth in this country want to do their bit, their share, in the future planning of this country. They have these problems, and the problems of our youth seem to be transmitted automatically to the youth of other nations. The youth of other nations that were present at the White House Conference on Youth sounded out in the same manner on the same problems that our youth did. In other words, I say that youth worldwide do a splendid job of communicating between themselves, and I can't say the same for adults, worldwide. We don't communicate as well as youth.

Q: Then, where youth is concerned, it is indeed one world. How do they communicate? Is it through frequent travel, or what?

Adm. M.: I guess it's a great many things. Travel, music - a great deal is transmitted in the music that youth listens to today.

Q: You mean the ballads and the...

Adm. M.: Yes, Sir, and all the wild music, the folk music, everything that they listen to today in the United States is also listened to overseas, in foreign countries. And, you might say, that the youth groups there from foreign countries were repeating the same things that our youth was talking about.

Q: There's an interdependence, then, between the groups. Do all youth rely upon them for ideas, as well as they rely on ours?

Adm. M.: I think that it's a mutual exchange. They rely on each other. They get together and communicate and they seem to agree on all the problems and issues, the frustrations, confronting the world today. It's very interesting to observe that. They spoke about the same problems facing our youth, and they look to the United States for help - please help us too in the solutions to all these problems.

Q: Why do they look to us for that kind of help? Don't they have reliance on their own abilities?

Adm. M.: I believe that the answer to that is that we have been helping the nations of the world ever since World War II. Remember Mr. Truman's Point Four Program?

Q: Yes.

Adm. M.: Well, then the Marshall Plan. Since then we've distributed our aid to beef up their economies, get a viable economy going. We've helped them in military aid. We've helped them in agriculture.

In many things, we've been a world leader - the world leader - in helping nations, and I believe that the world today keeps looking at the United States to continue this help. We have had a great many ideas. We've distributed a great many dollars, worldwide. We've also given them our technology. We've sent thousands and thousands of pamphlets on research throughout the world. You might say the United States has been a give-away nation, and they're expected to do this.

Q: Admiral, were there a great number of so-called hippies at the conference?

Adm. M.: Yes, Sir, there were a great number of what you might call hippies, they wore long hair, beards, mustaches, but they were a smart group of boys who contributed throughout the conference.

Q: What does this say about the changing life habits of the younger generation in our country, and in the world?

Adm. M.: Well, it was very significant to me. The youth in this country have changed and are continuing to change in their life style habits. I believe they're smarter, they're more decisive, they're better educated, and more universal in their thinking than we were when we were growing up. I believe they're more compassionate for their fellow man, worldwide. They are more concerned with world affairs today than we ever were, and I say this even growing up in the Navy and visiting foreign ports. They don't like to be signed up in the armed forces for an unpopular war in Vietnam. They feel it isn't worth giving their lives to continue that battle over in Indochina. They're deeply concerned with all the problems facing society and they want to contribute in the decision-making to the solution of these problems. You might say, a word of caution, youth may be demanding too much today in a hurry. They want to get there fast. But I think we'll just have to wait and see if this is a good opinion of what's going on today.

Q: One of the observations about our civilization has been that this is a "now" generation. We have become accustomed to expecting things to happen now, not ten years hence, and the youth are no different from many adults in that sense. We've been nurtured in that idea. Does this make for hasty decision and hasty actions? What does it do to our concepts?

Adm. M.: I don't have the answer to that, but you say, well, maybe all of us are trying to get - trying to move too fast and get the solutions to these problems right now. I see the youth demanding that, some adults too, but I'm afraid that the adults, in looking back at this over-all youth problem, don't want to be bothered with these changes that are now existing and will continue to change in the life style habits of youth in contrast to our era. I say the world is changing, customs and habits are changing, the domestic scene is rushing by us at break-neck speed, and it appears to me that adults today dislike these changes from the norm in which they were reared. Many of them don't want to re-adjust to these changing times to accomodate youth. On the other hand, many of them say "why not put youth in their place and tell them to adjust to our way of life?" And, of course, as you recall, when we were growing up we were supposed to be seen and not heard, and this thought was given to me just yesterday by a very knowledgeable Admiral, and I was surprised that he didn't want to recognize the fact that youth was changing.

Well, unfortunately for people who do not want to recognize this fact, it's a little bit too late. The youth movement has passed a great many people by. It's here. It's going to contine changing right along, and I believe that the adults of this country have got to turn to, catch up, and find out what's going on.

Q: Admiral, with the delegates there and your conversations with them, do they have a tendency to discount the value of experience,

H. L. Miller # 9 - 533

which is what some adults rely on?

Adm. M.: No. The youth were very receptive to the experience that was certainly evident in the adult groups that were present at the conference. Likewise, I think all youth and adults listened to the specialists who were there, the experts in their particular areas. It was four days of continued listening and searching for the answers to the problems we have today. And I think they did a pretty good job in picking the brains of everybody who was there.

Q: Would you talk about the role of the ethnic groups and the division into ethnic groups?

Adm. M.: Well, we had several ethnic groups there, and one of the objectives of the conference was to get all ethnic groups, everybody of the 1,500 who were there, to sound out, to contribute to the conference, to exchange ideas, to present the problems, and, you might say, present experience that was there to alert everybody to the issues and the frustrations that are present in this country today. I think they did a good job of listening to all the various groups. Now...

Q: Can you be specific about, say, the Chicanos, or one group like that? I mean what did they do, how did they make their views known?

H. L. Miller # 9 - 534

Adm. M.: Well, you see, all ethnic groups - the Chicanos, the blacks, the group of Italians, Greeks, Poles, Indians, the women - they all had caucuses and they had a spokesman for their particular caucus.

Q: This was the intention of the over-all planning, was it, or was it spontaneous?

Adm. M.: This was planned, and so on the final day all of these ethnic groups were represented on the platform and they told the 1,500 delegates, in brief, their problems and recommendations for solutions. Everybody had a chance of being heard. I didn't realize that there were that many ethnic groups in this country, but it was very good. One of the groups - the blacks - told us that even though it was recommended that marijuana be legalized, they didn't go along with that. They said that they had too many problems already in the ghetto today.

Q: Was the black caucus a large segment of the conference?

Adm. M.: There were about 10 or 15 that comprised the black caucus, but in the end the blacks and the whites and the Puerto Ricans and everybody blended. They were integrated into the various groups of the conferences, and I think it was a huge success.

Q: Isn't that the American way?

Adm. M.: Yes, but at times it's difficult in a conference of this size when people try to use political ploys in getting themselves heard or getting recommendations into the record that are not accepted universally by the delegates. So one has to watch these little side plays that take place at every conference in the world.

Q: I was rather surprised when you talked about the ethnic groups including the Greeks and Italians and so forth, because I thought that the younger generation of people with that background were being absorbed into the American scene and no longer sought refuge in the tongue of the father, but were using English as their means of communication.

Adm. M.: So did I, but I found out at this conference that we did have quite a few ethnic groups who really presented some telling information on how they felt in this country. They are not absorbed like you think. They still want to hold onto the traditions and customs, a great many traditions and customs and ways of doing business of their ethnic groups, and this is what surprised me.

Q: I read that one of the great concerns of this youth conference, as it was planned, was ways and means of implementing the resolutions, the ideas, that were generated at the conference. Could you talk about that?

Adm. M.: There were several proposals made. I made a couple myself. One-for all of us to go home and preach the gospel on the White House Conference on Youth and get everybody in the country marching and doing things, and, of course, that was impractical. The next one was holding a White House conference every two years or four years, so that we would be looking at these problems more frequently and doing something about them, other than this ten-year period that they now have.

Another proposal was to put the present White House conference staff under Mr. Shultz, who was really the executive officer of the President. Mr. Shultz is programing and budget. You see, to implement these recommendations, you have to have money and you have to have people, and you have to have a real powerful office to tell, or ride herd on the various offices of the government who have to implement these recommendations, such as Health, Education, and Welfare, Transportation, the Department of Defense, et cetera. If it was placed under Mr. Shultz, they have a god-papa there who would really be influential and powerful and be able to get something done. And then, say, after a year's time - at the most two years' - I'd say one year is the best, have another conference and at that conference, have Health, Education, and Welfare, Transportation, Department of Defense, and all the offices concerned, come to that conference and present the recommendations that they have implemented, and also future planning on other recommendations that were made. This way, they keep their feet in the fire and something has to be done. They have to answer to 1,500 delegates that were there last year, or a comparable grouping from around the country that will listen to and want these things done.

Now, another proposal or an idea is to have a state conference on youth in each one of our 50 states, with the ethnic groups there, the population, the geography, the cities and the rural areas, so that the governor and the legislative body of that state will know, first of all, what's going on in the state, and secondly, what the problems are. Those are, in the main, the proposals on implementation for this conference.

Q: Those recommendations from the youth conference are essentially for the executive, are they not?

Adm. M.: That's right.

Q: Was the Congress taken into consideration in any way?

Adm. M.: Yes, Sir. We know that you can say, "Now, Mr. President, we want all these things done", but he can't get to first base unless Congress appropriates the money and gives him the money and people to get all these recommendations implemented.

Now, there were Congressmen and Senators there in various task forces. They were present. They contributed. They listened.

Q: I read about Mr. Brock being there, but he's a neophyte in the Congress. Were there any men of longer standing and more influence?

Adm. M.: I think the Congressmen who were there, some of them very influential, were all interested. They participated. They listened. They voted. So, regardless of their stature, they still can have a tremendous influence on the implementation of these recommendations.

Q: This report from the conference will ultimately reach the President, will it not?

Adm. M.: Yes, Sir. They expect to have a report out in condensed form in about a month. The big Congressional Record type of report that will have all the studies in it and a great deal of conversation and all the recommendations, will be put together at a later period of time. Finally, I believe, they intend to put out a bigger condensation of those studies in the report into a third publication.

Q: This is intended for the executive. At the same time, I read that the preamble which is to accompany the recommendation was addressed to the people of the United States. Why is this?

Adm. M.: I wasn't on that task group. Probably because they felt that it should - the preamble should - soul-stir the people, that they would write their congressmen or write the President, and tell them that they believe all these things should be done.

Q: Was there any indication from Mr. Richardson or any other administration spokesman that there would be some tangible results, that there would be some answers, response, given by the executive to these recommendations?

Adm. M.: Yes, Sir. Mr. Richardson said that they would look over the recommendations very closely, he knew that they probably couldn't approve every recommendation, but they certainly would give every recommendation serious consideration, lots of study, and there would be results, there would be implementation of quite a number of them.

Q: Did this seem to be a satisfactory answer to the youth delegates?

Adm. M.: That was at the opening session, and I think so. I think for probably 1,450 it was a good answer. For the 50 who didn't want to listen to anybody, it probably was the wrong answer.

Q: There was one delegate who was quoted - he was the representative of the Governor of Pennsylvania - as saying that the delegates had evidenced a lack of real concern and he called the caucus boring. He must have been one of the 50!

Adm. M.: He might have been one of the rock-and-rollers. We had a rock and roll band up there and some of them liked to spend some of their evenings really beating it hard on the dance floor.

Q: I believe among the recommendations made by the conference, only one really was in support of a presidential policy that had to do with the draft.

Adm. M.: There were three or four considered very important recommendations of the conference. One was for the all-volunteer Army, and that got a standing ovation.

Q: Had they gone into the practical aspects of the whole problem?

Adm. M.: Well, the Department of Defense feels that, I think now about 1973, they can have an all-volunteer Army, and they are planning and taking measures to go in that direction.

The second recommendation was legalizing the use of marijuana, and we've discussed that before.

The third recommendation on the last day that received a standing ovation was to get out of Vietnam now.

Q: Not December 31st, but now!

Adm. M.: Now. And I think the fourth big recommendation was to make the age of 18 for the youth of this country as majority. They'll all be adults on their 18th birthday, and would have all the privileges that an adult has right now in every state and throughout the government.

Q: So this goes far beyond the proposed amendment permitting voting in all categories at the age of 18?

Adm. M.: Yes, Sir.

Q: One article I have here says that - it's titled "U.S. Youth Chooses the Radical Path." It's long been the popular view that the average American youth, given a chance to speak out, would reject the radical views of what has been called a vocal minority and would support programs and policies of their elders. Would you comment on that as something that came out of the conference? Is that a fair assessment?

Adm. M.: I don't think so. I think that, as far as this conference concerned, the majority certainly didn't go along with any minority groups that wanted to dominate any issue. They held their cool very well. I thought that the youth were very considerate. I thought they weighed all the issues very well. They make up their own minds. They presented the problems and the issues that they feel are the big ones in this nation, and certainly the adult group, I know, didn't consider all these problems before this conference. That's why I say I think the youth has passed the oldsters by, that the adults have to catch up and find out what's going on in the youth world. I still go back to the changes in the life style of youth, and the adult world hasn't caught up with that, hasn't realized that all this is taking place.

Q: Well, what is the predominant note in the youth world? Is it one of compassion?

Adm. M.: Yes. They are helpful, but the youth today wants to know - and this is in the armed forces, too - what, where, when, how why. They're asking questions and they're not getting the answers, and this is something that we have got to look into and continue to work on and worry about. We have got to give youth the answers to the questions that they have today. They're not getting them.

Q: Did this come new to you, or had you understood this prior to the conference?

Adm. M.: I understood a lot of it prior to the conference, but it came home very hard from all ethnic groups now, all groups, not just the white boys, and in my thinking, from here on in, when we talk about problems from, say, one particular group, we've got to think of all ethnic groups in this country. We haven't. I don't believe we have. In other words, I think that all the age groups, all the ethnic groups that we listened to are going to keep me thinking positively for the rest of my life, and I didn't think that way before I went to that conference.

Q: Well, now, Sir, when you have so many facets to consider and so many points of view to consider in the solution of a problem, will this not make for a watered-down compromise in many cases?

Adm. M.: No, I think that was certainly proven at this conference. You had one viewpoint, say, from the blacks. You had one viewpoint from the whites. But the success of the conference was getting those groups together, exchanging ideas and working out the best solution for both, and this can be done. It was proven up there. It was proven up there day after day, for four days. It was done, and we came out with very few minority reports. You might say those recommendations, in the main, were agreed to by a vast majority.

Q: What was the judgment on the conference by the bulk of the delegates? I know you think it was a great success. Was it a consensus?

Adm. M.: Well, I talked to several youths, I talked to several adults, and everybody that I spoke to considered the White House Conference on Youth tremendously successful. You might say they all said they wouldn't have missed it for anything in the world. They felt that they were making history and that they would look back on this as a very significant contribution to the future of this country, and I believe it. I think that the conference is going to contribute significantly to the future development of this country.

Q: You look upon it as something of a watershed, then?

Adm. M.: Yes, Sir.

Q: This depends upon implementation, does it not?

Adm. M.: Yes, but regardless of how much it's implemented, it will provide an awful lot of background and recommendations that have to be considered from now and for ever more in the future of this country. It's there. It's on paper. You can't duck it. It will be good - those recommendations will be good for communities, states, the armed services, everybody, to look at. There's some wonderful background material, lots of wisdom that went into that over-all conference.

Q: Did you have a chance to talk with the leadership of the conference? Were they pleased?

Adm. M.: Well, you see, they were looking to us - asking us, what we thought, because naturally they were trying to get a feel from us on whether or not the conference was a success. They were watching it every day, but I think they are convinced that it was a very successful conference, and tomorrow when I talk to some of that staff on the phone I'll find out.

Q: You came back, I imagine, with certain resolves?

Adm. M.: Yes, Sir. I'm going to talk to the governor of Alaska today up in Washington - Bill Egan - and I'm going to suggest to Bill that he have an Alaskan conference on youth if he wants to know what's going on in the country, with his Eskimos, Indians, whites, blacks, et cetera. I'm also going to write a letter to Governor Mandel of Maryland and suggest the same thing.

Next week, I am going to tell some of the delegates of the Maryland legislature who will be meeting at my Naval Air Test Center, Patuxent River, Maryland, with me and my top managers, both civilian and military, and the county commissioners, on the problems that are facing our community down there. I'm going to give them a run-down on the White House Conference on Youth, what we did, or what we tried to do, and suggest to them that they might have one for St. Mary's County because there are many problems. And, Number Two, maybe they will speak to Governor Mandel on a youth conference for the state of Maryland.

Q: You really are in a strategic position, you can implement some of these ideas!

Adm. M.: Yes, Sir, we can. Now, let me tell you what I said yesterday right at my own establishment at the Naval Air Test Center, listening to the military side of the house and the civilian side of the house, I said, OK, we have these problems of youth speaking from the military half, and they want to know where, when, how, why, and I added, let's not overlook the young civilian engineers that we have on this base. They have the same problems and they're looking at you older engineers and saying, why don't you listen to us? I said it's here. I know that's here. So, you can implement a lot of this no matter where you are, depending, of course, upon the position that you hold.

Q: It can begin right at home!

Adm. M.: Yes.

Q: Thank you very much for this interesting discussion of this conference and what it has meant to you.

INDEX

for series of

Interviews

Rear Admiral Henry L. Miller

U. S. Navy (Retired)

Volume II

Astronauts: resume of Navy Test Pilots who have become astronauts,
    p 485-7.

USS BAINBRIDGE: nuclear-powered frigate, p 371.

Bao Dai: Emperor of South Viet Nam, p 306.

Barrel Role Mission: Began in December 1964, to bomb and strafe
    supplies on the Ho Chi Minh Trail, p 352; p 354; p 356-7; p 362.

USS BENNINGTON - CV: On YANKEE STATION (Feb. 1965), p 363.

USS BON HOMME RICHARD: a unit of CarDiv 3, p 346; 355.

British HARRIER Airplane: p 454-5; p 483.

Buddhist Problems - South Viet Nam: p 331, 333.

BuPers: p 417, 419, 422-23.

CANDID CAMERA OPERATION: p 363.

Carrier Division #3 (CarDiv 3): Miller assumes command in August,
    1964, p 345; account of his command, p 346 ff.

China - People's Republic: U.S. planes over North Viet Nam told
    to stay clear of the border, p 361.

CHINFO: Miller serves from April 1966 to October, 1968, p 387 ff;
    launches a major effort to sell idea of nuclear power, p 389 ff;
    Combat Art, p 391-7; reproductions, p 397-400; movie making
    to tell the Navy's story, p 400-403; DIAL NAVY news service,
    p 404-5; sponsors a speech laboratory, p 409-410. Fleet home
    town news program, 412; the on-board public affairs program,
    p 413-4; aids in recruitment programs, p 415-6; use of Navy
    League and Naval Reserve Chapters, p 423-4; minority group
    program, p 428 ff; Global Strategy course at Naval War College,
    p 431-2; Public Affairs Seminar, p 433-34; aircraft carrier

H. L. Miller

cruise program, p 434-5; the Navy and Public Relations - comments, p 445-448, 450.

Cinc Pac Weapons Demonstration: p 355, 358.

Civil Guard - Republic of Niet Nam: training put under Com USMAC V, p 323.

Civilian Irregular Defense Group - South Viet Nam: put under Com U SMacV for training purposes, July 1962, p 323-4.

USS CONSTELLATION: unit in TF 77, p 347, p 355, p 358.

USS CORAL SEA: planes take part in FLAMING DART I, p 359; FLAMING DART II, p 360-1, 362.

Da Nang: U.S. Marines landed at the base, March 8, 1965, p 362.

Defoliation Program: Used in Viet Nam to uncover Viet Cong along river banks, p 323.

Diem, Ngo-dinh: President of South VietNam, p 306; p 309-310; declares a state of emergency, Oct. 19, 1961, p 310; Buddhist demonstrations against Diem government, p 331-33; killed on November 2, 1963, p 333-4.

Dirksen, Senator Everett: assists Chinfo in making a movie, p 401-3.

DIXIE STATION: station in South China Sea for combattant units, - USS ENTERPRISE goes into action for first time there - Dec. 2, 1965, p 382-3.

USS ENTERPRISE: Miller and staff embark on her for trip from Norfolk, p 371; p 374; Miller discusses advantages of nuclear power, p 376-81; takes up her position on DIXIE STATION and goes into combat, Dec. 2, 1965, p 382-5; in Hong Kong for R and R, p 385; Miller relieved in Feb. 1966 by Adm. Walker, p 386; at Newport News Shipbuilding for refitting, p 476-8.

H. L. Miller

The ENTERPRISE: weekly newspaper in St. Mary's County, Maryland - p 420-1.

Enthoven, Dr. Alain C.: one of the principal advisers to Secretary of Defense McNamara, p 444.

Estes Park, Colorado: see entries under WHITE HOUSE Conference on Youth.

Felt, Adm. H. D.: as CincPac was present at SecDef Conferences, p 317, 325; his policy for Viet Nam (1962), p 327; conference of May, 1963, p 330-331; August, 1963 instructed by JCS to prepare for evacuation of non combatants from Vietnam, p 332; trip to Saigon on Nov. 1, 1963, p 333-4; acts as military adviser to Secretary Rusk at SEATO meeting in April, 1963, p 337; retires as CincPac July 1, 1964, p 339.

FLAMING DART Missions: begin in February, 1965, p 359-60; subsequent missions, p 362, 366.

Ford, Glenn: narrates a TV film for Chinfo, p 402.

USS HANCOCK: planes take part in FLAMING DART I, p 359; takes part in FLAMING DART II, p 360, 362, 366; participates in HOT STOVE, p 370-1.

Hanzlik, Mr.: director of the staff, White House Conference on youth, p 493.

Harkins, General Paul: takes over MAAG in Vietnam - becomes Commander, U. S. Military Assistance Command, Vietnam (Com US Mac V), p 315, 319; at SecDef conference, July 1962 given task of training the Civil Guard and the Civilian Irregular Defense

H. L. Miller

Group in Viet Nam, p 323-4; his estimate of the problem in Vietnam and probable duration of war, p 324-6; states that death of Diem had little effect on military campaign, p 334-5; Westmoreland becomes his Deputy on Jan. 13, 1964, p 336.

Ho Chi Minh: p 305, 308-10, 316.

Ho Chi Minh Trail: YANKEE STATION Mission designed to check supplies, p 349 ff.

Hudson, Rock: p 401.

Ignatius, The Hon. Paul: Secretary of the Navy, p 437; objects to costs of commissioning Carrier JOHN F. KENNEDY, p 438; finally agrees on cost, p 440; portrait of Secretary Ignatius, p 441-2.

Industrial College for the Armed Forces - Alumni Association: Miller serves as President in 1967-8; p 450.

Intelligence - Camera Coverage: subject for discussion at SecDef Conference, July 1961, p 323.

USS JOHN F. KENNEDY - CV: Commissioning of, p 437 ff.

Johnson, The Hon. Lyndon: as Vice President (1961) makes a trip to South Vietnam, p 310. p 340-1; his White House begins to direct Naval Forces after Gulf of Tonkin incident, p 344; orders retaliatory strikes against barracks at Don Hoy, p 359; p 444.

Johnson, Admiral Roy: CincPacFlt, p 370-1; assigns Miller and staff to bring new carrier ENTERPRISE to Western Pacific, p 371.

H. L. Miller

Junk Force: topic for discussion at SecDef Conference, July, 1962 - p 319.

Kennedy, The Hon. John F.: p 309-10; 330-331; 333-334.

Khanh, General Ngu-yen: takes over control in Saigon on Jan. 30, 1964, p 335; p 341-2.

USS KITTY HAWK: p 383-4.

Krulak, Lt. Gen. Victor H.: (Brute): in 1962 serves as special assistant for counter insurgency in Viet Nam, p 318; p 321-322.

Laos: neutral status of country, p 352-354; see also entry under Yankee Station.

Lodge, The Hon. Henry Cabot: becomes U. S. Ambassador in Viet Nam, (June, 1963), p 331-2; replaced by Gen. Maxwell Taylor, June 1964, p 339.

Lovell, Captain Jim: relates story of Apollo 13 at Symposium of Test Pilots, NATC, p 484, p 486.

MAAG: Military Assistance Advisory Group: See entries under General O'Daniel; also - Dec. 1961, U. S. Army helicopter companies in VietNam for transportation purposes, p 311; 313-314; Gen. Harkins takes over in early 1962 and title is changed, p 315; MAAG disentablished - USMacV Commander, Westmoreland assumed all its missions and functions, p 338.

USS MADDOX - attack on in Tonkin Gulf, p 340.

SS MANHATTAN: Tanker used in experiment at Prudoe Bay, p 487-8.

U. S. Marines: first involvement in Vietnam with helicopter support, March, 1962 - p 315.

H. L. Miller

MARKET TIME: name given surveillance patrols off coast of South Vietnam, p 363-4; U.S. Coast Guard joins navy in these operations, p 364.

McDonald, ADM. David Lamar: as CNO shows interest in having Adm. Miller report on strikes and carrier operations in the South China Sea, p 372.

McNamara, The Hon. Robert: Briefed at CincPac Conference in December 1961 on situation in Vietnam, p 311-12; at conference - CincPac in July, 1962, p 316 ff; accepts estimate of General Harkins on duration of the Vietnamese war, p 325-6; President sends him and Gen. Taylor to Saigon in September, 1963, p 333; attends SecDef Conference on Vietnam on November 20, 1963, p 334; accompanies Mr. Cone to Saigon in Dec., 1963 to assess over-all effects of coup in November, 1963, p 335; names Major General Stillwell to serve as Chief of Staff to US MacV. p 336; p 373-4; p 387-389; speaker at commissioning of the CV- John F. Kennedy, p 437-8; p 441; portrait of Mr. McNamara, p 443-445.

USS MIDWAY: refitting with assistance of NATC, p 479.

Minh, General Duong-Van: (Big Minh): takes over as head of military revolutionary council (Nov. 1963), p 334; ousted in coup on January 30, p 1964, p 335.

Naval Air Development Center, Warminister: p 464.

Naval Air Station, Brunswick, Maine: p 465.

Naval Air Test Center - Patuxent, Maryland: Miller takes over Command in October, 1968, p 453-490; type of projects undertaken by the Test Center, p 454 ff; average number of plane types being tested, p 457-8; weather factors, p 460-1; Navy Test Facilities, p 462 ff; schedule for testing new planes, p 467-8; history of office of coordination of test and Evaluation for the Naval Air Systems Command, p 470-473; Navy industrial funding for NATC, p 474; illustration of how NATC assists in readying a carrier in drydock for refitting - the ENTERPRISE, p 476-8; the MIDWAY, p 479; the test pilot - a discussion, p 479 ff; success of the symposium for Test pilot reunions, p 484-5; "home of the astronauts", p 485.

U. S. Naval Institute - Board of Control: Miller serves as member of Board from 1966-71, p 451.

Naval Tactical Support Center for A/S Warfare - Adak, Alaska: p 468-9.

Navy Avionics Facility - Indianapolis, Ind.: p 462.

Navy Engine Test Facility, Trenton, N.J.: p 462.

Navy Missile Center - Point Mugu, California: p 462, p 466.

Navy Ships System Command, Panama City: p 464.

Navy Test and Evaluation Unit, El Centro, California: p 465.

Navy Test Facility - Albuquerque, N.M.: p 462.

Navy Test Facility, Lakehurst, N.J.: p 463.

Navy Test Facility, Philadelphia, Pa.: p 464.

Navy Weapons Laboratory - China Lake, California: p 462, 464, 466.

Nhu, Ngo Dihn: p 309; accuses CIA of trying to foment a coup against his brother (Oct. 7, 1963), p 333; killed in coup on November 2, 1963, p 334.

Nitze, The Hon. Paul: Adm. Miller briefs him on naval activities in the South China sea, p 372-3; p 388-89; p 390-1.

Nolting, The Hon. Frederick E., Jr.: 1961 - arrives in Saigon as U. S. Ambassador, p 310; replaced by Ambassador Henry Cabot Lodge in June, 1963, p 331-32.

North Vietnam; ground defenses and equipment, p 368-9.

Nuclear Power: Miller launches a major effort in the field when he becomes CHINFO, p 390-91.

O'Daniel, Lt. Gen. John W.: President Eisenhower names him as Chief of U. S. Mission to South Vietnam (1955), p 306; details U.S. Military Advisers to units of Vietnam army, p 307, 309; briefs SecDef on Vietnamese attitudes, p 312.

Odyssey House: in New York City - dedicated to task of rehabilitating drug addicts, p 504-5; Jim Murphy from Odyssey House acted as adviser to the Task Force on drugs, p 504-5.

Prince Sihanouk: p 332.

RA-5C - North American: photo reconnaissance plane, p 367-8.

USS RANGER - CV: flagship of Adm. Miller in CarDiv 3, p 346; p 356; planes from ship takes part in Flaming Dart # 1, p 359; Flaming Dart # 2, p 360; p 362; p 366; participates in Hot Stove, p 370-1.

Richardson, The Hon. Elliot: p 539.

Rickover, Adm. Hyman G.: Miller talks with him at time he takes USS ENTERPRISE to South China sea - promises to send reports, p 375; Miller, as Chinfo, works with him to sell idea of nuclear power, p 389-391.

Riley, VADM Herbert D.: Director of Staff, JCS - 1962, p 318.

ROLLING THUNDER MISSIONS: designation for U. S. bombing attacks on North Vietnam installations, p 365-6.

Rusk, The Hon. Dean: attends SecDef Conference in Hawaii on Nov. 20, 1963, p 334; at SEATO conference in Manila, Apr. 1964, p 337.

Russian Spy Ships: p 364-5.

SEATO: Council at Manila (Apr. 1964) calls for defeat of Viet Cong in South Vietnam, p 336-7; see entry under CincPac Weapons Demonstration, p 355.

SecDef Conferences at CincPac: Conference of July 23, 1962, p 316-7; topics of discussion, p 318-324; October 1962 conference, p 325-6; optimism, p 328-30; Conference of May, 1963, p 330; conference on Nov. 20, 1963, attended by Secretary Rusk, McNamara, etc.: p 334; support for military and exonomic aid to Big Mihn and the revolutionary council, p 335; June 1-2, 1964 conference, p 339.

Sharp, Adm. U. S. Grant: takes over as CincPac, 1964, p 339-40.

Shepherd, RADM Alan: Graduate of Test Pilot School, 485.

Sikes, The Hon. Robert L. F.: Member, U.S. House of Representatives; as member of Armed Services Committee helps get appropriation for Combat Art, p 425.

Stillwell, Major General Dick: named (March, 1964) as Chief of Staff to U S MacV, p 336.

South Viet Nam - Pilot Training: p 329-330.

U. S. Special Forces - South Vietnam: U. S. puts in Special Forces teams (1960) to help the Vietnamese, p 308.

Strategic Hamlet Program: initiated in Vietnam in February, 1962, p 313-314; subject for discussion at SecDef Conference in Hawaii, July, 1962, p 316.

Sylvester, The Hon. Arthur: Assistant Secretary of Defense for Public Affairs, p 389; p 406.

Task Force 77: Miller assumes command, p 345 ff., p 362.

Taylor, General Maxwell: Oct, 1961 arrives in Saigon as special adviser to President Kennedy, p 310; p 324-5; his interests at the Oct. 1962 SecDef Conference on Vietnam, p 326-7; President Kennedy sends him with SecDef in September, 1963 to talk with Diem, p 333; p 339, p 343; p 443.

Thailand: Military Assistance program for - laid out at SecDef Conference, July, 1962 - p 319.

Thompson, Brig. Gen. Sir Robert: British general who waged successful campaign against the communists in Malaya - later adviser to President Diem, p 314.

USS TICONDEROGA: unit in TF 77, p 347; p 355; p 383.

Tonkin Gulf Resolution: p 341; attack on the DDs NORTON and Edwards, p 342.

Viet Nam: resume of recent history - p 325 ff; optimism expressed over situation at SecDef Conference in October, 1962, p 328-9 ff.

VXN-8 Squadron: oceanographic squadron based on Patuxent, p 487-8.

Walker, RADM Thomas J.: relieves Adm. Miller in command of the
    ENTERPRISE TASK FORCE, p 386.

Watkins, Captain George: starts a public speaking seminar, p 410-411;
    p 485.

Westmoreland, General Wm. C.: Jan. 13, 1964 becomes Deputy on
    MacV staff, p 336; replaces Gen. Harkins as Mac V, p 337;
    names Gen. Throckmorton as Deputy, p 339.

WHITE HOUSE Conference on YOUTH: Estes Park, Colorado, 1971, p 491-
    547; Miller assigned to the task group on drugs, p 497; efforts
    at control, rehabilitation and education in the armed services,
    p 506-7; p 510; recommendation for legalization of marijuana,
    p 513-14; question of the military as delegates to the conference,
    p 523-525; ethnic groups, p 533-535; ideas for implementing
    the recommendations of the conference, p 536-7.

Whizz Kids: p 444-5.

Yankee Station - Yankee Team: Missions from Carriers (Yankee Station)
    began in September 1964 - photo reconnaissance over Laos,
    p 347-351; p 355-6; p 359; p 362, p 364; p 383.

Yates, Capt. Earl Preston (Buddy): Captain of CV JOHN F. KENNEDY,
    p 437-8; involved in problems of commissioning, p 441.

Zumwalt, Adm Elmo: p 372; p 418-419; p 436-7; p 483.

In Reply Refer to No.

CV8/A16-3
Serial 0015

U.S.S. HORNET (CV-8)

SECRET
DECLASSIFIED

April 28, 1942

OF10/Ld

Care of Postmaster,
New York, New York
San Francisco,
California.

From: Commanding Officer.
To : Commander-in-Chief, U.S. Pacific Fleet.
Via : Commander Carriers, Pacific Fleet.

Subject: Report of Action, April 18, 1942, with notable events prior and subsequent thereto.

Reference: (a) U.S. Navy Regulations, 1920, Article 712.

1. In compliance with reference (a), the following report of action is submitted:

(a) On 1 April, 1942, while HORNET was moored at the U.S. Naval Air Station, Alameda pier, sixteen Army B-25 bombers were hoisted to the flight deck and there parked. Under the command of Lieut. Colonel James H. Doolittle, U.S. Army, the B-25 Detachment consisted of seventy officers and one hundred thirty enlisted men. Lieutenant H. L. Miller, U.S. Navy, attached to the detachment as carrier take-off instructor also reported aboard for temporary duty, intending to return to Alameda after a demonstration take-off for the benefit of doubting Army pilots. The idea was abandoned when all planes were spotted for take-off and it was found that sixteen bombers could be comfortably accommodated, leaving a take-off run of 467 feet for the first plane. The advantage of having an extra plane for attack outweighed the desirability of demonstrating a proper take-off.

(b) At 1000, April 2, 1942, Task Force Eighteen, consisting of HORNET, NASHVILLE, VINCENNES, CIMARRON and Desdiv 22, stood out of San Francisco in a fog which reduced visibility to about 1000 yards. Once clear of the swept channel a northwesterly course was set. Air coverage was provided by Commander Western Sea Frontier until late afternoon. Navy blimp L-6 delivered two boxes of navigator's domes for the B-25s. Vessels of the Task Force were notified

- 1 -

CV8/A16-3
Serial 0015

DECLASSIFIED

OF10/Ld

April 28, 1942

Subject: Report of Action, April 18, 1942, with notable events prior and subsequent thereto.

------

of the mission by semaphore message late in the afternoon, and the crew of this vessel were informed by loudspeaker. Cheers from every section of the ship greeted the announcement and morale reached a new high, there to remain until after the attack was launched and the ship well clear of combat areas.

(c) On 6 April a strange type of numeral code was heard on 3095 kcs, strong signal (type of code: 69457 R 73296 R 47261 R). Japanese broadcast stations were continually monitored in order to establish program continuity. Any departure from their usual arrangement while HORNET was in the combat zone could have been construed as a warning of danger.

(d) Weather conditions were generally bad throughout the voyage. Heavy seas and high winds, coupled with rain and squalls, reduced the danger of being sighted but prevented cruiser aircraft from conducting flight operations. At times speed of the force was reduced to prevent structural damage to the CIMARRON. Destroyers fueled on 8 April.

(e) On April 9 instructions were received to delay rendezvous with Task Force 16 until 13 April. Reversed course and slowed to comply. Attempted to fuel HORNET from CIMARRON but had to defer the operation because of heavy seas. CIMARRON lost two men overboard in the attempt; one was recovered by life ring and heaving line, the other by MEREDITH. A man previously lost overboard from VINCENNES was also recovered by MEREDITH in a prompt and efficient manner. On 10 April CIMARRON fueled both cruisers. On 11 April set course 255° true for rendezvous with Task Force 16. On 12 April fueled HORNET and topped off cruisers and destroyers. CIMARRON efficiently fueled two destroyers simultaneously under adverse weather conditions. At 1630 LCT 12 April, radar transmissions were detected from 230°, distant 130 miles. Contact was made with Task Force 16 at daylight 13 April. From 2 April until junction with Task Force 16 no contacts of any kind were made.

(f) Various minor difficulties were experienced with the B-25s from departure until launching. Generator failures, spark plug changes, leaky gas tanks, brake trouble, and engine trouble culminated in the removal of one engine to the HORNET shops where it was repaired, then reinstalled. Planes could not be spotted for take-off until after final fueling because their wings overhung the ship's side. The high winds encountered

CV8/A16-3
Serial 0015
SECRET

OF10/Ld

April 28, 1942

Subject: Report of Action, April 18, 1942, with notable events prior and subsequent thereto.

---

caused vibrations in all control surfaces. Constant surveillance and rigid inspections were required to make certain the planes were properly secured to the flight deck.

(g) B-25s were spotted for take-off on 16 April. The last plane hung far out over the stern ramp in a precarious position. The leading plane had 467 feet of clear deck for take-off.

(h) On 18 April at 0800 orders were received to launch aircraft. Army crews, who had expected to take-off late in the afternoon, had to be rounded up and last minute instructions. Engines were warmed up, HORNET turned into the wind and at 0825 the first plane, Lieut. Colonel Doolittle, USA, pilot, left the deck.

(i) With only one exception, take-offs were dangerous and improperly executed. Apparently, full back stabilizer was used by the first few pilots. As each plane neared the bow, with more than required speed, the pilot would pull up and climb in a dangerous near-stall, struggle wildly to nose down, then fight the controls for several miles trying to gain real flying speed and more than a hundred feet altitude. Lieutenant Miller, USN, held up a blackboard of final instructions for the pilots, but few obeyed. That the take-off could be made easily when properly executed was shown when a B-25 made a straight run down the deck, lifted gently in an easy climb and gained altitude with no trouble.

(j) Plane handling on the flight deck was expeditious and well done. One plane handler lost an arm by backing into a B-25 propeller. A high wind of over forty knots and heavy swells caused HORNET to pitch violently, occasionally taking green seas over the bow and wetting the flight deck. The overall time for launching sixteen bombers was 59 minutes. Average interval, 3.9 minutes.

- 3 -

CV8/A16-3
Serial 0015
SECRET [DECLASSIFIED stamp]

OF10/LA

April 28, 1942

Subject: Report of Action, April 18, 1942, with notable events prior and subsequent thereto.

- -

(k) From April 13 to April 16, little of note occurred; weather continued to be heavy and squally, with generally poor visibility, which of course contributed to the success of the mission. ENTERPRISE maintained air patrol. Steaming on westerly courses.

(1) On April 17 all heavy ships were topped off and oilers and destroyers were detached. After fueling, cruisers and carriers continued their westerly advance at various high speeds (20 - 25 knots). 2000 position April 17: Lat:38°-33'N; Long. 157°-54'E. At 0310 April 18 made radar contact on unknown object, distance 3100 yards abeam. At 0313 course was changed by TBS to 350° T. At 0411 the ship was called to General Quarters and course was again changed to west. At 0507 course was changed into wind for launching of ENTERPRISE planes. At 0522 changed course to 270° T. At 0633 changed course to 220° T. At 0738 sighted enemy patrol craft of about 150 tons bearing 220°, distance 20,000 yards. At 0748 changed course to 270° T. At 0755 NASHVILLE opened fire on patrol vessel which was also bombed and strafed by ENTERPRISE planes. The vessel was still afloat when out of sight astern; NASHVILLE remained behind to destroy it. 0800 Position, April 18: Lat. 35°-26' N.; Long. 153°-27'E. At 0800 received orders from Comtaskfor 16 to launch bombers. At 0803 changed course into wind and prepared to launch; steaming at 22 knots, course 310° T. Crews manning planes and numerous lashings being removed from planes consumed several minutes. At 0825 launched first B-25 (Lieut. Colonel Doolittle pilot). Second plane launched 7 minutes later. Launchings have been previously discussed. Last bomber launched at 0920, after which HORNET reversed course to 090° T. and joined disposition. At 1100 word was received that enemy aircraft contact had been made by Japanese at 0830 (-10 time) in our approximate position at that time. At 1107 NASHVILLE rejoined. HORNET aircraft being made ready for launching. At 1115 launched 8 VF. At 1410 small enemy craft sighted 15,000 yards on port beam. NASHVILLE proceeded and destroyed this vessel. At 1425 an ENTERPRISE VSB crashed dead ahead of this ship while flight operations were being conducted. NASHVILLE recovered plane personnel. At 1445 Japanese language and English language broadcast announced the raid on Japan. No enemy aircraft sighted at any time. General Quarters stations were manned throughout the day.

- 4 -

CV8/A16-3
Serial 0015
DECLASSIFIED
OF10/Ld

April 28, 1942

Subject: Report of Action, April 18, 1942, with notable events prior and subsequent thereto.

- -

(m) The remainder of return trip was uneventful except for the loss of one VSB - both occupants were seen to sink - one with the plane and one unconscious alongside the plane. Entered Pearl Harbor morning April 25.

2. The Commanding Officer desires to state that the morale of the crew was exceptionally fine. All officers and men performed their duties in a completely satisfactory manner. No individual was outstanding or deserving of special commendation, and there is no reason for censure. Morale was somewhat lowered after danger of enemy air attack had diminished; a majority of the officers and men were quite surprised that no further action against enemy bases was contemplated, and were obviously disappointed. It is believed that attacks should be made as frequently as possible on raiding missions to keep morale and "action exhilaration" in a high state.

3. Submarines used in conjunction with such an attack would be highly valuable. They could cover the retreat of the attacking force and could possibly eliminate the patrol vessels in the track of the attacking force, permitting the latter to reach a more favorable launching point without being discovered.

M. A. MITSCHER.

A16-3

UNITED STATES PACIFIC FLEET
FLAGSHIP OF COMMANDER CARRIERS

Serial 0024

Pearl Harbor, T. H.,
29 APR 1942

DECLASSIFIED

C-O-N-F-I-D-E-N-T-I-A-L

1st endorsement to
CO HORNET Serial 0018
of April 28, 1942.

From: Commander Task Force SIXTEEN.
To: Commander-in-Chief, U. S. Pacific Fleet.

Subject: Report of Action, April 18, 1942, with notable events prior and subsequent thereto.

    1.   The Task Force Commander considers that the successful transportation and launching of the Army bombers under the continuous adverse weather conditions which prevailed reflects great credit to the Commanding Officer, HORNET, Lieutenant Colonel Doolittle, and the Army personnel involved.

    2.   The radar contact at 0310, April 18, distance 8100 yards abeam, mentioned in paragraph 1(i) of the basic report, is at considerable variance with presumably the same contact as reported by ENTERPRISE radar. At the time the ENTERPRISE was one mile astern of the HORNET, course 090 true. At 0310 the ENTERPRISE radar reported contact on two surface vessels bearing 090 true distance 21,000 yards. The contact was plotted to a minimum range of 18,000 yards, and disappeared from the screen at 27,000 yards, bearing 031 true.

W. F. HALSEY

Copy to:
CO HORNET.

SECRET
Declassified

U.S. NAVAL AIR STATION
Pensacola, Florida.
May 7, 1942.

*Copy to
R.Adm. Switzer
Com Nav Phil.*

From: Lieutenant Henry L. Miller, U.S. Navy
To: Captain D. B. Duncan, U.S. Navy.
Subject: Temporary additional duty assignment, report on.

1. On March 1, 1942, I was assigned to temporary additional duty to perform the following mission: To train Army pilots in carrier takeoff procedure employing B-25 aircraft. *at Eglin Field, Florida*

2. The narrative of events and operations subsequent to March 1st follows herewith: *On March 1, 1942 I reported to the B-25 detachment at Eglin Field for the above duty.*

Prior to formulating take-off procedure a study of characteristics and performance of the B-25B airplane and engine was made. Initial take-off procedure was based on the assumption that a maximum number of planes would be taken on board the carrier and that maximum allowable distance for take-off would be three hundred fifty (350) feet in a forty (40) knot wind with the plane loaded to 31,000 pounds, 2000 pounds over designed maximum load. A field was set aside for the exclusive use of the B-25 detachment. Runways were painted with a yellow stripe so that pilots could practice holding left wheel on the yellow line throughout the run. Flags were set at 250 feet, 400 feet, 450 feet, 500 feet, 550 feet, 600 feet, 650 feet and 700 feet.

On the first day with load of about 27,000 pounds, Captain Jones took the plane off at (50) miles per hour *Indicated air speed* using the following procedure:

    Flaps - Full down 45°
    Stabilizer - 3/4 tail heavy.
    Feet on brakes - brakes held on.
    Co-pilot opened throttles to 44".
    Pilot released brakes simultaneously, eased
back on yoke to get nose wheel light; then, as plane gathered speed, the pilot kept easing back on yoke until the tail skag was about two (2) feet off the runway, at which point he held it until the plane flew off.
    Immediately after take-off, the pilot pushed the nose over and rolled the stabilizer forward. He had to keep both hands on the yoke and fly the plane. The co-pilot worked the landing gear, throttles, and engine revolutions, after which the pilot bled the flaps up gradually.
    The distance was not measured on this run.

(1)

Declassified

May 7, 1942.

SECRET.

Subject: Temp. Add. duty report, Lt. H. L. Miller
- -

The above procedure was what was finally decided upon after experimenting with different flap settings, stabilizer settings and power settings.

To obtain the data which is recorded below, one man took stop watch time for 250' and time of take-off; one man measured distance of take-off; one man, myself, stood behind the pilot and took the airspeed on take-off. I also watched the pilot's technique so that constructive criticism could be given. Captain Jones and 2nd Lieut. Cray acted as instructors in showing the pilots exactly what to do. From the beginning, it was necessary to make the pilots constantly check the ball in the center and to insist on smooth flying throughout the takeoff:

Preliminary Training.

This was given merely for all pilots to get the correct procedure in mind. Also to obtain our best performance data. [Results are tabulated in Annex Afirm.]

Intermediate Training.

This training was given to ease the pilots into correct procedure with a greater load. [Results are tabulated in Annex Baker.]

Final Training.

This training was given to demonstrate to the pilots the procedure with the plane loaded for the mission assigned. [Results are tabulated in Annex Cast.] *On the last flight, last take-off (24 Bats) we crashed. No one hurt. Plane did not burn. Power Take-off was in a skid and emergency power not applied.*

On several occasions when only one or two planes were used, brakes heated up fast. A turn was made around the field with the landing gear down to remedy this situation.

The following details cut take-off distance considerably:

    1. Nose wheel straight.
    2. Release of brakes simultaneously.
    3. Same amount of power on both engines: i.e. 44".
    4. Getting nose wheel light initially.
    5. Not dragging tail skag on the runway.
    6. All pilots got considerable practice in takeoffs with wind as much as 90° to the runway. As each pilot progressed in take-off procedure, additional obstacles were placed in his way so that he would be able to take care of any

- 2 -

Declassified

SECRET.

May 7, 1942.

Subject: Temp. Add. Duty Report, Lt. H. L. Miller

situation which might arise on the "Big Day".

All pilots, with the exception of a few conservatives, caught on quickly. Doolittle, Gray and Jones were particularly outstanding. It was found that constant practice had to be given because pilots were prone to switch back to the conventional take-off.

Practice was given at Eglin Field, Florida, and at Willows, Calif., which is eighty-five (85) miles north of Sacramento, Calif.

Prior to going on board, lectures were given to officers and men on Carrier Deck Procedure, Safety Precautions, Naval Customs and Traditions, and Living Aboard Ship.

When the unit finally got aboard ship, it was found that with sixteen (16) planes, a take-off distance of four hundred sixty (460) feet was available. An extra plane was taken aboard, which was the sixteenth plane, for Lt. Joyce and myself to fly off on a demonstration run. However, when it was found that four hundred (460) feet were available, all sixteen (16) planes were taken on the trip.

Prior to the day of attack, all B-25-B's were dispersed along the deck.

On the day of attack the only change to the original take-off procedure was to keep the nose down (nose wheel still light) until the plane was past the island (stack and bridge); then, normal procedure was used. However, due to high wind across the deck, stabilizer was put in neutral after the first three (3) planes took off.

The first plane off (Doolittle) made a nice take-off. Second plane kept his nose in the up position too long and nearly stalled the plane. After the third plane took off pilots were shown via blackboard at the starting line to put the stabilizer in neutral. Succeeding take-offs were all good except one in which pilot did not have his flaps down. Either that or they worked up. He got away with it. Flaps on three (3) other planes were up, but ground crew caught it before take-off. Flight deck crew also straightened nose wheel before take-off.

Only casualty prior to take-off was a cracked nose glass in one plane caused by the rudder of another. Neither plane was held up. One sailor got an arm cut off by a propeller. It is believed that towing planes out of spot with tractor

- 3 -

Declassified

SECRET
Subject: Temp Add. Duty Report, Lt. H. L. Miller   May 7, 1942

would get them out with less risk to both planes and men when a forty (40) knot wind is blowing over the deck. It is

Take-offs were made under the most trying conditions. The ship was pitching badly. Fly One Officer released plane when ship was on down roll and between heavy pitches. There were intermittent rain squalls during the entire launching operation. Pilots held the left wheel on a white line which was painted on the deck. They did a mighty good job of it.

3. Recommendations for Future Operations with same type airplane:

1. Nose wheel pins, to keep nose wheel locked straight while plane is coming out of the spot aboard ship, should be left in place <u>until plane is out of spot.</u> Pins were made for this purpose but were not used because the Army Engineer Officer ordered them taken out before we could stop it.

2. A capable Engineer officer should be assigned to keep a constant check on the planes while aboard ship. The officer assigned for that duty on the ship should see that the planes are in all respects ready for flight operations. For the attack one plane (Capt. Jones) took off with a leaky bomb bay tank. He was given an additional fifty (50) gallons of gasoline in tin cans. Two planes (Lt. Lawson and Lt. Smith) took off with 24-volt generator out so that turret would have to be operated by battery. The right engine of one plane (Lt. Smith) was overhauled aboard ship. One plane (Lt. Watson) required a change of plugs on rear bank right engine just prior to take-off.

3. Spare batteries should be provided to be used while regular plane batteries are being charged. Spare generators should be taken along. Two (2) spare sets of plugs per engine should be provided. One hundred (100) more gallons of gasoline per plane should be provided.

4. A Finance Officer should be assigned to the detachment for regular payment of funds to the officers and men. This will maintain better security of the mission. Too many people wanted to know why the crews were supposed to be paid all over the country. The men were paid by the Navy aboard ship.

5. Greater secrecy should be maintained in the organization and administration for the assigned mission. Too many civilian and Army personnel knew what was being done, or seemed to know. Too much loose talk was heard from time to time. Overhaul and repair bases wanted to know too much.

Declassified

SECRET
Subject: Temp. Add. Duty report, Lt. H. L. Miller

May 7, 1942.

6. More experienced Navigators should be assigned for such an exacting assignment.

4. Conclusions:

a. 7. During the time aboard ship officers and men of both Services lived and worked together with commendable cooperation and unity of purpose. The Commanding Officer and personnel of the U.S.S. HORNET did everything possible to provide for the health and welfare of the combat crews and to insure the success of the mission. The Navy had the greatest respect and admiration for the Army combat crews who reciprocated this feeling. However it is recommended that naval aircraft Carrier Pilots be assigned to future tasks of this nature.

b. 8. Take-off procedure for forty (40) knots of wind down the deck:

    (a) Flaps full down - 45°.
    (b) Stabilizer in neutral.
    (c) Nose wheel straight.
    (d) Left wheel on white line.
    (e) Pilot hold brakes, then open throttle to 44". Co-pilot lock throttles in this position.
    (f) Pilot hold yoke to get nose wheel light on deck.
    (g) Pilot release brakes simultaneously and keep nose wheel light on deck until past the island. Then ease yoke back to get the nose up slowly until the tail skag is about two (2) feet off the deck. Hold this attitude until the plane flies off.
    (h) Immediately after take-off, pilot push nose down and adjust stabilizer. Co-pilot pull up landing gear, adjust throttles and engine revolutions, after which pilot bleeds up flaps. Pilot must fly the plane constantly while making take-off. Co-pilot handle throttles, etc.

4. Note: Two or three sets of hoisting gear for B-25 airplane are on the HORNET. In addition, two sets are at the Sacramento Air Depot.

H. L. MILLER.

c. 9. B-25B airplane, 31,000 lbs. can take off in 250' in a 40 kt. wind, using 44" M.P. On day of attack average run was about 350'. *Naturally every pilot was conservative.*

c. 10. Another recommendation: Planes should be out of check and overhaul two days before going aboard. Some of the planes on this mission got out of the Sacramento Air Depot on the day they were hoisted aboard; consequently a good test hop was impossible.

H. L. MILLER.

It was an exemplary performance by an outstanding group American boys who gave their all to fight a war. At the hour take-off, every officer and enlisted man aboard the Hornet would

Pilot	MP	Flap	Load	Wind	A.S.	Remarks	Time Dist.
York	30" then 44"	35°	appx. 26,000#	cross 45° 20 mph	70 mph	Did not come back fast enough on yoke. Strong cross wind. 30" released brakes then slow getting up to 44".	492'
"	"	"	"	"	75-80	Hard to get nose up. Did not have stabilizer back far enough. Strong cross wind.	552'
Hilger	30"	"	"	"	79	Touched again after take-off. Slow getting up to 44".	550'
"	"	"	"	"	74-78	Let nose drop after take-off. Slow getting up to 44".	560' appx.
Joyce	40" then 44"	"	4 men fwd, 1 man aft, 6 100# bombs De-Icers	1 mph	75	Too long on ground with nose wheel. Released at 40" while still easing throttle on to 44".	750'
Gray	44"	35°	appx 26,000#	7 mph	78	Jerky. Pilot swerved on take-off and was slow catching it.	804'
"	"	"	"	6 mph	70	Pretty good.	610'
"	"	"	"	"	"	Had to catch a turn of nose wheel with brakes at start	545'
Beth	"	"	"	5 mph	"	Excellent take off	495'
"	"	"	"	3 mph	78	Seemed okay.	640'
"	"	"	"	"	70	Good.	636'
Hallmark	"	45°	"	"	"	Seemed to hold it on ground a hair too long.	600'
"	"	"	"	"	75	Pilot started slow but rapidly got the dope on this procedure. Poor start.	775'
"	"	"	"	"	"	Little slow getting nose up.	610'
McElroy	30"# then 44"	"	"	"	70	Good procedure.	554'
"	40" then 44"	"	"	1 mph	80-85	Pilot had trouble easing up to 44" and keeping nose straight	990'
"	"	"	"	"	74	Pilot had trouble easing up to 44" and flying plane at same time	800'
"	40"	"	"	"	70	Pilot had 45" left engine and 41" right Plane was cocked around on take-off.	500'
Watson	"	"	"	3 mph	80	After release of brakes, pilot let nose drop.	665'
"	40" then 44"	"	"	"	65	Held nose on ground too long. Pilot had trouble easing both throttles to 44" evenly.	602#

Results of Preliminary Training (cont'd)

Pilot	M.P.	Flap	Load	Wind	A.S.	Remarks	Dist.
Watson	44"	40°	appx 26,000#	3 mph	62 mph	Released brakes and yanked up nose too high at start.	570'
						Note: Pilots seemed to have a great deal of difficulty trying to fly the plane smoothly when they used 30" or 40", released brakes, then opened throttles to 44". Hence, it was decided to start out initially with 44" manifold pressure. Col. Doolittle agreed that this was sound procedure.	
Holstrom	44"	45°	appx 26,000#	1-2 mph or none	75	Pilot was practicing by himself at beginning. His distances were 940'-910'-944'. When given procedure he readily got it and distance was cut to 810'; then to 510'	810'
"	"	"	"	"	80		
Daniel	"	"	"	3 mph	75	Held nose down a little too long.	510'
"	"	"	"	8 mph	"	Distances for take-off before instruction were 820'-931'-918'. This plane did not seem up to par. Pilot had a hard time gathering speed.	754'
Joyce	"	"	"	11 mph	"	Did not get nose up soon enough or high enough.	552'
"	"	"	"	"	"	Did not get nose up soon enough.	560'
"	"	"	"	"	"		550'
Farrow	"	"	"	none	75	Poor start. Nose wheel not straight. Touched twice.	690'
"	"	"	"	3 mph	"	Ran too far forward on nose, then yanked back. Tail wheel hit deck.	663'
"	"	"	"	"	"	Tail down too much but procedure improved.	600'
Steward	"	"	"	"	"	Am not including his data. He did not go with group.	
Hite	"	"	"	1-2 mph or none	74	Could not keep nose straight. Lost time and distance on takeoff.	678'
"	"	"	"	1-2 mph	70	Good procedure.	575'
Hinman	"	"	"	14 mph	70	Jerky. Tried to shove nose down too much.	445'
"	"	"	"	12 mph	65	Procedure Okay.	431'
"	"	"	"	"	75	Held on too long.	441'
"	"	"	"	13 mph	70	Tail was a hair too low.	430'
"	"	"	"	15 mph	75	Take off was made between gusts of wind.	450'
Smith	"	"	"	12 mph	70-	Tail off deck exact amount. Good procedure.	439'
"	"	"	"	"	75	Could get nose up one second earlier.	
"	"	"	"	13 mph	"	Excellent. This pilot has the news! Wind helps get weight off nose wheel.	365'
"	"	"	"	"	"	Excellent.	295'
"	"	"	"	12 mph	"	Excellent.	294'

Pilot	H.P.	Flap	Load	Wind	A.S.	Remarks.	Dist.
Hoover	44"	45°	appx. 26,000#	14 mph 20°-30° cross	70-	Good Wind. Good procedure for first time up.	312'
"	"	"	"	15 mph 20°-30° crosswind	75	Seemed good take-off. Wind died down during this period. Pilot stated he could not get power out of engine. Dragged tail skag on deck.	530'
"	"	"	"	"	"	Dragged tail skag on deck.	470'
Bates	"	"	"	"	"	Seemed Okay.	440'
"	"	"	"	"	"	Good procedure	450'
"	"	"	"	"	"	Okay.	450'
"	"	"	"	"	"	Nose down too long.	480'
"	"	"	"	16 mph 20°-30°	"	Nose down too long.	520'
"	"	"	"	"	"		500'
Bower	"	"	"	12-15 mph crosswind	"	Got tail down too far. Dragged tail skag on runway.	470'
"	"	"	"	"	"	Same	470'
"	"	"	"	"	"	Nose down just a bit too long.	450'
"	"	"	"	"	"	Nose down too long, then yanked back.	430'
"	"	"	"	"	"	Nose down too long.	500'
"	"	"	"	"	"	Nose down too long, then yanked back, and dragged tail skag on runway.	430'
Lawson	"	"	"	"	"	Nose down too long.	460'
"	"	"	"	"	"	Nose down all way.	560'
"	"	"	"	"	"	Nose still down too long.	450'
"	"	"	"	"	"	Okay procedure.	410'

Annex BAKER

Results of INTERMEDIATE TRAINING.

Pilot	M.P.	Flap	Load	Wind	A.S.	Remarks	Dist.
Jones	44"	45°	6 100# bombs. 2 men aft, 4 fwd. Full gas	30° cross 7 mph	75 mph	Poor start. Plane got cocked around on take-off. Nose was held down a little too long. Plane left ground as soon as nose came up.	535'
"	"	"	same except 5 men fwd	60° cross 7 mph	"	Good start. Radio man on toilet seat. One man on high turret.	550'
"	"	"	"	"	78	Poor start. Nose wheel cocked around.	600'
"	"	"	4 500# bombs 2 men aft, 4 fwd, full gas	45° cross 9 mph	80	Nose would not come up. Poor start.	750'
"	"	"	Same, but 2 men by toilet	"	73	Easier getting nose up. Poor start and touched brakes once along run.	700'
Smith	"	"	4 500# bombs. 2 men aft, 5 fwd, full gas	60° cross 10 mph	75 – 80	Pilot stated it was harder to get speed up with this weight. Difficult to keep plane straight in cross wind.	700'
"	"	"	"	"	"	Same	700'
Farrow	"	"	Same except 4 men fwd	45° cross 9 mph	75	No ammunition. Farrow made about six landings previous to this. Data was not recorded: Lt. Miller was not there.	688'
"	"	"	4 500# bombs. 3 men aft, 5 fwd, gas full less 100	"	80	Pilot did not get his nose up in time. Farrow flies plane smoothly though. He seems to have the news.	705'
McElroy	"	20° after release down 45°	Same except 120 gal short	Slight cross 11 mph	75 – 80	Slow coming back on yoke. Could have got plane offsooner.	685'
"	"	"	"	Slight cross 9 mph	75	Did not hold it off when he had nose in take off position.	720'
"	"	"	"	Slight cross 10 mph	74	Seemed like a pretty good take-off.	668'

Note: Full gas equals bomb bay plus wing tanks.

Annex BAKER

Results of INTERMEDIATE TRAINING (cont'd)

Pilot	M.P.	Flap	Load	Wind	A.S.	Remarks	Dist.
Gray	44"	20° then 45°	4-500# bombs 5 men fwd, 3 aft, Full gas less 120 gal	Slight cross 10 mph	80 mph	Gray and co-pilot Hinman said 45° flap at start was better. Co-pilot might push flap handle wrong way after start of run. Flaps got all way down at 450 ft.	618'
"	"	30°	"	Slight cross 12 mph	76	Wind seemed to be picking up. Pilot dragged tail skag on mat.	710'
Hinman	"	45°	Same except less 200 gal.	Slight cross 13 mph	75	Nose down too long.	650'

Note: Full gas equals bomb bay plus wing tanks.

It was found that all pilots readily caught on to heavier load take-offs, and because time was at a premium, final training with full load was begun.

Doolittle, Jones, Greening, York, Hilger and Gray made additional preliminary and intermediate test take-offs which were not recorded. All pilots made short take-offs from time to time just to keep in practice.

Results of FINAL TRAINING

Pilot	M.P.	Flap	Load	Wind	A.S.	Remarks	Stabilizer	Dist.
Hoover	44"	35°	Full gas 5 men fwd 1 aft, 4 500# bombs 800# ammunition	14 mph	70 mph	Poor start. Pilot cocked plane around. Lost time and distance.	tailheavy 3/4	750'
"	"	"		13 mph	"	Same	1/2	740'
"	"	45°		14 mph	65	Seemed like a good takeoff. 45° cross wind, gusty.	tailheavy full	720'
"	"	30°		"	72	Cocked plane around on takeoff this and next run.	same	660'
"	"	40°		"	68	Lost time and distance. Wind seemed lighter for this takeoff.	same	750'
"	"	35°		15 mph	75	Pilot said both of the runs felt tailheavy to him 60° crosswind.	3/4	700'
"	"	45°		14 mph	68	60° crosswind	same	750'
Daniel	"	35°	Same except 3 men fwd, 1 aft	90° cross 14 mph	78	Plane flew pilot all over mat due to crosswind of 90°	same	750
"	"	45°		90° cross 15 mph	65	Could have pulled back a little sooner.	same	680'
Watson	"	35°	Same except 2 aft	90° cross 17 mph	60	Dragged tail skag on deck for 30°	same	750'
"	"	45°		90° cross 14 mph	55	Just touched tail skag lightly once	same	660'
							T.O. Time	
Greening	"	"	Full gas 3 men fwd, 1 320# ballast. 4 500# bombs	7 mph appx.	80	Held nose down much too long. Did not haul yoke back enough.	14 sec.	990'
"	"	"		8 mph	75-- 76	Got yoke back but took a running start. Said brakes wouldn't hold.	13 sec.	800'
"	"	"		9 mph	74	Better. Put. stab. back farther to 3/4ths.	14 sec.	830'
Hinsman	"	"		11 mph	75-- 80	Good start. Nose up too much. Dragged tail on runway.	14 sec.	750'
"	"	"		"	74	Good start. Was off in 650' but did not hold it.	12½ sec.	720' MPH 250'
Holstrom	"	"	Same except 4 men fwd	9 mph	70	Held nose up then released. Good start, rough procedure.	12½ sec.	680' 55mph
"	"	"		11 mph	68	Good start. Handled nicely.	10½ sec.	640' 55
Beth	"	"	same	"	75	Did not get nose up quite soon enough. Rough technique.	12½ sec.	700' 55
"	"	"	same	"	69	Good start, good procedure. Perfect take-off.	11½ sec.	630' 50
Hite	"	"	Same	"	70	Good start, good takeoff.	11½ sec	680' 50
"	"	"	"	12 mph	74	Good start. Tail down too much.	11 sec	635' 52

Note: Full gas equals bomb bay and wing tanks.

Pilot	M.P.	Flap	Load	Wind	A.S.	Remarks	T.O. Time	Dist
Gray	44"	45°	Full gas 4-500# bombs	15°-20° cross 8-10 mph wind & rain	74 mph	Dragged tail skag. Poor start	17 sec.	785'
Bower	"	"	"	"	"	Poor start. Dragged tail skag	13	770
"	"	"	"	"	80	Poor start. Jerky. Touch tail skag	16	810
Lawson	"	"	4 men forward 1300# ballast	"	74	Jerky. Poor start. Pulled and pushed yoke.	14	715
"	"	"	"	"	"	Cross wind. Left wheel off at 575'. Jerky coming back on yoke.	15	740'
"	"	"	"	"	"	Won't get nose up. Nose wheel cocked on take-off	15	740'
Bates	"	"	"	"	"	Won't get nose up.	13	640'
"	"	"	"	"	75	Won't get nose up. Could have been off in 500'	12	600'
Smith	"	"	"	"	76	Nose down a hair too long	12½	640
"	"	"	"	"	73	Nose down too long. Yanked it off, dragged tail skag and wheels were off 150' before tail	14	740
"	"	"	"	"	75	Got lots of speed then yanked it off, dragged tail skag and lost speed	15	750
Hallmark	"	"	"	"	77	Did not seem to gain speed on this run even tho nose was down. Nose cocked around for take-off.	14½	750
"	"	"	"	"	74	Lots of rain. Wind died down, did not get nose up enough for takeoff. Nose cocked around	14	700
Hinman	"	"	Full gas 4-500# bombs	None	70	Lost time and distance on straightening out after release of brakes. Shows what an initial wind will do to help straighten out.		995
"	"	"	3 men fwd 750# ballast	cross 30° 7c8 mph	70	Same. And tail not down. dragged last 100'		900
"	"	"	"	"	70	Same. And tail okay 12'		850
Doolittle	"	"	Same except 4 men fwd	cross 20° 10 mph	75	Brakes slipped slightly. Lost time and distance getting straight. Left engine came back to 42". Nose up then pushed down.		950'
"	45"	"	"	"	"	Better procedure, but can still get tail down a little more. Nose was late coming up.		850'
"	46"	"	"	"	"	Bad start. Jerky procedure.		870'
"	45"	"	"	"	"	Nose up and down twice on takeoff.		810'
"	"	"	"	"	"	Bad start. Nose wheel cocked. Used brakes to straighten out		850
"	"	"	"	"	78	Bad start.		900'

Annex CAST

Subject: Temp. Add. Duty Report, Lt. H. L. Miller, May 7, 1942

Results of FINAL TRAINING (cont'd)

Pilot	M.P.	Flap	Load	Wind	A.S.	Remarks	Dist.
Gray	44"	45°	4 500# bombs, 800# ballast. 5 men fwd. full gas	45° cross 9 mph	75 mph	Had trouble holding brakes. Pilot said nose would not come up without stabilizer back at least 3/4ths.	710'
"	"	"	"	"	80	Pilot did not have trouble keeping left wheel on yellow line, which was painted on runway. Tail skag hit on runway last 100'.	750'
"	"	"	"	"	70	Nose cocked around on take-off. Good procedure but pilot eased nose up too fast. Wind died down about 5 mph for this run.	710'
Holstrom	"	"	"	70° cross 10 mph	74	Good procedure. A little trouble keeping straight due to crosswind and nose wheel cocked.	850'
"	"	"	"	20° cross 10 mph	78	Better run, but pilot lost distance by hitting tail on deck.	750'
Joyce	"	"	"	12 mph	80	Did not get the nose up soon enough. Cool air, therefore much better prop efficiency and lift.	750'
"	"	"	"	"	74	Same remarks as above.	685'
Smith	"	"	"	"	74	Did not get nose up soon enough. Poor start.	816'
"	"	"	"	10° cross 8 mph	78	Did not get nose up soon enough.	770'
"	"	"	"	2-3 mph	65	Hit tail on runway but used better procedure. Runway very wet. No tendency of tires to slip on runway.	750'
Daniel	"	"	"	15° cross 12 mph	70	Could not get nose soon enough due to loading of plane.	720'
"	"	"	"	"	75	Did not get nose up soon enough. Veered off yellow line. Poor start. Lots of rain.	820'
"	"	"	"	45° cross 8 mph	65	Kept plane in straight line. Touched wheels twice after take-off.	700'

RESULTS OF FINAL TRAINING (cont'd)

Pilot	M.P.	Flap	Load	Wind	A.S.	Air Temp.	Dist.	Remarks
Gray	44"	45°	Full gas plus crawlway tank. 4 men fwd, 1 man aft.	20° across 5 mph	76 mph	60° F	950'	Good start. Tail just right. Got plane off then settled back.
"	"	"	500# bombs.	7 mph	"		850'	Good start. Good procedure.
Bates	"	"	900# ballast aft. 100# ballast fwd.		75-80 mph	63°	800'	Jerky procedure. Good start. Still jerky procedure but much better. Pilot has improved greatly on technique.
"	"	"		5 mph			850	Good procedure. Plane crashed after takeoff due to pilot taking off in a skid with right wind down, and holding nose up too long after takeoff. No casualties.
"	"	"					850	

Note: It was found that DeIcers made no appreciable difference in takeoff. Additional takeoffs were made at Willows, Calif. with light load for several of the pilots, so that their procedure would be refreshed.

Note: The whole-hearted cooperation of all pilots contributed materially to the ease with which the procedure was learned.

- 4 -

Talk by Commander Henry L. Miller, Commander, Carrier Air Group SIX at Propeller Club Luncheon 21 June 1944.

Gentlemen, the first part of my story sounds like the Mutual Admiration Society of Navy and Merchant Marine getting together for a lengthy pat on the back. Nevertheless those of us who have been out that way seeing the supplies pile in, have taken off our hats to you people who build those ships for the Navy and you who operate those ships to get the men and materials to us. We know that the Armed Forces have taken most of the help and realize the shipping industry is operating on a shoe string, that is why we in the Navy just wonder how you do it.

Mr Wheeler suggested that I talk on some war experiences in those battles in the Pacific, so I'll go ahead with a few until I see someone throw in the towel.

My first job in the Big Time was pretty easy. Back in February of '42 I received the assignment of training General Doolittles' pilots to take off from a carrier to hit Tokyo. It was thrilling work for me because up to that part of the war, I was instructor at the Naval Air Station, Pensacola, Florida and I at least felt that with this assignment I was finally getting into some contact with war. After a free ride on the Hornet to the Jumping off spot for the Bombers, I returned to the U.S.A. and in August got orders to a Fighter Squadron as Squadron Commander. Our assignment was aboard the new navy cruiser hull carrier. After training like a bunch of <u>beavers</u> for several months during which time I got to be Group Commander in addition to my Squadron Commanders job, we headed for the Pacific and the war with the Japs. We weren't long in getting started. While other carriers were hitting Marcus Island, we covered a landing force that built an air strip on Baker Island, after which we hit Tarawa and

-1-

Makin. From there, we started to play the South Pacific circuit where the going was really tough. After four (4) strikes on Bougainville, to keep those airfields neutralized while our forces made landings at Empress Augusta Bay, Admiral Halsey ordered us on an all out strike against the strongest spot in the South Pacific, Rabaul. The Japs had a strong cruiser and destroyer force there just ready to come down and knock off our small force at Empress Augusta Bay. We with a big carrier, killed that deal by sinking or seriously damaging eight (8) cruisers and two (2) destroyers in Rabaul Harbor. That strike was pretty rugged. Everything in the Pacific after that was anti-climax. The A.A. was so intense that it seemed as tho one could step out of his plane and walk down from 20,000 feet to the ground. In addition, there were 75 - 100 Jap fighters in the air, of which our task group shot down about twenty-five (25). One of my pilots protected the Group Commander of the big carrier. He shot down one (1) Jap fighter and came back with 288 bullet holes in his plane. The Hellcat looked like a sieve. They even shot the wrist watch off his wrist and the throttle out of his hand. He was ready to go in to battle again about ten (10) days later. We hit Rabaul again about a week later, then started for Nauru Island which we beat up pretty badly while the other carriers were hitting Tarawa. From Nauru, we proceeded to Tarawa where we helped out while the landing forces were taking that island. When that job was in the bag, we proceeded to Pearl Harbor at which place the pilots got some much needed rest before going on the Marshalls Operation. Civilization really looked good to us for a change, plus fresh vegetables, a can of beer, and those wonderful island steaks. The people in the islands were very generous in their hospitality and did much in providing a home-away-from-home for the pilots over Xmas.

In January, we hit the Marshalls with the whole works. Our assignment was the islands of Wotje, and Taroa. In three (3) days of bombing and strafing, those islands looked pretty moth eaten and the Japs took an awful pasting. It looked pretty easy, so off we went to the Northwest part and started in on Eniwetok where after bombing the place to pieces, we supported the landings. When the air strip was smoothed over at Eniwetok, some of us were given the opportunity to fly in and land and see the damage that we had done. One and one half (1½) hours on that island and our hearts went out to the Army, Navy and the Marines who had to live on the place. It was full of holes from bombardment, full of dead Japs, and full of just plain dirt. I didn't feel clean for a week.

Our next operation was close ahead. We joined up with the rest of the Carrier Navy, the BB, CAs, and DDs and proceeded to find out what the Japs had at Palau about 500 miles from the Phillippines. The U.S. Navy that we saw was really an impressive sight. There were ships as far as the eye could see. The day before we got in there, the Japs picked us up and of course sent quite a few totpedoes plane attacks against us that nite. Well, they never got back to tell the folks about what they saw because our fighters and ships gun fire knocked them all down. Our task force got quite a few ships, shore installations, and about 90 Jap planes on that operation. On the way back, we made raids on Yap and Woleai islands, left our calling cards, and returned to our base.

Hollandia was next on the list. We worked with General McArthur in bombing the spot and supporting the landings. The hardest part of that work was the weather. It seems as tho there are always a maze of thunder storms around there and one just has to get by them some way. At times it is nip and tuck but fortunately we didn't lose any planes on that account. With the greater part of the Navy down in the Southwest Pacific it seemed to be a pretty good idea to give Truk a jolt as we went by. So on 29 and 30 April, we spent quite a few hours dropping bombs, strafing ground installations, and shooting down planes at that Jap stronghold. It looked pretty sick when we left. Every island in that atoll that had anything of value on it was bombed. On the second day, all the planes were given the big island of Dublon at Truk for a target, that spot was really plastered. We had cleaned out all the planes in the air and on the ground the previous day, so there was no air opposition the next day.

Truk was the last job for our Air Group. After 9½ months of combat, we returned to the states for some rest, then to reform and go out again. I was given a bigger Air Group, and at present we are in a training status trying to get to the point of being a hot outfit before going out to the Big Time.

Our Air Group was together for 18½ months. During that period, we lived, and fought together most of the time. An outfit like that really gets pretty close, in a way, just as close as any family. When the time comes for breaking up and going back for a rest, one certainly hates to do the parting. We had a fine bunch of boys who got along together beautifully. If we lost one after all that we had been thru, it was pretty hard to take. As a comparison, a husband sees his family after the days work is done. We were together for 18½ months almost every day, all day.

The war game always has its amusing side. One squadron in the South Pacific had a young pilot, who was trying to make good, going down to Guadalcanal for some supplies so they told him to try and bring back some beer. This youngster put about four (4) cases of canned beer in the wings of his plane just aft of the ammunition boxes and proceeded to return to his base. On the way, he figured that a strafing run on this Jap island would finish up a good day so down he went. The pilot realized the plane was hit after he pulled out of his strafing run and had a hard time sitting it down at his home base. However, with the whole squadron waiting for the beer, he felt quite the hero until they opened up the wing and found that a 90 millimeter shell from the AA had gone thru the four (4) cases of beer.

On one job where we were supporting the landings on an island, we listened in on the tank circuit. The lead tank called another and said "Hey Joe, I've got all the Japs pushed back on this corner, how's to tell the other tanks to come up here and give me a hand". Joe called back and said "I'll be right there but those other guys are all down in the south end hunting souvenirs". The great American boy!

One of our really crack Group Commanders who is just now coming back for a rest got so enthused over an attack that he forgot to use his bean for a couple of minutes. The following conversation tells the story. Lets call the characters Singing Sam and Barry.

"Barry this is Singing Sam, go ahead" -- No answer.

"Barry this is Singing Sam, answer me" -- No answer.

Very indignant now --

"Barry, this is Singing Sam, when I call you, answer me" -- Still no answer --

a long pause, then "Barry, this is Singing Sam, if you don't hear me, turn on your radio"!

If the ships are fortunate in dropping the hook at the right base, one can usually find enuff nurses for a dance. Just before we hit Palau, we were at one of those bases and the boys were making up for lost time. Two carriers had a party, then came our turn. Our pilots wanted to have the best one that was ever put on, so for three (3) days, they went tearing around the countryside bartering real eggs and real round potatoes, no foolin', for dates with the nurses. It was pretty tough going because the nurses at this base had lots of Army, Navy and Marines who were more or less permanent settlers on this island. Party day came around and only about 12 of the pilots had dates. Nevertheless, they went ahead with the arrangements. Down-stairs of this so called club was fixed up with the food (a buffet supper), soft lites, sweet music (from a makeshift quartet who were pretty good), and all sorts of nite club effects. Up-stairs, they had the big orchestra, which was borrowed, the bar, dancing, tables, and even a photographer. Everything was all set but the gal situation, when lo and behold, two hours before the big Event a hospital ship steamed into the harbor. Our boys were out there in boats before they anchored and when the orchestra played its opening number, in marched about 25 brand new fresh caught nurses with our pilots just beaming behind them. The other two Group Commanders turned around, looked at me and said "O.K. Miller, you win".

Thank you gentlemen for your kind attention, it was certainly a pleasure to be here. ---

INDUSTRIAL COLLEGE OF THE ARMED FORCES
Washington, D. C.

Economic Mobilization Course
1952-1953

REQUIREMENTS BRANCH

INDIVIDUAL REPORT NO. 170

SUBJECT: OIL FOR THE LAMPS OF FREEDOM OR FREE-WORLD OIL
REQUIREMENTS

Prepared by: Henry L. Miller
Commander, USN

Date Submitted: 19 January 1953

CONTENTS

	Page
INTRODUCTION	1
I. FREE-WORLD REQUIREMENTS	3
A. Petroleum Demand	3
B. Prediction of Requirements	3
II. FREE-WORLD SUPPLY	4
III. FREE-WORLD REFINING CAPACITY	5
IV. FREE-WORLD RESERVES	7
V. TOTAL MOBILIZATION	8
A. Total War Requirements	8
B. Total War Supply Problems	10
C. Iron Curtain Requirements for Total War	13
VI. FUTURE OUTLOOK ON OIL	14
A. Incentive to Produce	14
B. Future Estimates and Synthetics	17
SUMMARY	20
CONCLUSIONS	21
BIBLIOGRAPHY	23
APPENDIX I	25

INTRODUCTION

1. As of the end of 1952, the free peoples of the world have further fortified themselves against a common enemy in the possession of the most essential commodity of war and peace--petroleum. Petroleum has truly become a world industry-- and yet, it has just started in the full realization of its potentialities.

2. Supplies, which for more than half a century largely centered in one country, have spread until nearly half of the output comes from scattered areas outside the United States. Seventy percent of the world's proven reserves are now located in the newer areas.

3. Refining has become a major industrial enterprise in many countries. War rehabilitation and the postwar objectives of better living for all people have been and will continue to be based on petroleum.

4. Since 1946, Russia and her satellites are credited with increased crude oil production 519,000 bbl. daily. The gains elsewhere in the free world have totaled 4,296,000 bbl. daily, or eight times greater. The increase in Texas alone for the six-year period has been twice that of the iron curtain countries. Gains in the Middle East, despite the shutdown in Iran, are two and one-half times greater.

5. Russia now has at her disposal less than 10 percent of the world's petroleum output. This is hardly more than a start in fueling a major conflict. At the same time, it should be apparent that the controlling responsibility of our country and its friends is to see that this 90 percent position in petroleum supplies is maintained and protected.

6. All this necessitates a new statesmanship among free nations that understands the responsibilities and opportunities of this dominance in oil as the base for prolonged world peace.1/

7. This report will consider the problems of free-world requirements of petroleum to make this prolonged peace a reality. It will also summarize the free-world supply, refining capacity, and reserves. The first part of the report will cover the years of 1952, 1953, 1954, and 1955, assuming that the Korean conflict will continue during those years and that no global war nor an additional "Korea" will break out. The projections of the oil forecast for the above years assume no worldwide economic depression. The remainder of the report will consider requirements for total war and the future of oil. See appendix I.

1/ "Petroleum--The Base for a Peaceful World". The Oil and Gas Journal, vol. 51, No. 33, p. 135, 22 Dec 1952.

I. FREE WORLD REQUIREMENTS.

　　A. **Petroleum Demand.**

　　　　1. Total petroleum demand of the free countries of the world for 1952 amounted to about 11,800,000 barrels per day (b/d). In 1946, the actual requirements were 7,110,000 b/d.[1] The United States alone is now burning up oil products at the rate of about 7,200,000 b/d. Predictions by the oil industry on future requirements after W. W. II fell far short of the actual demand. With the help of a boost in imports after W.W. II, the industry kept supply one jump ahead of the tremendous increase in requirements.

　　B. **Prediction of Requirements.**

　　　　1. How do they predict these requirements? Basically, as with any business forecast, they studied economic trends, industrial expansion, population shift and growth, capital investment in new plants and durable equipment, employment levels, total energy needs, transportation requirements and availability, and possibility of future war.

　　　　2. However, they failed to add in a boom instead of a recession, more cars and diesel locomotives, the Korean incident, and the shift to oil and gas by many users in heating and industrial plants.

　　　　3. Appendix I shows the free world total oil requirements up to and including 1955.[2] It shows a marked increase of roughly 600,000,000 bbl. per year.

---

[1] "Free World Demand Nears 12,000,000 Bbl. Daily", *The Oil and Gas Journal*, vol. 51, No. 33, p. 187, 22 Dec 1952.
[2] Ibid., p. 188.

II. FREE WORLD SUPPLY.

1. Total production of crude oil and allied products for the free countries of the world reached a level of about 11,949,000 b/d in 1952.[1]

2. Appendix I shows the predicted supply, including and excluding Iran. It indicates a great increase of supply which runs parallel with the increase in requirements over this period.

3. Oil supply is now in good shape. The one tough product to whip is aviation gasoline presently due to its high cost. Petroleum Administration figures indicate that the supply of aviation gas is currently running 20,000 b/d short of requirements. This situation should be righted by June of 1953. However, this product will continue on the marginal list for another couple of years because the oil industry does not want to convert refining capacity unless they are paid for the risk.

4. Supply of crude oil keeps pace with the needs only through the discovery of new fields. It is felt that the current program of 50,000 new wells per year, which the Petroleum Administration for Defense has laid down, will maintain an excess of crude oil under present world conditions.

---

[1] "Free-World Demand Nears 12,000,000 Bbl. Daily", The Oil and Gas Journal, vol 51, No. 33, p. 188, 22 Dec 1952.

III. FREE-WORLD REFINING CAPACITY.

1. Appendix I shows the refining capacity of the free-world for the years 1952-1955, and the number of refineries plus the crude oil distillation of these refineries in 1952.

2. Crude oil input capacity, on a basis of total world refining, is now nearing 14,000,000 bbl. daily. Of this total, about 13,000,000 bbl. daily are refined by the free world countries and only 1,000,000 bbl. daily by Russia and her satellites. The United States refines about 7,200,000 bbl. per day. The free world has 552 refineries, of which the United States has 329. Russia and her satellites have 84 refineries.

3. The largest refinary in the world is Abadan, in Iran. It refines 500,000 b/d, of which 18,000 b/d is aviation gasoline. If, and when, Abadan gets back into operation, it will be a long, slow process. Only a small portion of the Abadan refinery is now being utilized because of nationalization of the oil industry.

4. Only 12 new refineries will be built in 1954, with an additional 8 being projected for 1955-56.[1] The free-world's refining capacity for the next few years will still be inadequate to meet the requirements as to quality and quantity of certain products. This stems from the many different kinds of petroleum products required in both civilian and military use, including aviation gasoline and jet fuel.

---

[1] Tuttle, R. B. "Survey of Oil Refineries", The Oil and Gas Journal, vol. 51, No. 33, p. 303, 22 Dec 1952.

5. At present, several oil companies are cutting down on the numbers of greases refined. They are substituting lithium-based all-purpose greases. This step alone will greatly increase the refining capacity for other products.2/

2/ "Domestic Notes", Business Week, p. 96, 27 Dec 1952.

IV. FREE WORLD RESERVES.

1. Most of the increases estimated to have occurred in world reserves of crude oil in 1952 again were made in the prolific fields bordering the Persian Gulf.

2. Appendix I shows the free world crude reserves of 1952. The tabulation is based on available published data on reserves by geographic areas and also reflects opinions of various informed sources in the industry.

3. After the Middle East, the other most important country is Venezuela, followed by Canada and Mexico.

4. Estimates of crude reserves behind the Iron Curtain are largely guesses. Nevertheless, in accordance with current oil estimates they are overly optimistic. Available information on production in Romania indicates a steady decline. Increases have been given the other satellite countries.[1]

5. A good estimate is that the Iron Curtain countries now have about one-eighth of the world's oil reserve of about 118,000,000,000 bbl. This figure amounts to about 9,500,000,000 bbl., with the free-world having about 108,500,000,000 bbl.

---

[1] Duff, D. "Reserves Gain Largely from Persian Gulf Areas". The Oil and Gas Journal, vol. 51, No. 33, pp. 180-184, 22 Dec 1952.

V. TOTAL MOBILIZATION.

A. Total War Requirements.

1. The requirements for full mobilization in all out war are not as great as the free-world demand, refining capacity, or supply, as indicated in Appendix I, with the exception of aviation gasoline, which is noted below.[1]

2. The wartime requirements problem of POL in full mobilization arises, not from excessive consumption, but rather from requirements due to damage or loss of POL through enemy action.

3. Economically, we now have enough oil fields producing to satisfy the requirements of the free-world in all out war if civilian consumption is rationed to the tune of 2,000,000 b/d of crude oil.

4. From Appendix I, it can be seen that the following picture of world oil is apparent for total mobilization for war:

N & S America $\neq$ Europe & N. Africa & Middle East $\neq$
2,000,000 b/d civilian consumption = Enough to fight.

N & S America $\neq$ Europe & N. Africa & Middle East $\neq$
2,000,000 b/d civilian consumption = Enough to fight.

N & S America $\neq$ Europe & N. Africa – Middle East $\neq$
2,000,000 b/d civilian consumption = Not enough to fight.

In any case of the three above, there will not be enough aviation gasoline in the first six months of the war to go all out. However, the supply will catch up to the requirements after this time.[2]

---

[1] Coleman, Wilson H., Cdr, USN, POL Team, JLPG, Interview, Wash., D. C., 29 Dec 1952.
[2] Ibid.

5. To summarize the picture of free world requirements in total war, the following totals show what we have now and what military POL and AvGas is required through fiscal 1954:

Military Storage facilities   500 bbl. or more   30 June 1952

ZI	Overseas	Total U. S. Storage
29,865,916 bbl.	48,820,785 bbl.	78,696,701 bbl.

Requirements
   Thousands Barrels per day

	1952	(1st Half 1953	
Total Allied Military POL	445	538	---
U. S. Civilian	6630	7036	---
Foreign Civilian	3515	3747	---
Bunkers (mostly civilian)	1062	1032	---
Total	11,652	12,353	---

Total yearly U. S. Military POL   410,391 b/d 1952 — 519,190 b/d 1953 — 641,000 b/d 1954.

Total yearly U. S. Military Av Gas   98,650 b/d 1952 — 126,500 b/d 1953 — 137,870 b/d 1954. [3]

---

[3] Smith, Lt Col, USA, Munitions Board, Interview, Wash., D. C., 9 Jan 1953.

B. Total War Supply Problems.

1. As has been pointed out, the requirements of POL for total war are not as high as would be expected. Losses from enemy action would be made up through civilian rationing. However, many other precautions would necessarily have to be taken in order to maintain the required supply. These are enumerated below:

    a. "As of October 1, 1952 there were 2084 oil tankers of over 6000 Dead Weight tons in the world, totaling 30,809,024 dead weight (d.w.) tons. Russia had 19 of these totaling 180,769 d.w. tons. Tankers are totaled in terms of T-2 type tankers of W.W.II fame. The T-2 tanker, of 16,600 d.w. tons, 14.5 knot speed, was built in U. S. shipyards.

    "The 2084 tankers now available are listed as the equivalent of 1709.5 T-2 tankers.

    "There are presently the equivalent of 107 T-2's under construction or on order in United States yards of which only 53 are destined for registry under the United States flag."

    "We now have a surplus of tankers in the free-world. Estimated war losses indicate that for all out war, the U. S. should continue an accelerated tanker construction program."[1]

    b. Rationing.

It is estimated that from the over 7,000,000 b/d of oil now being used in the U. S., 2,000,000 b/d could be saved for military use from civilian consumption in all out war. This saving would come from gas rationing and house heating.

---

[1] Winterbottom, John J. "Tanker Tonnage Keeps Pace with Soaring World Demand for Petroleum Products", The Oil and Gas Journal, vol. 51, No. 33, p. 192, 22 Dec 1952.

c. Reactivation of Old Fields.

Old oil fields, which are now marginal to produce, would be reactivated in total mobilization. Navy oil reserves would also be opened for global war. This would greatly increase the domestic output.

d. Stockpiling.

It is planned to stockpile as much in the way of oil and oil products as is possible so that lifting of oil during the first six months of conflict would not seriously deplete our tanker tonnage before we could get our protective escort ships together. (Anti-submarine Warfare)

e. More Foreign Wells.

From Appendix I it is noted that foreign wells are very much in the minority. However, the Middle East has the greatest reserve of oil. Also, further exploration in other countries would no doubt reveal additional sources. Hence, foreign drilling will be encouraged in order to take some of the load from the United States. Total well completions, set by the Petroleum Administration for Defense at 50,000 wells per year, reached 46,000 for 1952.

f. Refineries and POL Products.

Crude oil necessarily has to go through several refining processes before it becomes a finished product. Refining capacity for crude oil distillate is now at a surplus and predicted requirements indicate that this surplus will continue.

Refineries are tremendously costly and they require functional design and construction for the particular kinds of gasoline and oil necessary for the consumer.

Aviation gasoline supply is currently short of demand. Greater refining capacity is required and plans for these refineries are projected. However, there will still be a shortage of aviation gasoline in the first six months of total war. The oil industry can refine the requirements now, but they are reluctant to convert because of the continuous conversion by the military to jet planes which will, of course, result in less demand for aviation gasoline.

 g. Pipe Lines.

Pipe lines are the great neutralizer for tanker shortages and for quicker transfer of oil. Over the long run it is also much cheaper transportation. It is contemplated to push a program of more pipe lines to offset any tanker shortage resulting from increased oil demands or from enemy losses. Current foreign pipe laying under way or projected, totals 11,010 miles. These include 2400 miles of crude oil lines, 1050 miles of product lines, and 7560 miles of natural gas lines. The United States has 1600 miles of crude oil lines underway and 7000 miles of natural gas lines. The United States now has 170,000 miles of pipe lines.

 h. Anti-Submarine Warfare (ASW)

In the event of total war, ASW forces would be expanded immediately in order to provide safe escort for the tanker fleet.

1. Reconstruction.

The problem of reconstruction of oil facility losses due to war damage is an ever present one in total war. It is felt by the oil industry that requirements will be met. Minor damage will be easily repaired.5/ At present, there is no program for the reconstruction of major damage in the oil industry, although it is in the talking stage.

C. Iron Curtain Requirements for Total War.

From the limited information on Russia and her satellites, let us look at her total war potential.

Russia and her satellites are producing over 1,000,000 bbl. of crude oil per day. Her civilian consumption cannot compare with ours because of:

    a. Few motor vehicles;

    b. Few oil heaters for domestic heating;

    c. Ability to move armies on foot;

    d. More jet fuels instead of hard-to-refine aviation gasoline.

In short, her present economy and military machine is not geared to oil like that of the United States. Germany lasted quite a while on a total production of 400,000 barrels a day.

It seems reasonable to admit that Russia could start a war on her present production, but she would have a most difficult task keeping her war machine going for any length of time.

5/ Doolittle, James H. - etc

VI. FUTURE OUTLOOK ON OIL.

A. Incentive to Produce.

1. From the statistics compiled in Appendix I, it can be seen that the oil picture is optimistic for the foreseeable future. What is this foreseeable future? It has been estimated by the experts that this future will end about the year 2000, but this, of course, depends on the ability of the oil industry to sustain production.[1] This ability to sustain production is greatly influenced by demand, the laws of various countries, the costs, and the price of oil---all adding up to the incentive to explore and produce. (Atomic energy as a source of power will be discussed in succeeding paragraphs)

2. Since World War II, the production of oil of the free-world has risen from 6,900,000 b/d to about 11,900,000 b/d. The oil industry explored and produced this tremendous increase because the price of crude was favorable for greater investment by the industry. The incentive was there, but new problems are now arising which may decrease production in certain countries.

3. The first of these is the demand of oil bearing countries to take the lion's share of the profits and leave the oil company with a bare minimum of profit on its investment. The inherent risk in every oil venture is such that a company does not want to invest great sums of capital unless the return will be a fair one.

---

[1] Doolittle, James H., Lt Gen, USAF (Ret.), Shell Oil Co., Interview, Wash., D. C., 30 Dec 1952.

4. The second problem is the wave of intense nationalism which is sweeping the world. These nations wish to be self-sufficient. They lean toward expropriating foreign holdings and giving little of the initial cost in return. It is difficult for them to realize that outside capital is needed to start industries in their countries.

5. The third problem is the poisonous use of this Nationalism which the Communists are exploiting in order to drive foreign interests out of a country. The Communists, through their propaganda, incite the poorer classes to demand exorbitant wages, expropriation of all foreign properties, or laws which are restricting and insulting to foreign nationals.2/

6. Examples of the above are many and varied. Fourteen years ago Mexico expropriated the foreign oil holdings and since that time she has had a difficult time sustaining her own oil requirements. As of 1952, Mexico has finally become an exporter again--although there are untold oil reserves in that country. Iran is another example. Her Abadan refinery, owned by the British, was taken over by the Iranian government. In Iran only a few of the rich were getting the oil profits, hence the effect on the rest of the country was negligible when she closed the British holdings.

7. Peru and Bolivia are demanding everything but the kitchen sink. At present in Bolivia, labor is practically

---

2/ Ibid.

dictating to all industry. Laws have been passed which continue to restrict managements prerogatives. The investment outlook is not favorable in these countries at present. The foreign investment situation is extremely critical in these countries.

8. It has been axiomatic that when foreign investments are made by oil interests, the rich get richer and the poor still remain poor. The government or private groups which hold most of the land are ruled by a few. The profits do not get to the people. Oil companies have put over $2.4 billion into expansion abroad. Saudi Arabia is one exception to the above. Its progressive development programs for the country are showing the people that oil is their economic salvation.

9. We have a major problem in our own country. In the United States an estimated 40,000,000,000 barrels of oil is in the tidelands in the Gulf area and off the coast of California. Some exploration has been going on for years. President Truman made the tidelands a Naval Oil Reserve on 15 January 1953. Because of the millions of dollars which the oil industry has already put into the tidelands and because the new Administration promised State control in their platform, it seems probable that the new Congress will have to decide this issue.

10. The oil industry is intensely interested in the Point 4 program of the State Department. It is felt that through the capital investment program, which Point 4 is

initiating, foreign countries will change their laws and stimulate the interests of private capital in foreign holdings. In the oil industry, capital and know-how are available to any country which will give it security of holdings and a fair return on the investment.

11. It is also felt that no communist troubles, labor troubles, or law troubles would be encountered if some formula could be worked out to get the majority of the profits working for the betterment of all people in a foreign country. As an example of the effect of oil royalties on foreign countries, I cite the $000 million in royalties which the Arab nations received in 1952. This dwarfs the entire activities of the World Bank and the Point 4 program.3/ Iraq had more income from oil alone than its entire national budget. Saudi Arabia has an extensive development program for its peoples using oil income.

B. **Future Estimates and Synthetics.**

1. It is estimated that, with the continuing rate of consumption, crude oil obtained from the ground will last for another 50 years. Natural gas will also be depleted in that time. What comes next?

3/ "Washington Outlook", Business Week, p. 04, 27 Dec 1952.

2. One project is to improve recovery methods in existing oil fields. Present methods bring up only 25 to 35 percent of the oil in any deposit. If technologists can work out ways of getting more oil from the ground, billions of barrels can be added to our known reserves at no finding cost.

3. It has been said that John L. Lewis is the best man the oil industry has ever had for keeping the production of oil at an all time high. He brought the price of coal up, also the number of strikes to interrupt production, and, of course, the high price of heat and power for many industries and homes.

4. Oil shale is the next synthetic which shows promise of conversion. There are vast deposits of oil shale but the cost is still excessive. It first has to be mined. Labor costs are prohibitive. The shale then has to be crushed, then retorted so that the oil is cooked out of it. Until a simpler process of extraction and retortion is found, oil shale will be an unattractive synthetic due to its productive costs.

5. By far the most promising of the present sources of synthetics is tar sand. Tar sands are found all over the world, with one of the largest fields in Athabasca, Canada. New processes of extraction make tar sands very attractive. Brazil, Venezuela, and Canada have large deposits from which the oil can either be washed or dissolved. This will give an oil which is of high sulphur content and almost free of hydrogen.

6. Looking far into the future, when and if science and technology develops the breeder reactor in the atomic energy field, then uranium can be used more efficiently than any other energy producing substance. Carbon and hydrogen can then be extracted and combined for oil fuels. The Atomic Energy Commission is now making a special effort to get private capital to invest in research and development in the industrial use of atomic energy. Oil is one commodity which will have an important part in this field. The oil industry even now is making a major contribution to the finding of uranium for atomic energy uses. With the gamma ray log, a radio active device already being used in oil well drilling, readings for uranium traces are taken for the first 500 feet of drilling.

7. Solar energy is next on the list, but considerable research has to be done before radiation from the sun can be harnessed to supply our energy needs.

SUMMARY

From the world outlook on oil today, the free world requirements are not as great for the next 3 years as the predicted supply or refining capacity. It is assumed that the Korean war will continue and that there will be no world wide depression or further conflicts during that time.

Educated guesses predict that we will have well-drilled oil till the year 2000, after which synthetics will have to be used for energy sources.

For total mobilization, in global war, the free world will have more than enough petroleum only if they hold the Middle East and can get the available OIL supply from the Middle East to the areas where it is needed.

This will involve more tankers, pipe lines, refineries, wells, stockpiling, reactivation of old fields, rationing, and reconstruction of oil facilities due to war damage.

The Iron Curtain countries have about 9,500,000,000 bbl. and the free-world countries have about 108,500,000,000 bbl. of the world reserves of crude oil.

CONCLUSIONS

It is concluded that:

1. Under present world conditions, the free world requirements will not exceed the world supply or refining capacity of petroleum products for about 50 years, after which synthetics will have to be used.

2. The shortage of aviation gasoline is not due to refining capacity, but to the former price on that commodity and to the conversion of reciprocating engines to jet engines.

3. The refining capacity of petroleum products can be increased greatly if the lithium based all-purpose greases are produced and used in greater quantity.

4. The world reserves of fuel can be greatly increased if foreign countries allow private capital to develop their oil resources under favorable conditions and not under the threat of nationalization.

5. For global war, the free world will have more than enough if the supply from North and South America and the Middle East can be brought to the areas where it is needed.

6. Global war will require an increase in tankers, pipe lines, refineries, and foreign wells, reactivation of old fields, civilian rationing, stockpiling, and reconstruction of oil facilities due to war damage.

7. This study focuses attention to the major mobilization problems of holding the Middle East, holding tanker losses to a minimum (better ASW), the need for civilian rationing, and in the event the Middle East is lost--drastic civilian curtailment of consumption.

8. Jet aircraft, which today use five times more fuel than a reciprocating engine aircraft, will not raise the military requirements of fuels in total war five times that of W.W. II simply because we will not have the numbers of aircraft that we had in W. W. II. The reason lies in the present cost of aircraft. A fighter, bomber, or even a training plane costs roughly ten times more today due to the higher costs of materials and labor, and the tremendously complicated electronics and fuel systems in these aircraft.

BIBLIOGRAPHY

1. Biggs, Burton B., RADM, USN. *Petroleum and Gas.* Wash., D. C., ICAF, 2 Nov 1950. 19 p. (L51-46)

2. Doolittle, James H., Lt Gen, USAF(Ret). *Petroleum--World Reserves, Production, Manufacture and Use.* Wash., D. C., ICAF, 1 Mar 1949. 43 p. (L49-93)

3. Duff, D. M. "Reserves Gain Largely From Persian Gulf Areas", *The Oil and Gas Journal.* vol. 51, No. 33, p. 180-184, 22 Dec 1952.

4. "Free-World Demand Nears 12,000,000 bbl. Daily", *The Oil and Gas Journal*, vol 51, No. 33, p. 135, 22 Dec 1952.

5. Harvard University. Graduate School of Business Administration. Mobilization Analysis Center. *Requirements Survey. Part III, Vol. 1, Department of the Navy.* Wash., D. C., Dept of Defense, Jan-Mar 1951. 75 p. (HU RS Pt. III, v. 1) (Classified)

6. Harvard University, Graduate School of Business Administration. Mobilization Analysis Center. *Requirements Survey, Part III, Vol 2, Department of the Navy.* Wash., D. C., Dept of Defense, Jan-Mar 1951. 275 p. (HU RS Pt. III, V. 2) (Classified)

7. King, Marcus R., Col, USAF. *World Petroleum Situation.* Wash., D. C., ICAF, 17 Oct 1951. 21 p. (L5-38)

8. Kintberger, L. S., Cdr, USN. *Methods of Determination, Presentation, and Evaluation of Petroleum Requirements by the Munitions Board.* Wash., D. C., ICAF, 17 Jan 1951. 8 p., typewritten (Individual Report No. 192, 1951)

9. "Loss of Oil in Iran Vexing for Britain", *The New York Times*, 6 Jan 1953, p. c-75.

10. "Petroleum--the base for a peaceful World", *The Oil and Gas Journal*, vol 51, No. 33, p. 135, 22 Dec 1952.

11. "Truman Order Saving Tideland Oil for Navy Expected This Week", *The Washington Post*, 11 Jan 1953. p. 1.

12. Tuttle, R. B. "Survey of Oil Refineries", *The Oil and Gas Journal*, vol 51, No. 33, p. 303, 22 Dec 1952.

13. U. S. Munitions Board. *Munitions Board Requirements Manual*. Wash., D. C., 1 Feb 1950. 111 p. (US 263 R43 1950)

14. "Washington Outlook," *Business Week*, p. 64, 27 Dec 1952.

15. Winterbottom, John J. "Tanker Tonnage Keeps Pace with Soaring World Demands", *The Oil and Gas Journal*, vol 51, No. 33, p. 192, 22 Dec 1952.

Dear Jack —

This is what WHCY is all about. The ten problem areas are listed. On the last page — a brief on what the reports will consider.

Sincerely
Hank

White House Conference on Youth

P.O. Box 19, Washington, D.C. 20044

CONCEPT

The 1971 White House Conference on Youth comes at a time when young people are increasingly questioning the relevance and responsiveness of all major institutions and are seeking a greater opportunity to participate in the decisions that affect their lives. There are unmistakable signs of a growing alienation between a substantial segment of our youth and our institutions, with young people becoming increasingly skeptical about the will or the ability of the "establishment" to cure the problems that beset the Nation.

The Conference is a process of interaction and communication between young people and adults in positions of authority in various institutions, both governmental and nongovernmental. The goal is to find new approaches to the major issues concerning young people today and to open up channels for youth to become more involved in the decisions that affect their lives.

Since the first White House Conference on Children and Youth was called by President Theodore Roosevelt in 1909, conferences have traditionally been held every ten years. The past six conferences have served to focus national attention on the needs of children and youth, and they have also affected legislation and the social fabric of the Nation.

This Youth Conference marks a departure from the traditional White House Conferences on Children and Youth. For the first time there will be a separate conference on youth, with young people playing a major role in the development, deliberations and follow-up process of the Conference. Young people also played a significant role in the White House Conference on Children, which was convened in December 1970.

DESIGN

The White House Conference on Youth is approaching its objectives through the discussion of specific issues determined to be of greatest concern to young people today. The ten issues are:

1. Foreign Relations
2. Environment
3. Race and Minority Group Relations
4. Drugs
5. Education
6. The Draft, National Service, and Its Alternatives
7. Poverty
8. Legal Rights and Justice
9. Economy and Employment
10. Values, Ethics and Culture

The delegates will make recommendations in these areas. To help them in their deliberations, ten youth-adult task forces are preparing background papers. Each task force is comprised of four adults and eight youth. The adult members are prominent individuals with expertise and policy-making authority in the task force area. The youth members represent the divergent viewpoints, backgrounds and concerns of young people across the Nation. Each task force is co-chaired by a youth and an adult member. These task forces began working on their reports in September 1970. Each report will cover the following objectives:

1. Identification of the current status of the issue area as it relates to youth.

2. Prediction of the status of the issue area as it will relate to youth during the coming decade.

3. Identification of the consequences for youth and society if certain policy actions are or are not taken.

In addition to researching the above objectives, each report will propose recommendations in two areas:

a. To what extent and how should young people be involved in the decision-making processes of the Nation's institutions?

b. What substantive policies or programs should be considered or implemented by private and governmental institutions, given the shared desire to reach certain goals?

These recommendations will be put on the Conference agenda for consideration by the delegates along with additional recommendations solicited from all delegates.

The ten task forces met together for three days in late August 1970, at the University of California at Irvine. At this meeting, the 120 task force members planned the research procedures for their reports and chose the issues within each area on which they would focus. Each task force scheduled at least three meetings during the fall and winter to discuss the progress of its research and to meet with various young people around the country. These meetings are being held at a wide range of locations and the reports will be completed by early March.

At Irvine the task force members also met in committees to discuss and make recommendations on other aspects of Conference planning. These committees addressed the questions of special events at the Conference, international participation, a citizen outreach program, delegate selection and Conference location and format. The recommendations from these committees have been incorporated in the Conference plans, including the proposal that the Conference be held outside Washington, D.C., in an informal setting conducive to serious, substantive work with a minimum of distractions.

PARTICIPANTS

The Youth Conference will involve 1,500 delegates; 1,000 young people and 500 adults. The youth delegates will be a broad, representative group of the Nation's approximately 40,000,000 youth between the ages of 14 and 24. The profile of the youth will accurately reflect national youth population statistics and thus there will be working youth, poor youth, young housewives, military youth and others in addition to youth in school. Youth delegates have been selected from a pool of nominees submitted by State Committees on Children and Youth, national organizations, task forces, and self-nominations. Each youth delegate will have a sponsor to defray travel costs; the White House will cover the cost of room and board during the Conference.

The youth delegates were chosen according to the current youth population statistics on age, sex, current status in the work force, geography, and education in order to get a broad representation of young people.

The 500 adult delegates will be leaders from the Nation's institutions. These adults have been selected on the basis of their ability to effect change in their respective institutions and society. For each task force issue area, a small screening committee composed of individuals highly knowledgeable of the area and representing different viewpoints was convened to assist in preparing a master list of adult nominees. Adult delegates have been chosen to reflect as accurately as possible the power structure relating to each issue area.

In addition to the 1,500 adult and youth delegates, 100 international participants will be invited to the Conference as special delegates. They will represent the viewpoints of youth and adult experts in other nations during Conference deliberations. A small number of adult observers also will be invited to attend the Conference sessions, including representatives from the State Committees on Children and Youth.

The delegates will be asked to participate in an outreach program in their own communities during the six weeks prior to the Conference. Delegates will receive the reports of their respective task forces, summaries of all task force reports, bibliographies and related information for Conference preparation, details on the Conference concept and role of the delegates, and other information or questionnaires that the task forces may wish to include.

PROGRAM

The Youth Conference will be held at the YMCA Conference Center at Estes Park, Colorado, between April 18-22. Delegates will work primarily within their assigned task forces, meeting in discussion groups and in larger task force sessions. Each task force at the Conference will make specific recommendations directed to the institutions influential in its issue area and propose strategies of implementation for those recommendations. The program, however, will also provide delegates the opportunity to participate in the activities and discussions of other task forces in order to permit the full interaction of ideas. In addition, there will be free time for using the numerous recreational facilities at the Conference Center.

The four-day meeting will result in a slate of recommendations put together by young people and adults directed at the Nation's institutions and related to priority programs and youth involvement. The Conference proceedings will be published and presented to the President.

TASK FORCE REPORTS

The Foreign Relations Task Force report will discuss the U.S. national interest, the U.S. role in international organizations, and the role of youth in foreign policy formulations.

The Environment Task Force will review the current crisis in the environment, including a prediction as to how youth, in particular, will be affected if the Nation does not address itself to the problem, and will make recommendations directed to both youth and institutions.

The Race and Minority Group Relations Task Force will consider racism, both individual and institutional, and their various manifestations.

The Drugs Task Force will consider problems of drug abuse: consequences of use and abuse, treatment and rehabilitation, law enforcement, education and prevention, research, nonchemical alternatives, and the marijuana dilemma.

The Education Task Force will examine the following subjects as they relate to high school and college: the purpose of education, public attitudes, equality of educational opportunity, relevance of educational systems and programs, student participation in decision-making, and special problems concerning handicapped students and students who have dropped out of school.

The Draft, National Service, and Its Alternatives Task Force will evaluate proposals for revision of the draft, various national service schemes and an all-volunteer military force.

The Poverty Task Force will address itself to the nature of poverty as it affects youth, the extent of youth poverty, the reasons this Nation continues to countenance poverty, government anti-poverty programs, and make priority recommendations for eradicating poverty.

The Legal Rights and Justice Task Force will concentrate on three areas: the age of majority, the relationship between youth and academic institutions, and the administration of justice with respect to youth.

The Economy and Employment Task Force will consider the national economy, changing youth attitudes toward work, the overall nature and priorities of the future economy, and institutional barriers to youth involvement in the economic system and in the economic decision-making process.

The Values, Ethics and Culture Task Force will consider two basic approaches: a sociological look at youth's attitudes and values in the present society; a framework for an ideal society as they perceive it and the values and goals on which it would be based.

DECLASSIFIED

STORY OF "FIGHTING TWENTY-THREE"

Fighting Squadron TWENTY-THREE (VF-23) was commissioned on November 16, 1942, at what was then the Naval Reserve Aviation Base, Willow Grove, Pa. The Commanding Officer was Lieutenant Henry L. Miller, USN, and the Executive Officer was Lieutenant Harold N. Funk, USN.

It was to be a twelve (12) plane fighter squadron with a complement of twenty (20) pilots, and three (3) A-V(S) officers. The initial planes which were assigned to the squadron were F4F-4's. The squadron was part of Air Group TWENTY THREE, with its ultimate destination, CVL-23, the U.S.S. PRINCETON, a converted 10,000 ton cruiser, then under construction at the New York Shipbuilding Company, Camden, New Jersey. The Commanding Officer of the Air Group, at the time, was Lieut. Comdr. George B. Chafee, a TBF pilot.

The original complement, as finally completed in December 1942, consisted of the following officers:

- Lieut. Henry L. Miller
- Lieut. Harold N. Funk
- Lieut. Samuel J. R. Froelick
- Lieut. Claude C. Schmidt
- Lieut. Charles M. Kenyon, A-V(S)
- Lt(jg) Richard J. Hofler, A-V(S)
- Lt(jg) James R.O. Rickard, A-V(S)
- Lt(jg) James A. Smith, III
- Lt(jg) Leon W. Haynes
- Ens. Oscar H. Cantrell
- Ens. Albert W. Robbins
- Ens. Richard P. Selman
- Ens. Robert Jefferson Young
- Ens. John J. Redmon
- Ens. Leslie H. Kerr
- Ens. Walter John Kirschke
- Ens. Joe H. Webb
- Ens. James W. Syme
- Ens. Jack D. Madison
- Ens. Jack M. Abell
- Ens. Robert S. Tyner
- Ens. David H. Olin
- Ens. William G. Buckelew

The enlisted personnel of the squadron totalled eighty-seven men; the leading chief was William Carlin, ACMM, a veteran of the United States Navy of almost continuous standing since the First World War.

The facilities at Willow Grove were all incomplete; the only building which was complete was the Officers Quarters. The rooms were very comfortable with each officer occupying a room. Along with the condition of the grounds, the terrible weather prevented the commencement of any training program, so that operations were held to a minimum.

War Diary of Fighting Twenty-Three

November 16, 1942. Lieut. Henry L. Miller, USN, assumed command and posted the watch. Officers aboard. Lieut. Harold N. Funk, USN, Executive Officer.

November 17 - Routine inspection of squadron area.

November 18 - Routine inspection of squadron area.

November 19 - Ens. Leslie H. Kerr reported for duty.
November 20-22 - No activity.
November 23 - Ens. Albert W. Robbins reported for duty.
November 24 - No activity.
November 25 - Ens. Joe H. Webb and Ens. Jack D. Madison reported for duty.

- 1 -

CONFIDENTIAL

November 26 - Lt(jg) Leon W. Haynes, and Ens. Robert J. Young reported for duty.
November 27 - Ens. Robert S. Tyner and Ens. James W. Syme reported for duty.
  Operations during this period of time merely consisted of flying around
  the area for purposes of familiarization. This was done in an SNJ.
November 28 - Ens. David H. Olin reported for duty.
November 29-30 - There was no activity to speak of; occasional flights in the SNJ,
  and getting the squadron personnel in order were the main jobs.
December 1 - Lt(jg) James A. Smith reported for duty.
December 2 - Lt. Samuel J. R. Froelick reported for duty.
December 3-6 - There were occasional flights when the weather permitted; other-
  wise activity was held to a minimum.
December 7 - Ens. John J. Redmon reported for duty.
December 8-16 inc. - the temperature was down to 20° F. Ceiling was zero, and the
  area surrounding the field was also closed in.
December 17 - Lieut. Miller and Lieut. Funk returned from Norfolk with two new
  F4F-4's. We had our first fighter planes; now the question was, will it
  ever clear up so as to be able to fly them.
December 18 - Lieut. Miller departed for Parris Island, Marine Air Station, S.C.
  He had heard about a good training base there, and no one was using it.
December 19 - Lieut. Claude C. Schmidt reported for duty.
December 20 - Temperature was down to 10° F.
December 21 - Lieut. Miller returned from Parris Island. He accidentally had run
  into a friend who was Commanding Officer of the Air Station down there, so
  the chances of moving the squadron down began to brighten up.
December 22 - Ensign Walter J. Kirschke reported for duty.
December 23 - It was getting warmer, temperature was up to 32° F.; however every-
  thing was closed in around the field.
December 24 - Ensign Richard P. Selman and Ens. Oscar H. Cantrell reported for duty
December 25 - A Merry Christmas to ALL.
December 26 - Day after Christmas - - what can you expect? Right!
December 27 - Rain, fog and smoke. There was a pilots' conference, and it was
  understood we would move to Parris Island in a few days.
December 28 - Lieut. Charles M. Kenyon and Lt(jg) James R.O. Rickard reported for
  duty.
December 29 - Lt(jg) Richard J. Hefler and Ens. Jack M. Abell reported for duty.
December 30 - There was the usual rain and fog, with a ceiling of 100 feet.
December 31 - The squadron received two more F4F-4's from Norfolk. Ensigns Webb
  and Kerr flew them in.

January 1, 1943 - A HAPPY NEW YEAR TO ALL.

January 2 - Lieut. Pincetich flew Lt(jg) Smith and Ensigns Syme and Kirschke to
  Norfolk for the purpose of picking up new F4F-4's for the squadron.
January 3 - Ens. Syme and Young left Norfolk for Willow Grove. Ens. Young was our
  Navigation Officer, but for some reason or other, Syme convinced Young that
  he (Syme) could fly that course blindfolded - (he really knew the way). Well,
  today the squadron had its first forced landing case. Syme was lost, so
  landed in a cornfield in Virginia, and was surrounded by friendly natives.
  Young had gone a little farther and made an airfield in Charlotteville, V.
    Also on this eventful day, Lt(jg) Hefler, who was indoctrinated as an
  Intelligence Officer, was ordered to proceed to Parris Island with the colored boys, and establish a BOQ. His experience in such matters was nil,
  but he left in spite of it all.
January 4 - Lieut. Funk departed for Charlotteville to rescue our lost Ensigns.
January 5 - Ensigns Young and Syme returned home in the SNJ-4; and Lt(jg) Haynes
  departed for Parris Island.
January 6 - 1000 - all of the squadron planes departed for Parris Island, arriving at 1700.
January 7 - Flight operations commenced. The facilities were ideal, the weather
  was exceptional for flying, and there were no other squadrons present.
    So the long grind commenced. Hefler turned out to be an exceptional
  BOQ manager, with the able assistance of Lewis, our first class officers
  cook, so that when we all arrived, each had his private room, and a
  dinner-de-luxe.
January 8 - Friday - We must have brought the rain with us, since due to the weather flight operations were held up; however, the vans with our material arrived so all hands were kept busy.

CONFIDENTIAL

January 9 - Saturday - Our first Saturday at the Marine Base. The rain continued, so we were all busy unpacking and prodding Hofler to get us an "in" to the nurses' quarters. It seems that he met one of the nurses on the train, and had already fixed himself up for dates. The procedure was to attend the movie, then go to the officers' club, so we were informed. As to how the squadron would fit into the picture remained to be seen.

January 10-31 inclusive - Ground school was established, much to the disgust of all pilots, with a long comprehensive schedule worked out in detail to acquaint our boys with all types of ships, aircraft and fighter direction procedure. Kenyon was picking up the fine points of making out a schedule and realizing the problems of getting a flight off on time.

Occasional rains would periodically hold up operations. Whereupon the enlisted personnel would deluge the personnel office with requests for leave to visit their aged parents, or an ailing cousin.

Lieut. Curtis, the signal officer on the PRINCETON, arrived in order to conduct field carrier landing practice. The first of a series of trips to Norfolk to pick up parts was made by Ensign Madison. The proposed overnight trip turned out to be a lengthy one, due to the flying conditions in the North. Ensign Abell ran into a little difficulty in a soft-ball game, and sprained his ankle, so he hobbled around the office for a week.

Lieut. John J. Becker, who was to be in charge of the V-4 Division aboard the PRINCETON arrived; he was to see that all planes were always ready to fly, no matter how many crack-ups they had.

February - found the squadron well established at Parris Island. The boys had become well acquainted with the various marine regulations and marines, - and the nurses. The squadron had a Captain's Inspection on the sixth; all hands were at their best, so that the Captain was well pleased.

The operations schedule was running true to form, gunnery runs were being conducted every day, and carrier landings on returning to the field. The USS PRINCETON was to be commissioned on the 25th; most of the boys wanted to see the ceremony, - or was it Philadelphia? - However only the Captain and Lieut. Kenyon went up, since operations had to continue at Page Field.

March - turned out to be a tragic month for the squadron. On the 15th, Ensigns Robbins and Selman were killed when the SNJ they were flying crashed at Hilton Head Island, south of Page Field. A week later, on the 23rd, Ensign Young was killed when his F4F-4 landed on the water, turned over, and trapped him in the cockpit.

On the first part of the month all the pilots proceeded to Norfolk and qualified on carrier landings, then went on to Philadelphia to qualify for catapult shots, and take in the City.

On March 1st, Lieut. Miller was promoted to Lieutenant Commander. Also the story broke about Doolittle's bombing of Tokyo, i.e., the means used; whereupon Lieut. Comdr. Miller gave us a detailed story, since he had trained the pilots on carrier takeoffs, and went on the HORNET with them on their historical trip.

Later in the month, the Charleston radar station had eight of our planes placed on an alert status, since unidentified planes were reported off the Coast.

April - The Air Group Commander, Lieut. Comdr. George B. Chafee received orders to report as Air Officer on the USS CABOT. Lieut. Comdr. Henry L. Miller, as senior officer present, became the Air Group Commander.

Night flying and night carrier landings were being held. However, the planes kept the marines awake, and frightened the ladies at the O. Club, so the General ordered that the carrier landings cease, which somewhat curtailed our night operations. Fortunately, however, most of the night flying schedule had been completed by that time.

In spite of occasional differences of opinion between the marines and the Air Group, we gave the marines a party at the VOQ to show our appreciation for the use of their facilities. As to the complete success of the party, no doubt remained in anyone's mind, and memories of that memorable occasion still linger and are frequently referred to.

The Commander in Chief of the United States Army and Navy visited the Marine Base on April the 14th. All planes of the Air Group were flown in parade formation, as President Franklin D. Roosevelt inspected the balance of the officers and enlisted personnel of the squadron.

CONFIDENTIAL

April - continued -

From the middle of the month, until April 26, the squadron experienced a series of crash landings. First it was Ensign Kirschke who was forced down in a swamp on Hunting Island; then Ensign Tyner was forced down on the beach on Hunting Island; and within two days Ensign Buckelew and Ensign Madison had the unfortunate experiences of making respective forced landings in swamps. Fortunately none of the pilots were injured.

To add to all the excitement of this month, Ensign Jack Abell decided to get married. The wedding was held at the Marine Base Chapel, on the 12th, with Lt(jg) Smith, III, as best man. The bride was Mildred Marie Fariss of Roanoke, Virginia, a little girl that Jack had been after for years, and finally won.

May - Since most of the training schedule had been completed by this time, the squadron was working on polishing up the rough edges and working with the Scouts and Torpedo planes on group tactics.

On May 1st, Ensign Madison decided that he should be a married man, so took as his bride the former Helen Harrell of Moultrie, Georgia. Ensign Cantrell was best man, and the ceremony was performed at the Marine Base Chapel. One week later Ensign Tyner decided that he was not to be outdone by Abell and Madison, so took as his bride the former Joannie Tyson of Lansdale, Pennsylvania. Bob had met her during our short stay at Willow Grove. Ensign Syms was best man, but did not succeed in getting more than one drink of champagne into Bob, who is an abstainer. However, you can be assured that a good time was had by all.

On the 18th we received our orders to leave Parris Island, and proceed to Pungo, an auxiliary field near Norfolk, Virginia. Pungo turned out to be quite a spot. We lived in quonset huts for the few days that the squadron was based there, and dined in an annex of the general mess. Fortunately Virginia Beach was but a few miles away. The boys became acquainted with a Navy Nurses Rest Home, so made frequent trips to the Beach in the Pungo milk wagon.

During our sojourn at Pungo the squadron qualified aboard the USS PRINCETON, while she was in the Chesapeake Bay, before docking at Pier 7 in Norfolk on the 25th. The planes were flown to Norfolk and hoisted aboard the carrier on the 27th, and at 1500 on the 28th the ship was under way for her shakedown cruise in the Gulf of Paria, Trinidad. However just before leaving, Lieut. Froelick was ordered to the hospital, so was detached from us.

We arrived in the British West Indies on June 1, 1943, entered the Gulf of Paria, and anchored at the Port of Spain, Trinidad. The following day was the start of a gruelling training period which set records in carrier landings for a shakedown cruise. The squadrons completed 1242 landings, day and night. The cruises in the Gulf of Paria were not without incidents however, since on the 2nd day three of our pilots lost themselves and landed at Carupano, Venezuela. Neither of the three, Ensigns Abell, Buckelew, or Tyner, knew or understood Spanish, but through some means, as yet unknown to us, explained where they came from, and were able to communicate to the squadron that they were safe and having a fine time.

On June 6th Ensign Cantrell was lost during a routine flight, and was not found. It is difficult to say what might have happened, so it is best not to venture an opinion.

Liberty was something we did not experience much of while in Trinidad. We were granted one liberty per week, between 1100 and 1800. Consequently whoever was fortunate to be on the liberty section was ready to disembark at 1100 sharp, and head directly to Maqueripe Beach Club, where one could swim and visit their bar or to Port-au-Spain and the Queens Park Hotel Bar, where the Planters punches were 24 per and delicious.

On the 29th of June we left the B.W.I. to return to Philadelphia. Every one was in high spirits in spite of the fact that all were tired from the strenuous exercises of the cruise, and looked forward to seeing the States again, and getting a few days leave.

July 3 - The USS PRINCETON was 150 miles at sea when it launched the Air Group which flew to Willow Grove and landed at 0900. The Air Station had certainly changed, since our departure in January. There were trees, lawns, paved streets, etc, instead of the mud and slush which we experienced earlier in the year.

- 4 -

CONFIDENTIAL

July 3 - continued -

Half of the officers and enlisted personnel were granted six days leave, and upon their return the balance were to leave. No sooner had the planes landed than all those departing had disappeared, headed toward all parts of the United States, - Florida, California, Washington, and even Boston; New York was kept in reserve as the place to visit, after returning from leave, every night upon the squadron being secured.

New F6F-3's were turned over to the squadron, and all planes were made ready to go aboard. The pilots had checked out in the F6F-3 while on the shakedown cruise, at Edinburgh Field, Trinidad. The new droppable belly tanks were tried out and found to be satisfactory.

Three new fighter pilots reported to the squadron: Ensigns Howard, Coyer, and Hill; and Ensign Parent, a gunnery officer, was also assigned to the squadron.

On July 1, in a wave of promotions, all of the former ensigns in the squadron were made junior grade lieutenants, so our new ensigns were alone in their particular rank.

July 20 - By 1400 all squadron personnel had to be aboard; to say the least it was a difficult task breaking away from New York, its cafes' night life, music, and beautiful girls. How Lieutenants Tolman and Rickard made it still remains a mystery. Lieut. Hefler, the romantic one, left his beloved Isolde with tears in her eyes and a milk shake in her hand. But we all made it in spite of Lieut. Hubbard's efforts to get the above gentlemen on the inebriated side during their sojourns in the Big City. At 0500 the 21st, the ship was under way, destination unknown.

Later in the day it was learned that we were to go to Panama. Ground School was held daily for all pilots, and combat air patrols were flown by the squadron, alternating the duty with the USS BELLEAU WOOD, who was with us.

We passed through the Panama Canal on July 26th. It was not too warm and all hands enjoyed themselves watching the procedure of taking us through the locks and passing through the canals and lakes. That evening we were granted liberty in Panama! The old hands who had been there previously made certain that all the known places were visited. So much happened during the liberties there that to attempt to correlate all events is an impossibility. However the high lights were: the famous drink known as the "Blue Moon", which consisted of a one-ounce jigger of orangeade - as we later discovered - and which cost one good American dollar; the famous girls who frequented the local bars would order these while you got high on imitation whiskey. Then there was the famous Chinese girl, known as Lilly Vong at Refugios Place. Lt(jg) Synn was taken aback with her Indian dancing, and decided that she was the only one for him, and it was to be done the hard way, without the famous Blue Moon! Did he succeed? As yet no one knows, and Synn won't talk!

On the 28th the PRINCETON, BELLEAU WOOD, and LEXINGTON received orders to depart from Panama, and as we later found out, to proceed direct to Pearl Harbor. The members of the squadrons who were unfortunate enough to hail from California expressed their views of deep disgust in their bad (?) luck of not being able to see their native state, if only for one day.

As we left Panama, Lieut.(jg) Olin suffered an appendix attack, and was operated on that afternoon. That evening Harry felt better and was glad it was over with and out.

Mail was received, and everyone was happy, that is, until the official mail was opened, wherein one particular letter inquired about and gently suggested that our former F4F's were "missing parts". Thereupon Lt(jg) Korr, our material officer, exclaimed in exasperation: "The monkey-wrenches be damned, let them buy others!"

By this time strict censorship had been invoked, so as a result, cries of murder, mayhem, and mutiny were being cast at the squadron censors, in spite of all out efforts towards explanations that it was not proper to tell your wife and/or sweetheart where you were, or where you were going, even though she'd love to be in Honolulu with you.

CONFIDENTIAL

During the long direct trip to Pearl Harbor, Lt. Comdr. Fuoss and Lieut. Chamberlin conducted fighter-director classes, and combat air patrols were alternated between our ship as the duty carrier, the LEXINGTON and the BELLEAU WOOD. Whenever the B.W. would launch her group a few seconds sooner than ours, the Air Officer would immediately conduct a session, to put it mildly, and the next day we would shatter all existing records, and thus maintain the reputation as the Peerless P.

On the 7th it was learned that the Air Groups from the three carriers would attack various targets on the Island of Oahu, in order to determine the alertness of the Army's defense. After the extended cruise from Panama, this was welcome news, since we would be ashore again. Consequently all were preparing for the dawn launchings on the 9th. The simulated attacks were successfully carried out, with no interceptions by Army fighters, and our planes landed at Barber's Point, at 0900. This Naval Air Station had recently been completed, consisted of 26,000 acres, runways thousands of feet in length; transportation was available, beds with Simmons Mattresses, and an Officers Club classified as very favorable, except for the little matter that other Air Groups were already in possession, and it was a bit difficult getting by them to the bar.

The Army Interceptor Command immediately placed the squadron under its jurisdiction, and every morning at 0300 one of our divisions was on an alert call, and generally scrambled. This continued for a period of three weeks, which gave the boys an opportunity to see beautiful Hawaiian sunrises.

Confusion and rumors were the order of the day for the next three weeks. Every day ComAirPac would incite new stories on the future of the Air Group. However between rumors, operations were carried on with fuel consumption tests and gunnery hops being stressed; occasional liberties were granted in order to give the boys an opportunity to give Honolulu the once-over. Waikiki was out of bounds, due to the dengue fever epidemic.

On the 21st we were informed that we were practically on our way to war so visit the medicos and get your tetanus shots. This we did with reluctance in spite of the fact that we should be accustomed to them by now. But for some reason or another the needles seem to get duller and duller. The enlisted personnel were taken to Ford Island, Pearl Harbor, to go aboard.

For this cruise the USS PRINCETON was to carry the Flag; Rear Admiral Radford and his staff were going aboard. As a result rooms and offices were being confiscated right and left; everything was in a state of last minute turmoil.

Our SBD dive bombers were to be left behind, along with three of our boys who were in the Naval Hospital at Aiea Heights. Lt(jg) Olin, and Lt(jg) Buckelew were to have their tonsils out; and Ensign Parent developed a case of yellow jaundice. Twelve fighter planes and pilots from Fighting SIX, Butch O'Hare's squadron, were to be attached on temporary duty with our squadron. When the planes were hoisted aboard on the 23rd, there were 24 F6F-3's and 9 TBF's aboard the PRINCETON when she left Pearl Harbor on the 25th at 0930 for a mission of war. Our Fighting SIX pilots were: Lt. Crews, Lt(jg) Loesch, Lt(jg) Trimble, Lt(jg) Altemus; Lt(jg) Odenbrett; Lt(jg) Palmer, Lt(jg) Coleman; and Ensigns Nyquist, Godson, Robbins, Philippe, Davis, and Roberts.

Later in the day the pilots were called into a conference, and our mission explained. We were to supply air coverage, along with the USS BELLEAU WOOD during the occupation of Baker Island, until the airfield was constructed. Never having heard of Baker Island, the Intelligence Officers, Hallowell, Hefler and Hubbard (in alphabetical order) immediately broke out maps, charts, slides, etc, and informed us that the island's only occupants were the beautiful Gooney birds, and guano; that it was 1235 miles SW of Pearl, at Lat. 0°12' N., Long. 176°30' W., a few miles from the Equator, and we would be there at least a month. What would the heat be like? Japanese planes were reported to be patrolling that area, so the pilots were happy and anxious for a Tallyho.

- 6 -

CONFIDENTIAL

On the 26th, Combat air patrols and fighter direction were the exercises for the day. The USS PRINCETON was the duty carrier, so we launched four of our planes. When the planes were recovered, Lt(jg) Loesch, who was in Fox-1 (The Imp), made a bad landing and went over the port side. Lt. Cdr. Miller, the Air Group Commander, has as yet not recovered from the loss of his famous Imp. After seven days of routine patrolling and proceeding at a slow speed, we left the convoy which proceeded on to Baker; while we remained off, and provided air protection. At 2357 or 1157 P.M., on the 31st, we crossed the Equator. This was the first of a series of crossings during our stay in that area. When we finally left we had crossed 34 times. The Crossing Ceremonies were belayed until later, when we had left the danger area.

On September 1st, at 0602, the first CAP was launched over the Baker Islandings. The patrol returned without incident. At 1200 we launched Dixie Loesch's division of Ens. Nyquist, Lt(jg) Coleman, and Ensign Robbins, for a CAP over the landings. At 1314 a Jap float plane bomber, known as Emily, was intercepted by Loesch and Nyquist, and was destroyed in ten seconds. The boys only made one run each and the Japs hit the water.

The PRINCETON was refueled on the 2nd, while the BELLEAU WOOD was the duty carrier, and carried on its patrols without incident. On the third of September we sent out our routine patrols. At 1201 Lt. "Sandy" Crews took off with a six-plane flight: Ens. "Junior" Godson, Lt(jg) "Jock" Odenbrett, Ens. Roberts, Lt(jg) Coleman, and Ens. Philippe. While over Baker another Jap bomber was intercepted by Coleman and Philippe, and after a mad running fight, the boys made the Japs hit the water and crash. The PRINCETON had two to its credit, and the BELLEAU WOOD had none.

It looked as though the Japs were very regular and prompt about arriving over the same area on odd days at 1300. Consequently everyone wanted that particular hop, and the BELLEAU WOOD squadron was claiming favoritism was being given the PRINCETON group. Whereupon the Admiral allowed the BELLEAU WOOD boys the patrols over Baker. As luck would have it, on the 8th, Lieut. Funk and Lt(jg) Kerr were patrolling miles away from the Baker patrol, when, lo and behold, a Jap plane approached from a different direction; and number THREE Jap hit the water in short order.

Lieut. Comdr. Hatcher flew to Canton Island and brought us mail, - Happy Day. It certainly broke the monotony, and gave us news; Lt. Funk received orders to report to San Diego and assume command of a fighter squadron. He was addressed as Lieutenant Commander, so everyone was congratulating him and wishing him luck. However, rumor had it that before returning to Pearl we would attack Tarawa, a Jap held island, in the Gilbert Islands; so Mr. Funk was reluctant to leave immediately. Since he wanted to be in on that attack, his orders were temporarily forgotten. To add to all the excitement, Ensign Davis, on the 8th of September, in an early morning takeoff, failed to get his plane, Fox-3, airborne, hit the water just off the bow of the carrier, and caught fire. Davis escaped miraculously and was picked up by a destroyer. His face and hands were burned, but he was glad to be aboard, and was up and around upon arrival at Pearl.

On the 11th, it was definitely learned that we would attack Tarawa. On the 17th we crossed the 180th Meridian of longitude. This placed us in the four quadrants of the earth, in the short space of time of four months.

D-Day was the 18th of September. At the last minute it was decided that Makin Island was also to be attacked. Lieut. "Sandy" Crews and his wingman, Ensign "Junior" Godson volunteered to escort the TBF's. They were launched at 0330 and carried out a successful attack, strafing and setting four float planes afire. The Tarawa attack was launched at 0430, and successfully carried out; the boys evaded terrific AA fire and enjoyed strafing Japs who were jumping into fox holes all over the place. Later in the day, Lt(jg) Haynes took off for a CAP with his division consisting of Lt(jg) Altemus, Lt(jg) Madison, and Lt(jg) Syme. At 1513 (3.15 P.M.) a Jap torpedo plane was intercepted by the boys, and it was only a matter of seconds before the plane was shot down by Syme and Madison. The Fighting 23 boys had shot down every enemy plane they had met, and as yet Fighting 24 on the BELLEAU WOOD had none to its credit. So you can imagine their consternation.

CONFIDENTIAL

With a successful attack behind us, and all the boys present, the Task Force Commander sent us the following message: "Congratulations to all hands. Your alertness to meet the enemy in any way he chose to fight was one of the many highlights of the day. It was well done."

The Force was headed back to Pearl Harbor, and a much needed rest. King Neptune and his Royal Court came aboard on the 21st; the events leading up to Neptune's appearance were hectic, to put it mildly. In spite of the fact that the Pollywogs (those miserable creatures who had never entered into the Royal Domain before) outnumbered the shellbacks ten to one. For days before Neptune's appearance you would see Pollywogs with various assortments of haircuts about the ship. The Shellbacks would catch an unwary pollywog and give him the royal trimming. But the worm was to turn!

On the evening of the 20th the loudspeaker blared forth for Lieut. Kenyon to man Fox-1 on the flight deck. That only had one meaning; Chuck was to get a haircut! To the astonishment of the Shellbacks, Chuck remained in the Ready Room, along with a room full of rarin'-to-go pollywog pilots, officers, and enlisted men. They invited the honorable Shellbacks to come forth and see what they could do about it. The result was a terrific melee; chairs, dishes, backpacks, chartboards, shillales, and Shellbacks were reeling and flying back and forth across the room. Shellbacks would be dragged into the room (in such number as could be most efficiently and adequately indoctrinated), worked over a bit, and bound up. Schmidt was standing on a cruise box inside the door, and as a Shellback would enter, he was tapped on the noggin with a shillala; whereupon Kirschke, who made Illinois a winning football team, and Webb, our man from Texas, would toss him to waiting pollywogs. Fortunately for the Shellbacks, the Admiral happened by and ordered peace and quiet restored, - until the official initiation the next day.

Later that evening we were all duly served with our subpoenas, listing individual offenses which had been committed during one's sojourn with the ship or squadron, and also notified what you were expected to wear and perform in the presence of Neptunus Rex. Costumes varied from the Queen of the May as depicted by Lt. Cdr. Hatcher, to Winter Flight gear, baby dresses; Hubbard was the Chicago Real Estate shark selling the Stevens Hotel to an unsuspecting civilian; some wore a gas mask and towel; others had binoculars made from rolls of that certain kind of paper; the Air Officer wore diapers; Symo was the most gorgeous blond girl we had seen in ages; Madison, a Texas cowhand; Marsh organized a band consisting of himself, Scott and Fratus, and led the parade of Pollywogs; Pincotich had a drill team dressed as wooden soldiers; then came the Queen of the May with her court, consisting of Lieut. Funk, Schmidt, and the TBF pilots, Lt(jg) Norris, and Ens. Cox, who danced around their queen madly and hilariously. Neptunus Rex was well pleased with the performance and accepted all new hands into his Royal Domain after we had run the gauntlet of going through a long double line of paddles manned by eagerly waiting shellbacks.

When the Task Force neared Pearl on the 22nd, the Air Groups were flown to Ford Island. Half of the squadron, Schmidt, Haynes, Symo, Webb, Kirschke, Korr, and Madison were sent to the Chris Holmes Rest Home, which is run by Commander Air Force Pacific, for squadrons returning from combat operations and located on Waikiki. It is a beautiful residence located on the seashore, and walking distance from the Royal Hawaiian. The management furnished the boys with beautiful bedrooms, palatable meals, anything to drink, and later in the afternoon Mrs. Gault, the hostess, would invite girls for dinner and a movie. Due to the blackout at 9.00 P.M., the girls would be escorted home before the curfew. The first group remained there until the 27th, when they were replaced by Mr. Hiller, Smith, Abell and Tyner. Hofler, Rickard and Kenyon took the cure on the 29th. Lieut. Funk was detached upon our arrival at Pearl, and took the first available air transportation to California.

During this time, Olin, Buckelew, Hill, Howard and Coyer were hard at work, flying a daily schedule with field carrier landings and gunnery being stressed.

CONFIDENTIAL

On October 1st, the long overdue ALNAV made its appearance. Haynes and Hefler finally were Lieutenants; to make matters worse for them, it happened that the Air Group was giving the Scouts a party. They had been officially detached from us and were headed South. The drinks however were not free (for the remaining Air Group) so everyone sought out the new Lieutenants; the result was an expensive day for the boys.

On the 8th, seven new Ensigns reported to the squadron. They had just arrived at Pearl from training, and needed combat training. During these few days, night operations were being conducted at Kaneohe; it was contemplated to move the squadron to Kaneohe in order to train our new pilots.

October 10th was a quiet, beautiful Sunday morning at Pearl Harbor. Plans were being made to move to Kaneohe. It was 0800 when Rickard answered what he believed was a call from a sweet young thing he met at Waikiki. It was the Air Officer; he wanted the Air Group Commander immediately; something was in the air; everything had broken down south and we were on the move. Lt. Cdr. Miller reported to the ship immediately, and shortly thereafter planes and pilots returned to Ford Island from Kaneohe. The seven new Ensigns were transferred to Fighting One in exchange for twelve of their experienced pilots; two were full lieutenants, Bascomb Montgomery, and Richard O'Connell; one (jg) Crockett, and seven Ensigns, Vaden, James, Matlock, Healy, McWilliams, Hahn, Boyd, Pupillo, and Muhlfeld.

Everyone was assigned something to do, so that by 2400 that day the non-flying personnel and equipment were aboard the PRINCETON, ready to leave. Lt. Smith, our Engineering Officer, performed miracles in getting the planes in condition; he was all over the field with his skivvy shirt showing, personally supervising every detail on all the planes.

On October 11th we left Pearl. The PRINCETON was headed toward the South Pacific. As we left the harbor, the Task Force that attacked Wake Island was preparing to enter. Unfortunately through no fault of ours, we had missed that job, but we were headed into something bigger, and we would get the South Pacific Duty over with also. Later in the afternoon the new pilots were qualified in carrier landings, along with Ensign Howard, Hill and Coyer, our three Ensigns who had been joy riding since leaving Philadelphia, because they were not qualified.

We crossed the Equator for the 35th time, on October 15th, and held the traditional crossing ceremonies the following day. Buckelew, Olin, Parent, and our new pilots were the center of attraction, and suffered more than the original bunch who were in the majority at that time, and had demanded (and received) leniency. Sunday, October 17th, we crossed the International Date Line, and the next day was Tuesday. Monday was a lost day, but we were paid for it anyway. On October 22nd, Ensign Howard had a barrier crash and broke his ankle. He was taken ashore when we arrived at Espiritu Santo in the New Hebrides on the 24th of October. Here we were given two new pilots from VF-12: Ensigns Mooney and Darby.

While at Espiritu some of the new pilots were flying at Bomber Three, others were aboard and sending all excess gear home under orders of the First Lieutenant, before leaving Espiritu on October 29th. During a combat air patrol on the 31st, Syme experienced engine trouble while hunting out an unidentified plane, and was forced to make a water landing. A destroyer was immediately sent out; it found him enjoying himself sampling all the nicknacks in his back pack.

On November 1st, we were ordered to attack Buka, and Bougainville (Bonis Field) in the northern Solomons. We attacked on the first, and again on the 2nd of November. In the pre-dawn take-offs of the 1st, Lieut.(jg) Olin failed to get airborne and went off the bow into the drink. Harry yelled like hell as he passed the carrier, and was picked up by a destroyer in a few minutes.

- 9 -

CONFIDENTIAL

During the same takeoffs, Lt(jg) Tyner had engine trouble and had to make a water landing. Fortunately a destroyer saw him and picked him up. During the attacks of the second day, Ensign Keener, a pilot from Fighting TWELVE but temporarily attached to us, was lost during a strafing run, and has not been heard from.

November 3rd, we received the following message: "Admiral Halsey has congratulated the Task Force on the strikes on Buka and says Well Done, and that as a result that Buka is not now contributing to Jap War Effort."

The Force had retired and was awaiting further orders. The evening of November 4th everyone was about to enjoy a movie, when the Air Officer was summoned; then the Intelligence Officers; and later word was passed to man torpedo elevators. Something was in the air, but they went ahead with the movie; after which all squadron officers were told to meet in the Ready Room. No one could believe their eyes and ears. Rabaul was to be attacked in the morning! It was to be an all-out, repeat all-out, attack on everything the Japs had in the harbor. This was the Big Time Lieut. Comdr. Miller had so often spoken of, but little did anyone realize it would hit the boys in such a sudden manner without any preparation. To put it mildly, everyone's nerves were on edge, and everyone was only too anxious to get any information the Intelligence Officers could dig up on the Jap bastion of the South Pacific.

After consultations and many changes, Lt. Kenyon produced the flight schedule for the attack on Rabaul, November 5th, 1943, - a day never to be forgotten by our pilots. Lt. Cdr. Miller led the squadron, and had in his division, Lt(jg) Syme, Lt(jg) Kirschke, and Ens. James. Lt. Claude Schmidt led the second division with Ens. Coyer, Lt(jg) Abell, and Ens. Pupillo. Lt. Smith led the third division with Lt(jg) Olin, Lt(jg) Webb, and Ens. Hall. Lt. Bascomb Montgomery had the fourth division with Lt(jg) Buckelew, Lt(jg) Madison, and Ensign Massey. Lt. Dick O'Connell was in the fifth division with Lt(jg) Kerr, and Lt(jg) Crockett. This was the order in which the boys took off from the PRINCETON at 0900 November 5th.

Rabaul, located on the northern tip of New Britain Island was protecting a good portion of the enemy's fleet which had been gathering there for a major Jap strike. As our planes approached, the harbor was protected by an umbrella of terrific anti-aircraft fire, the like of which our boys had never experienced before, and hope never to see again. Japanese fighter planes swarmed the sky, Zekes, Tonys, Haps, everything the enemy could make airborne. Our bombers dove with deadly accuracy, while our fighters filled the sky with falling Jap planes. Hell had literally broken loose, and planes filled every inch of the sky.

At 1250, as the first planes appeared over the carrier everyone was anxiously scanning the sky, counting planes, while others remained below to pick up radio reports on returning planes. As the first planes landed, reports looked bad, some had it that one complete division had been lost; but as the minutes passed, more and more planes were coming aboard. On the final count it was learned that Lieutenants Smith and O'Connell, and Lt(jg) Madison were missing. Reports on Smittie and O'Connell were meagre; no one could accurately account for what had happened to them. Jack Madison had started after a couple of Zeros, and reports indicate that he probably got them, but while after them, one got behind him and made his plane fall. When the boys left Rabaul, the place was an inferno. Cruisers and destroyers were hit, some sunk, while Jap planes were scattered all over the place, total wrecks.

- 10 -

CONFIDENTIAL

The official tabulation for the raid was:

	Definite	Probables	Damaged
Miller, Lt.Cdr.	Tony		Tony
Syme, Lt(jg)			Zeke
Schmidt, Lt.			Tony
Olin, Lt(jg)	Zeke	Zeke	
Webb, Lt(jg)			
Hill, Ens.	Zeke		Zeke; Betty
Montgomery, Lt.	1 Zeke 2 Tonys		
Buckelew, Lt(jg)	Zeke		Zeke
Madison, Lt(jg)		Tony	
Massey, Ens.	Zeke; Tony		
Kerr, Lt(jg)			Betty
Crockett, Lt(jg)	Zeke		
Totals	9 VF	2 VF	6 VF 2 MB

Tony)
Zeke) - Jap Zero fighter planes.

Betty - Jap medium bomber.

That evening the ship's flight surgeons broke out the brandy and the boys with nerves still on edge talked on into the night. The next day congratulatory messages were pouring in from all directions.

Admiral Halsey sent us a Well Done, that the PRINCETON and SARATOGA had performed a magnificent job. General MacArthur sent the following: Every Officer and man working with Admirals Sherman and Merrill deserves commendation. From the Commander of our Task Force to the PRINCETON: Msg Capt. Henderson. I am proud of the performance of your ship and Air Group on this whole trip. Both have demonstrated their ability to be full participating partners in the best combat team in the world. Adm. Sherman. From the Commander of our Cruiser Division: Please extend to the Air Groups from all hands our congratulations and great admiration for the outstanding job they have done, and the punishment they have dealt out to the Japs. We are proud to be with you. From General Arnold: The Army Air Forces congratulate the Navy for the magnificent day attacks by the carrier aircraft on Jap ships in Rabaul November 5th. The pilots established a record that other airmen will find difficult to equal. Please extend my congratulations to all concerned.

As the messages poured in, too much attention was not paid them, since the pilots were still tired as hell from the terrific ordeal, and everyone's thoughts were with our one and only Smittie, "Black Jack" Madison, and Dick O'Connell, who had failed to return. Everyone was missing these boys; they were the type that every squadron wants and is proud to have. We will never forget them.

Lt(jg) Crockett, who had been assigned the job of protecting the Air Group Commander of the SARATOGA, was reported doing well in Sick Bay. During the attack he and the Air Group Commander had been jumped by numerous Jap planes. Crockett's plane was riddled with bullet holes; 180 were counted on the port side only. He had been wounded, but still remained with the Commander, and shot down a Jap plane during the fight. To this day Crockett does not remember landing on the carrier after the attack; he was in such a weakened condition. The following message was received from the SARATOGA Group Commander: "Group Commander sends to Fighter pilot Number Three x Your courage, determination and loyalty will be a lasting inspiration to me x H H CALDWELL."

- 11 -

CONFIDENTIAL

Lieut. Schmidt's division performed the outstanding feat of protecting and bringing safely home 18 dive bombers from the SARATOGA. He had picked up the SARA planes upon the completion of their attack, and protected them from twenty Jap fighter planes that were attacking the bombers as they left Rabaul. Our boys claim they strained their eyes and were mighty happy to see their carrier and realize they were finally home.

On November 8th, we arrived at Espiritu Santo again. However, few were permitted to go ashore, since we were merely to take on supplies and leave again. We left again on November 9th. Our objective was to attack Rabaul again! Preparations were thoroughly made, and all details of the raid minutely gone over again and again. Here we borrowed a division from Fighting TWELVE. They were Lt(jg) Parker, Hughes, Russell, and Caldwell.

On November 11th, Armistice Day, Rabaul was again attacked! Our planes took off at 0545. Lt. Comdr. Miller was again leading the Air Group, and had in his division Lt(jg) Syme, Lt(jg) Webb, and Ens. Hill. Lt. Schmidt led the second division, and had with him Ens. Coyer, Lt(jg) Abell, and Ens. Pupillo. Lt. Haynes had the third division with Lt(jg) Tyner, Ens. James, and Ens. Darby. Lt(jg) Kirschke led the fourth division with Ens. Boyd, Lt(jg) Buckelew, and Ens. Massey; and Lt(jg) Parker had the fifth division with Lt(jg) Kerr, Lt(jg) Hughes, and Lt(jg) Russell. The attack was perfectly planned and executed. At 1045 the planes appeared over the carriers, all the divisions intact -- all were safely back!

The anti aircraft fire was just as bad, and the Japs had planes all over the sky, but our boys had learned from experience, and were just too damn good and wise for the unfortunate Japs.

The following was sent us: "Please convey to all hands in the Force my utmost admiration for their brilliant performance during their operations in the South Pacific. You have dealt severe blows to the enemy at Buka and Rabaul x Your first attack on Rabaul was another shot heard round the world. Your second equally effective, even though hampered by insufficient targets. I know you will carry out successfully your Central Pacific operations. Good hunting, and good luck. Halsey."

We returned to Espiritu on November 14th. Admiral Sherman gave the Task Force a party at the O Club, which turned out to be quite an affair. All the boys, even those who were not short snorters were getting signatures from Admirals Halsey, Fitch and Sherman. When that party was over, Lt. Cdr. Miller gave another cocktail party at Bomber 3 -- enuf said!

Crockett was dismissed from the Naval Base Hospital at Espiritu and returned to the Squadron on the 15th. Lt. Montgomery and Ens. Healy and Ens. Howard were detached from the squadron on the 16th, to report to Commander Fleet Air South Pacific.

On November 16th we left Espiritu Santo on another attack mission. We were to attack the Jap held island of Nauru, adjacent to the Gilbert Islands. The base was attacked on November 19, 1943, and the attack successfully carried out. Our boys had become most proficient in evading anti aircraft fire and strafing anything selected for them.

Claude Schmidt returned beaming all over the place; he had shot down a Jap Zero. He had really poured the lead into him, and enjoyed watching the Jap hit the water. Ens. McWilliams did not return with his division, and was believed lost, since Jap Zeros had jumped our boys and a first class dog fight ensued. However, it was not long before he was picked up on the radio, and shortly landed aboard. He was covered with grease from top to bottom, but had a big grin all over his face; he had a Zero to his credit also. All our planes were aboard, and the Japs were minus planes.

CONFIDENTIAL

Upon completion of this attack the following messages arrived: "From the Commander of the Task Force x Well Done to the Air Groups on today's strikes x This completes nine strikes by this Task Force in 19 days, which I believe is a record for carriers in this war x Again I say Well Done to this Force x "

On the evening of the attack, some Jap snoopers located our force and trailed us for quite some time, but would not close in. All hands were at General Quarters, and those on the flight deck watched the ships open fire on The Snooper. The fireworks would light up the area for miles. However it must have frightened the Nips, since they left and did not return.

Tarawa was being attacked and occupied by American Naval Forces. On November 23rd we met and escorted a large convoy headed toward Tarawa and then supplied the air coverage over the area.

November 25th was Thanksgiving. We were given a super lunch, turkey and all the trimmings, cake, ice cream, cigars and cigarettes; but it still would have been better were we at home. The occupation of Tarawa was successful, and on November 27th, at 0500, we received orders to perform all kinds of plane transfers. Saxation, our first class yeoman, who we discovered after the lapse of a year had been the checker champ of New York and is currently giving us checker lessons, earned the right to become a Chief today; he put out forty four sets of orders in fifty one minutes. We wonder if he derives his speed from the fact that he is a New York lawyer? And after all this speed and fuss, none of the orders were needed; - someone changed his mind fifty two minutes later.

What is to become of us? That remains to be seen. It looks as though we may head to some convenient port for a rest. Up to the present time we have crossed the Equator 36 times, and the International Date Line six times.

During the news broadcast later in the day the Chaplain read the following: "Heartiest congratulations on your success, and more power to you for the future. My warmest admiration to officers and men of all units, surface, ground, and air, taking part in this brilliant joint action. DeWitt Navy Staff College."

Saturday, November 27th. Claude Schmidt and his division ferried planes to another carrier. Upon landing he discovered that they intended to keep him for further operations. Upon making more inquiries, the more he was assured that he would not leave. Whereupon Claude asked permission to see Admiral Pownall. He is about as tall as Claude, so they had a heart to heart talk. Schmidt gave him all the details on Rabaul, and the 19 raids in eight days our boys had been on; after which the Admiral ordered him back to the PRINCETON with a recommendation that our boys had earned a rest. Claude asked the Admiral how the operations were proceeding, and he replied: "Fine, Fine, every Jap on the island has been killed."

Sunday, November 28th. Kirschke, Buckelew, and Hill ferried planes to the BELLEAU WOOD. Upon landing they were told that they would remain. Frantic calls for help availed them nothing, and the boys are still there. Three pilots from the LISCOMBE BAY came aboard. She had been hit by a torpedo and sunk.

Monday. Today is Sunday November 28th. Again having crossed the International Date Line. Word was sent us that our three pilots were transferred to a tanker and would either meet us or be taken to some port where we will go -- will they log the sack time! Ships from various forces have met and are refueling today. The forces around us would scare a Jap to death; it's the mightiest fleet in the world; secrecy prevents mentioning the number of carriers, battlewagons, cruisers, cans, etc., that are within seeing distance. It's really a magnificent sight, and one which makes one feel secure.

- 13 -

CONFIDENTIAL

November, 29th. Kirschke, Buckelow and Hill were transferred aboard today. We have been detached from our task force and ordered to proceed to Pearl Harbor, escorting returning ships. The convoy is to travel slowly, so that we shall not arrive until December 7th. The afternoons were spent playing volley ball, and one afternoon the Chaplain held a field meet on the flight deck, rope climbing, and line throwing. In a tug-o-war the Air Group enlisted men held their own, but were nosed out in the final tug.

On December 7th we arrived at Pearl. It seemed as though it took hours to get the O.K. to enter the harbor; finally the word was given, and as soon as we dropped anchor everyone was off for the rest home and various hotels.

The evening of the 8th the ship sent a representative to locate us and bring us tidings that we had to remove all our gear by 0700 the next morning, since the ship was leaving for the States, - minus the Air Group. What news!/@*?;/.

The next morning we were all down packing and packing in a mad rush, throwing things away. The ship's loud speaker was blaring forth for the squadrons to leave the ship immediately. Finally they tossed us off. There we sat on a stack of gear and listened to the heckling of the ship's crew as she pulled off for the States, - with Christmas around the corner!

For two days we remained around Honolulu, catching up on rest and social obligations that had been sadly neglected during our sojourn in the South Pacific. Leon Haynes was detached and found himself the quickest available transportation to San Diego, which had him home for Christmas.

We were finally ordered to depart for Puunene Naval Air Station, Maui, where we were to train during the absence of the PRINCETON. Hofler and Rickard were the first to set off, and had transportation, ready room, and rooming assignments all set when the rest of the squadron arrived.

All of our gear was placed on the SWAN, a minesweeper, and on arriving at Maui, to the disgust of all concerned, it was discovered that our gear had been ransacked and all our Christmas "spirits" removed. A hell of a fix we were in!

Lieutenant Commanders Fuhring and Curtis accompanied us to Maui.

Lt(jg) Syms having in his inimitable way made the correct connections in Honolulu, he and a small group were invited to spend Christmas at the Kukaiau Ranch, Nancy Russell's parents' place, on the big island of Hawaii. The balance of the Air Group were extended invitations to the Hinds Ranch, also located on Hawaii, next to the fabulous Parker Ranch.

Stories are still being retold about the various experiences enjoyed at these places. Louie Parent had a horse fall on his head; Hubbard surprised all at his prowess at Pheasant Hunting; Hofler was known as "the big bad wolf with a Dartmouth mind", while the same young lady, D. J. Gruin, referred to Kerr as a "mass of tangled inhibitions". Kirschke met Lanie, and the boys found out what a rodeo and branding was like.

While this was going on the other half of the squadron was hard at work. Lt. Cdr. Curtis was working the boys on field carrier landings, night and day. On December 14th, two new Ensigns reported for duty, - Ensigns Hendrickson and Weickhardt; and on December 16th Ensigns Nicklin and Brugger reported for duty with the squadron. These boys needed field carrier landings, and gunnery, so were unable to rest, since much work had to be accomplished in a short time.

Christmas and New Years were uneventful. Some of the boys were away on the ranches, and those remaining scattered off to the Officers' Club or various homes in Lahaina and Kahuli.

CONFIDENTIAL

Ensign Parker reported on January 3, 1944. He had left San Francisco on the Clipper, New Years Day. We checked him out in an F6F as soon as possible, but due to his inexperience it was thought advisable to leave him ashore when we prepared to ship out.

Commander George Chafee, our former Air Group Commander, appeared and made preparations to take our planes aboard his carrier for a couple of days and qualify all hands. All the planes flew out on January 7th, and qualified without incident. Claude Schmidt was assigned a bunk in Sam Froelick's room. He was the same old Sam of Parris Island days.

The PRINCETON was back from the States, so on January 10th we embarked for a few days' cruise to qualify new pilots. Just as we were leaving Pearl Harbor our Chief Yeoman Saxation opened what seemed like a routine envelope; but did it have a slow curve in it; -- Lt. Comdr. Miller was ordered detached and directed to report as Air Officer on a CVE! Wait until he flies aboard and gets that news!

The planes were to fly aboard. Ensign Eubank, flying a TBF, was the first to come aboard. As he approached and was allset to land, something happened which caused a terrible accident, and Ensign Eubank's death. The two passengers riding with him were rescued. It was our first fatal accident, and a very unfortunate one.

The next day, January 11th, Ensign Nicklin had a little bad luck coming aboard, and tore the tail off of his plane, but no one was injured; other than that everyone qualified without difficulty, and we returned to Pearl on the 13th.

A week was devoted to preparing the ship and squadron for the next combat mission. Planes were checked, new planes taken aboard, exchanges of enlisted personnel made. The foresighted brought aboard Coca cola, magazines and jars of candy. As to when we would be leaving no one knew, although our mission was surmised by everyone. Ensign Parker was temporarily transferred to ComAirPac on the 18th, since he was not considered qualified for carrier operations and combat as yet. This was a wise move, since he would not have been permitted to fly; as a result of which he would have lost all that time to practice.

At 1200 on January 19, 1944, we left our anchorage at Pearl Harbor for the Japanese held Marshall Islands. On leaving the harbor an Air Group meeting was held, and all were informed regarding our targets: Wotje, Maloelap, and Eniwetok.

Classes on plane and ship identification, and the Marshall Islands, were conducted by Lieutenants Hubbard and Hefler until January 27. During the first days out fighter director work was carried out by the carriers. On one particular day another carrier was given a "Well Done", while the Peerless P was conspicuously omitted. You can be sure that our gang were in there pitching from then on.

Two days later, while taking our planes aboard, we were missing a plane. After a frantic muster, it was discovered that Ensign Hahn was absent; when all of a sudden we discovered that he was trying to land on another carrier, -- by mistake of course.

D-Day was to be on 31 January 1944. On that particular day landings were to be made on Kwajalein Atoll and Majuro Atoll. However our attacks were to commence on the 29th.

On January 29th at 0555 our first strike against Wotje Island took off. Four divisions were on this attack, which was the first of three strikes for the day. Lt. Cdr. Miller's division consisting of McWilliams, Syme, and James was in the lead. Claude Schmidt with his division of Matlock, Aboll and Pupille was the next off; followed by Karr's division of Boyd, Olin and Nicklin. The last division off was Crockett's, with Vadon, Tyner and Hendrickson.

- 15 -

CONFIDENTIAL

During the day combat air patrols were flown all day. Kirschke's division of Darby, Buckelew and Hahn, and Webb's division of Weickhardt, Hill and Muhlfeld were the ones who drew the assignment. There were three sorties against Wotje this first day, and four combat air patrols. The anti aircraft fire was not as intense as anticipated, and after the first sortie, was considerably less.

January 30, 1944, we were all awakened at 0400, battle breakfast of steak, eggs, fruit and coffee was served. The pilots were briefed on a new target, and the first attacks of the day against Wotje and Taroa were launched at 0545. Today our fighter planes, along with the strikes against the Japanese were conducting combat air patrols over the Jap airfield at Wotje, to make certain that no Nip planes took off or landed. Lt. Cdr. Miller's division of McWilliams, Syms and James; Kirschke's division of Darby, Buckelew and Nicklin; and Webb's division of Weickhardt, Hill and Muhlfeld were assigned the patrols over Wotje. They would patrol for three hours, and return to our carrier. However, just before leaving a few strafing runs against Nip installations were generally in order.

The strikes against Taroa were conducted by Crockett's division of Vaden, Tyner, and Hendrickson; and later Kirschke's division; when Schmidt's division of Matlock, Abell and Pupillo, and Kerr's division of Boyd, Olin and Massey relieved the first patrols over the Jap airfield of Wotje. Throughout the day we had six patrols over the Nip base at Wotje, and four strikes against the enemy at Taroa. However it must be remembered that after each patrol the boys generally departed with a strafing run, so in all the Japs were kept quite busy.

The target at Taroa or Maloelap, also one of the Marshall group, was just south of Wotje, so we easily hit both bases simultaneously. Schmidt's division on its last patrol of the day went to Taroa and spotted for the cruisers that were bombarding the island. When that day was completed you can be certain that there were not too many lively Nips on that island.

D-Day was January 31, 1944. Our forces were landing at Majuro and Kwajalein Atolls. We continued our devastation of Wotje with strikes, patrols, and bombardment by cruisers. There were five patrols and three strikes over the island. During the last patrol, Lt. Cdr. Miller spotted for the cruisers that were bombarding, and from all reports the place was in shambles that evening. Today we had our first casualty of the operation. Lt(jg) Buckelew, while carrying out daring strafing runs against an enemy gun emplacement that he had spotted was struck by anti-aircraft fire which disabled his plane and forced him to make a water landing. Buck himself was not hit; he called Ensign Brugger, his wingman, and told him about his having to make the water landing. When the plane landed it disappeared immediately, and for some unknown reason Buck was unable to get out. Our planes circled for fifteen minutes, but without success.

This evening we received the following message: "Well Done x I have the best carrier pilots in the Navy.", signed, Admiral Ginder.

February 1. We retired to refuel. This gave the pilots an opportunity to catch up on some well earned rest.

February 2. We headed for Eniwetok Atoll, the western-most atoll in the Marshall Group. There we were to patrol and intercept any enemy planes trying to reinforce the Nip air bases in the Marshalls. Our forces had landed and the conquest was in the bag; but you can never tell, - the little Nips will try anything.

February 3. We attacked Engebi Island in Eniwetok Atoll. There were no enemy planes in the air, so a systematic destruction of their airfield was begun and carried on until February 6th. Sorties were conducted every day. The AA fire was reduced to nothing, and as a matter of fact the torpedo planes were taking passengers as observers towards the end; Hubbard, Hofler, and Hallowell taking trips and watching the bombs drop. They did admit that it was a hard trip just for a thirty-second look at the target.

- 16 -

CONFIDENTIAL.

At noon on the sixth we recovered our aircraft and left for Roi, our newly acquired base in the Kwajalein atoll.

From January 29th, until February 6th, we had carried out twelve strikes against the enemy and conducted ten combat air patrols over the enemy airfield which also included a strafing attack before leaving the target.

At about 0900 we arrived at Roi, which is on the northern end of the lagoon. From the distance we could see ships and ships in the lagoon. They were of all types and sizes. This lagoon is the largest in the world. It was an experience seeing it, and seeing all the ships we had there. As we entered we could see evidences of our landing forces in the various smaller islands in the entrance to the lagoon; tanks and landing boats littered the shores. You could see machine gun nests which were razed; some tanks were overturned, and marines were all over the place souvenir hunting.

The next day, Schmidt, Kerr, and Crockett were allowed to go to Roi and see the devastation. They came back with pockets packed with souvenirs and colossal stories. It seems the marines had cornered the market on Jap property and demanded terrific exchanges for a flag or sword. What they wanted above all was one of our .45 calibre revolvers. For that you would get a Jap sword. Next on their list was whiskey. For a bottle you'd get practically anything they had. Money meant nothing. By that time they had all of that that they wanted.

February 9th. We received a new operation plan. It was to occupy Eniwetok Atoll; so at 1400 we departed from Roi to carry out our orders. The Task Force was the same as we have had all along. Lt(jg) Kroeger and Ensign Cox and Lt(jg) Tyner were taken over to a ferry carrier, and will fly two TBFs and one F6F back to the PRINCETON. Ensign Boyd is still on another carrier. He will fly a Hellcat back to the PRINCETON tomorrow. He has been aboard that carrier since the 5th, when he bounced over the barrier on attempting a landing, and as he bounced over he gave it the gun and took off again. However, his tail hook was torn off by another plane's prop, as he took off, so he had to make a crash landing on the other carrier without a tail hook. That experience of Boyd's was really a thriller. So far it's tops, and we don't care to see any more like it, thank you.

Thursday, February 10th. We arrived at our assigned location off of Eniwetok Atoll, and launched our attacks beginning at 0900, with Lt. Cdr. Miller and Lt(jg) Webb's divisions going in first. Our next strike took off at 1115 with only Claude Schmidt's division going, and the third attack of the day taking off at 1315 with Kirschke's division following Lt. Cdr. Miller's division in for the attack. On this strike Kenyon decided to participate, so flew in with Lt(jg) Kroeger in a TBF. The anti aircraft fire was minimum and the place was still badly torn up from our previous visit.

Friday, February 11th. Still softening up Eniwetok Atoll for our contemplated landings. Engebi Island's airfield was bombed by our TBF's, and strafed by our Hellcats on two strikes. The place is in ruins, and no opposition is being encountered. Lt. Rickard rounded out the A-V(S) officers' trips by flying in on the first strike with Lt(jg) Spear.

We had another unfortunate accident today. Ensign Boyd on returning from the attack on Engebi, made a bad landing, struck the bridge, and went over the side. He was unable to get out of his plane.

Later this afternoon keep-away with the medicine ball was our form of exercise. Whoever is not in a standby condition generally gets up on the flight deck and limbers up, thereby staying in pretty fair condition.

February 12. Last night the Japs attacked Roi Island in Kwajalein Atoll. Our ship's operators picked their planes up, but General Quarters was not necessary. This morning Lt. Cdr. Miller, Lt(jg) Syms, Webb, and Coyer, and Lt. Schmidt's division of Abell, Tyner, and Ens. Weickhardt took off at 0700 and attacked Engebi. It was to be the last strike for the time being.

CONFIDENTIAL

On recovering our planes we left our intercept station and headed for Roi. Mail is expected, our first in a month. We wonder if it was one of the targets last night.

Tonight Dr. Fuhring broke out the "rations", and the boys are recollecting and comparing past raids.

Sunday, February 13, 1944. Today we returned to Roi, entered the lagoon at 1000, and immediately began refueling and taking aboard bombs. The Air Group was in condition 13, i.e., on thirty-minutes notice, so most of the boys caught up on sleep. Some took sun baths, and others tried their luck at fighting, but without much success. This afternoon the Catholic Chaplain from another carrier came aboard. Services were in memoriam of Jim Boyd. Later our exercises on the flight deck consisted of a little keep-away medicine ball, and at 1700 we weighed anchor and left the lagoon for the night.

Monday, February 14. We returned to Roi at 0900 and anchored in the lagoon for the day. Nothing was scheduled, so the boys spent the day sleeping and taking sun baths. As we left the lagoon for the night, one of our newest cruisers arrived and sent us word that she had mail for us. Consequently we can't wait to return to Roi in the morning and claim our long overdue mail.

Tuesday, February 15. We entered the lagoon again this morning, and anxiously awaited our mail. There were 339 sacks for the PRINCETON. Little by little it arrived, and as the squadron sacks came aboard they were immediately sent up to the office. The packages were in a terrible condition, and if they contained cakes or candy, it was worse. No first class mail arrived, which meant no letters! At 1425 we departed from Roi, and headed toward Eniwetok again, this time to capture the atoll.

Wednesday, February 16. Our attacks commenced early this morning, and continued throughout the day. Some anti aircraft was noticed, but it was spasmodic. The islands were well strafed and bombed, and are ready for the landings tomorrow. Ensign Cox of the TBF's was wounded in the neck in the first strike today.

Thursday, 17 February. Today is D-Day. Landings were made on two small islands adjoining Engebi, as our planes and ships bombed and bombarded the islands. Lt. Cdr. Miller was assigned the task of Air Coordinator with the ground forces. Landings were made according to schedule, and our transports entered the lagoon without difficulty. Ensign Pupillo on returning on the last hop of the day crashed into the barrier; no one was injured.

Friday, 18 February. Landings were made on Engebi itself today. Opposition seems to be of a minimum caliber. Our ships are now bombarding the rest of the islands in preparation to land on them. Ensign Janes crashed into the barrier today. It is beginning to look as though the boys are tiring.

Today, February 18, Eniwetok Island was captured by our forces. Lt. Cdr. Miller and Lt(jg) Webb were the air coordinators from our squadron who participated in the supervising of the landings; their flight lasted 5½ hours. It was the longest flight undertaken from the PRINCETON to date. Other divisions from the squadron, Lt(jg) Syme, Kerr, and Kirschke each leading one, participate in strafing the Nips after the landing forces had them cornered. The boys really enjoyed it today; there was AA fire, bombs falling, boats landing on the beaches and tanks roaming the island looking for Japs, - a Warner Brothers thriller could have done no better.

Sunday, February 20. The capture of Eniwetok was slower than expected; our forces were meeting with some resistance. During the day our six divisions each were given one combat air patrol over the atoll, and enjoyed watching the ground forces and tanks move in on the Nips. The transmissions between tanks were amusing, one particular tank complained that the rest which were supposed to be with him were gathering souvenirs. The tally from our other forces' raid on Truk was published today and enjoyed by all.

- 18 -

CONFIDENTIAL

Monday, and Tuesday, 21 and 22 February, were devoted to taking the remaining island on the atoll, Parry Island. Our boys were kept busy strafing Nip fox holes and snipers. Fuel was running low, so today, Wednesday, the 23rd, we refueled. Mail went off, but as yet none has made its appearance.

One year ago today, February 25, our ship was commissioned; Lt. Comdr. Miller and Lieut. Kenyon had attended the ceremonies. However, today we are a long way from Philadelphia here in the Marshall Islands, flying patrols over our latest conquest, Eniwetok Atoll, until the field is repaired and a squadron arrives to take over. Patrols have been cut down; we only had one flight today, which consisted of two divisions over the atoll.

February 26. Another day in the same area; more patrolling. We had expected to leave, but unforeseen circumstances made us remain. Today's schedule only called for one patrol over the atoll; the balance of the pilots stood by in a ready condition, and very bored with the whole situation. It's been six weeks that we have been without mail; one can well imagine our predicament, and there are no hopes of receiving any.

February 27th. Still on the same job. However today the Admiral allowed two planes to fly to Engebi and land. Hubbard returned with a TBF full of souvenirs, so tonight everyone is gathering something to take home.

February 28th. Today we were assigned the morning patrol. Lt. Cdr. Miller and his division led three other divisions off the deck. They came aboard at 1100, and the Task Force changed course, which heads us toward a harbor in the Marshalls. However, there we expect mail and provisions.

February 29th. After one patrol we departed for an atoll.

March 1. We dropped anchor at 1000 and immediately looked around for our long overdue mail. It soon came aboard, and all hands were swamped with forty-two days of mail.

March 2, 3, 4. all the mail was distributed at once, Ensign Parent and Nicklin being undisputed winners of the greatest loot, with forty letters each. We all took turns going to one of the small islands for a swim, and looking around for cats-eyes and various colored coral formations. We were probably the first white people to visit this little island, and honorably initiated it with a beer party. Some Navy nurses were located in a nearby island, but their doctor escorts upon seeing us immediately whisked them off. Kenyon, on returning to the ship, was sitting on the gunwale of the gig, all dressed, so Kirschke gave him a friendly tap, and over went Kenyon, clothes, coral and all.

March 8. At 0830 the ship weighed anchor. We are headed for Espiritu Santo, and as to what we will do after that is a great mystery. New planes were flown aboard by Lt(jg) Crockett, Olin, Tyner, and Ensign Nicklin.

March 9th. We crossed the equator for the 41st time, and conducted the ceremonies in accordance with the ancient tradition of the sea, Ensigns Hendrickson, Nicklin, Weickhardt and Brugger being the center of attraction. Hendrickson appeared as Alice in Wonderland, Nicklin as Charlie Chaplin, and the high chair pilot of the Navy, Weickhardt, as a beautiful hula dancer; and Brugger as one of our colored mess boys. King Neptune was Lt. Kelleher; the Queen, Lt. Whitney; the Royal Baby, Lt. Blackburn; Royal Judge, Lt. Cdr. Hatcher; Royal Prosecutor, Lt. Kenyon; Royal Barber, Captain Trumpeter, USMC; Royal Dentist, Lt(jg) Rapp; Davey Jones, Lt. Boiteret; and the Royal Doctor, Lt(jg) Schulman. Along with our pilots, the Executive Officer, Commander Murphy was the center of attraction; his most serious offense was impersonating a Naval Officer for 16 years and never crossed the line.

Today, March 10th, was omitted from our calendar; it is Saturday, March 11th. It was a quiet day, no flights were scheduled; so the boys devoted the day to sunbathing and sleeping.

CONFIDENTIAL

March 11th. Arrived at Espiritu Santo at 1520, and at 1525 we were all headed for the O Club. Two divisions flew ashore, and consequently got a half hour head start.

March 12th. Nothing doing; just recovering from last night. Lots of mail arrived.

March 16th. Lt. Cdr. Curtis is bouncing 12 new pilots just out of training. Attended LANGLEY party, which was A-1.

March 17th. Enlisted men sent aboard again; eight pilots still ashore; and we are on 6-hour notice.

March 19th. New pilots were being bounced in preparation for carrier qualification. Ens. Parker arrived from Pearl, having flown down to meet us.

March 20th. With various other ships giving parties, we decided to outdo them by sending out invitations to cocktails at the Officers' Club on San Juan Hill. We obtained the use of the LANGLEY orchestra for dancing, and took our small band to play for the dinner room which was beneath the bar and dancing floor. About 1700 while waiting for time to pass, at the club, the hospital ship, USS SOLACE, arrived in the harbor. Immediately Rickard and Hefler sent forth emissaries to obtain nurses for the party. When the party was finally under full swing, the committee of two had located and obtained between 35 and 40 nurses, between the hospital ship and various Army and Navy hospitals located in the near vicinity. Peterkin had obtained the use of nine vehicles with drivers, and Hubbard stationed himself at the door and greeted everyone from the Admiral to uninvited guests. The party was such a success, that instead of closing at 2200 as planned, it continued on until past 2300.

March 21st. The PRINCETON weighed anchor from Espiritu and cruised around the entrance to the harbor all day, during which time we qualified new pilots for ourselves and two other carriers.

Wednesday, March 22nd. Preparations were being made to get under way again; everyone was picking up necessary equipment, planes, and even clothing; since khakis could be purchased here. At 1600 we met our former dive bomber pilots who were returning from an Australian vacation, so a reunion and party was in order. Tolman, Maerki, Sullivan, Maloney, Tobey, and Hodden were all present. Of course the stories that developed were magnificent.

Today, the 23rd, at 0730, we left Espiritu for something big; everyone is guessing as to what it is, but no one is certain. This operation has been kept under cover better than average. Eight new pilots reported to us, all Ensigns, Parker, Supan, Hill, Munson, Blyth, Bledsoe, Waldron, and Phillian. Hefler and Hubbard immediately took them under their wing; and ground school was under way.

The following day, the 24th, lectures on Palau were given. It seems to be a good bet that we will strike there. However, Tally Ho Ack Ack, our Admiral Ginder's daily news report, did not give out any definite information, so it seems we will have to wait until our force is completely made up. The new pilots were given catapult instructions by Lieut. Elmo Runyan, and then taken up on the flight deck and taxied on the catapult to show them how it's done. The doctors issued first aid kits and gave them their first aid lectures tonite.

Today, 12 fighters carried out practice interceptions on planes from accompanying carriers; also pilots were given recognition instructions.

The 26th, we spent refueling our Task Force. There was an early morning anti submarine search, and a combat air patrol. They were landed by 1000 when the tanker came alongside. Here we are refueling at a spot that a few months back was controlled by the enemy, and we would not have dreamt of entering. Truk is only a stones throw away from us, but here we are.

- 20 -

CONFIDENTIAL

March 26. Our forces have been organized; the operations plans have come aboard, and we are headed for Palau and Yap. When you get on the flight deck and look around, one has a sense of security, since the greatest fleet in the world is before your eyes, and it's headed toward giving the Japs hell. A Jap snooper came in close today, within thirty miles, then left for home. It's doubtful if we will get in undetected, so the next two days will be looked forward to with interest. The pilots took it easy today, most of them sleeping or taking sun baths. At 1600 we had athletics on the flight deck, played keep-away with the medicine ball in the warm sun. Presently we were on the Equator. This is crossing number 42 for us, headed west. Consequently the heat is something to write home about. Ensign Woickhardt's new ship's orchestra entertained the crew on the flight deck. This evening it was a beautiful sunset. Too bad no girls were around to round out the evening.

Wednesday, March 29th. Was a quiet day until noon, when one of the carrier C.A.P. spotted a Betty coming in low and finished it off. About five o'clock the boys picked up a couple more Japs, and ended their flight; this was followed by the "H" carrier planes who downed another. Right after dark, the Nips came in full force, tracers were lighting the sky, and soon one Betty blew up right off our starboard quarter. This was immediately followed with our guns getting a Nip off of our stern, causing beautiful explosions and fires. Immediately after the second one, a third came over our bow, strafed our flight deck, and you can be sure all hands hit the deck. Hubbard, Rickard and Kenyon practically dug a hole falling so hard. The Nips kept coming in and the other ships were giving them warm receptions. All the pilots were ordered to bed, since tomorrow will be a hard day.

March 30th. Today is D-Day. We attacked Palau at 0630. Lt. Cdr. Miller took off and led Fighting Squadron 23 on the fighter sweep to clear the air of Jap planes. Ens. McWilliams, Lt(jg) Syme, and Ens. James were in his division. Lt. Schmidt led the second division with Matlock, Abell, and Hill. Lt(jg) Kerr led the third division in with Ens. Vaden, Lt(j) Olin and Ens. Hendricks. On arriving at the target a few Zeros were encountered, and in quick order two were shot down by Miller and McWilliams. The airfield was then thoroughly strafed. Attacks were carried out all day long without further incident, with the exception of Lt(j) Webb, whose motor cut out and he made a water landing next to a destroyer. At 8:00 P.M. when all planes were aboard and darkness had set in, the Nips again showed up to attack us with low flying torpedo planes. Ships opened fire from all directions, and tracers were going in all directions. This lasted a few hours, and finally those that were left decided to go home.

March 31st. The second day of attack on Palau, March 31. The fighter sweep took off at 0730 with Lt. Cdr. Miller, McWilliams, Syme, and James. Schmidt led the second division with Matlock, Abell, and Hill; Les Kerr the third with Muhlfeld, Olin and Hendrickson. The fireworks began early; on the way in Syme spotted a Betty and with a beautiful run shot it down. On arriving at the target, Zeros all over the sky greeted our boys. Olin and Hendrickson had to return with motor trouble; but the rest of the boys waded in with guns blazing and carried on dog fights for an hour without stopping. Schmidt's division waded in and in a few minutes had shot down eight Zeros. Abell after shooting down one, returned to base with Les Kerr who had engine trouble. Les already had shot down two however. After shooting down a Zero, Lt. Cdr. Miller and Ensign McWilliams strafed the airfield. Lt. Schmidt after getting two, stuck around with Ensign Hill who shot down three. Ens. Matlock with one to his credit. Likewise for Ens. James and Lt(jg) Muhlfeld.

On returning to base Claude discovered that Muhlfeld was badly wounded and also that their gas was dangerously low; so after frantic calls, landed on the nearest base.

CONFIDENTIAL

During all this melee, Lt(jg) Kirschke with his division of Lt(jg) Darby, Lt(jg) Massey, and Ensign Brugger were sent out on combat air patrol to intercept an approaching torpedo plane. The boys located the Jap, and in quick order shot it down. When all our planes were aboard and a count taken, it was discovered that Jimmie Syme was missing. Some believe that they saw him parachute, so searches are being made to try and locate him.

In the afternoon attack our group escorted our torpedo bombers to the target. Mr. Miller spotted a Zero and shot him down. Kirschke, Darby, Massey and Brugger; and Crockett's division of Vaden, Tyner and Weickhardt flew in also and strafed all installations.

Later in the afternoon Lt(jg) Kerr led his division into Palau to search for Syme, but without success. Ensign James returned to our carrier, and brought word that Lt(jg) Muhlfeld was all right, despite severe wounds. Muhlfeld and James each shot down a Zero, which made our day's total 15 Jap planes. For the first time in three nights we were not under attack. Consequently all hands got a well earned sleep.

The score is as follows:

March 30		March 31		
Miller -	1	Schmidt -	2	
McWilliams	1	Matlock -	1	
	2	Abell -	1	
		Hill -	3	
		McWilliams -	1	
		Kirschke's Div.	1	
		Syme	1	Betty
		Kerr	2	
		Miller	1	
		James	1	
		Muhlfeld	1	
			15	

April 1, 1944. At 0730 three of our divisions took off on the fighter sweep over Woleai, just east of Palau, and west of Truk. They were Lt.Cdr. Miller's division, Kirschke's, and Crockett's divisions. On the way unidentified planes were encountered, which threw our planes off course, and they never reached the target. The balance of today's attacks on Woleai were cancelled, so combat air patrols were flown. Despite distance and war, a dispatch arrived detaching Lt. Cdr. Miller; he has avoided reporting to the CVS for three months; the question is, can he put this one off?

April 2. This was a day of rest; the ship took on fuel, and Joe Hobb was returned to us from the destroyer that picked him up. Our combat air patrol took off for a short hop.

April 3. Lt. Comdr. Ralph Fuoss received orders today designating him Commanding Officer of Fighting Squadron 23, and orders came designating Lt. Cdr. Hatcher as Air Group Commander. The question remains whether Lt. Cdr. Miller will remain until Ralph is qualified, which may mean a few more weeks' delay, and maybe another operation. Tally Ho Ack Ack announced today that we are headed for our usual port in the Marshall Islands, and should arrive at the end of the week. Good News; it may mean mail for us. There was only one flight today, an early C.A.P. Lt. Comdr. Miller and Lt(jg) Coyer took Ensigns Parker and Blyth with them for a little experience.

April 4. This was all sleep and no work. It poured rain all day, so even the sun baths were curtailed. We again crossed and re-crossed the Equator, making our total equal 44 crossings.

- 22 -

CONFIDENTIAL

April 5. Rain all day; all flights cancelled.

Today is Holy Wednesday, April 5, again. We are headed toward the Marshalls, and have picked up the day we lost on going to Espiritu. Tomorrow we are due to arrive, so will be anticipating overdue mail.

April 6. The following message was received from the Task Group Commander: For Air Group and Squadron Commanders x I sincerely appreciate the cooperation and support given me by your commands during the operations now terminated x It will be a pleasure to serve with you on any and all future operations x signed, Ginder.

April 7th. Mail was delivered last night. Consequently today everyone was answering letters. Some of the boys went ashore and enjoyed a few beers under the palm trees. Muhlfeld was transferred to the USS RELIEF this afternoon; we should be able to pick him up at Pearl later, when we get there.

April 8th. Four new pilots reported to us today: Lt. Tripp, and Ensigns Sprinkle, Farnsworth, and Schellenberg. Everyone is taking things leisurely and doing a lot of sleeping.

April 9th. Easter Sunday. Sunrise services were held on the flight deck at 0630; then at 0800 Catholic mass was celebrated in the hangar deck. Later in the day most of the boys went to the beach for a swim and a drink of beer.

On Monday an Air Group outing was arranged, so that at 0900 all started to go ashore and set up an O Club in a vacant quonset hut, on one of the islands. A ball game between the married and unmarried officers ended in the fifth inning, with half the married ones leaving the game due to exhaustion, but with them leading. By 1300 we had consumed our supply of liquor. However other air groups arrived with their beverages just in time, so that the Bar continued to serve, and everyone had more than enough. Some had cameras; when a picture was to be taken of someone, before it was snapped, everyone had posed and gotten his face into the group. The party broke up around 1700 with everyone feeling their way through the coconut trees and helping each other out of the island jungle.

The next day was a quiet day after the outing; some made an appearance, and some did not.

April 13th. Preparations were being made in order to get under way. Lt. Cdr. Miller, Crockett, McWilliams and Tyner went ashore at 0630 in order to fly new planes aboard. The ship was under way at 1200. From the flight deck we watched the world's greatest fleet steam out of the lagoon; it was a magnificent sight watching each type of ship steam out in single file. We are headed south, and will take part in the biggest operations yet carried out in the Pacific; it will mean the end of the Jap in a certain area. The operations plan was being carefully studied, and lectures being prepared for the pilots. As the ship weighed anchor, great quantities of mail were delivered, so that everyone was in a happy frame of mind.

Friday, April 14th. One combat air patrol took off for a routine flight. When the boys landed they provided everyone with excitement. The first one aboard, John Hill, hit the barrier. Then came Parker, and practically repeated the story. Sprinkle followed, and blew out a tire. Lack of wind across the deck was the main trouble. Lectures on New Guinea are being given to all the pilots, along with the plans for the coming landing operations, which are to be of gigantic size. Our task group, of which Admiral Black Jack Reeves is in command, is composed of numerous types of ships, and large enough to handle any situation that the Japs may wish to throw against us.

- 23 -

CONFIDENTIAL

There was no yesterday, Saturday, 15th of April. It was omitted, and today is Sunday, the 16th, due to the fact that we are again headed West, and therefor are in East Longitude time again.

Surprise gunnery and bombing flights were ordered today by the Admiral, which gave the pilots an opportunity to get in form again. Due to the unexpected flights, all ground school classes were cancelled. Athletics were conducted on the flight deck; calisthenics; then keep-away with the medicine ball.

Monday, April 17th. Last night we crossed the equator for the 45th time. A combat air patrol was flown, and gunnery flights were scheduled. The weather has been perfect, so everyone is acquiring a sun tan.

April 18th. Today was Group Commander day. Each group commander from the various squadrons called on each other, and made final plans for the attacks on New Guinea. Lectures on the targets, and plan of attack were held, so all the pilots are familiar with the whole plan by now.

Wednesday, April 19th. Our radar operators picked up a strange plane about 0300 this morning, which sent all hands to their battle stations, and started an active day. At 0600 a tanker came alongside and refueled us. It was done in record time, since the Task Force had to be refueled today. Les Kerr, Weickhardt, Olin, and Blyth took off for a routine combat air patrol. They were catapulted, since there was no wind. However, it was not long before a snooper was picked up, and the boys took after him. As soon as the Jap twin-engine torpedo plane was sighted, he was a dead Jap, and at 1315 he splashed.

We are still a couple of days from our target, but these Nips are persistent guys, so we are expecting more before arriving. Tonight's message from Admiral Reeves: From 58.3 to Princeton: Congratulations.

20th. Last night we re-crossed the Equator for the 46th time, and remained north of it all day. Since yesterday's shooting down of the Jap plane, all the boys are anxious to get in the air and do a little shooting themselves. Two divisions drew patrols today, but no Nips showed up to accommodate them. The high light of the day was a submarine contact inside our screen that sent all hands to their battle stations, and set all the ships zig-zagging frantically; but nothing turned up.

Final lectures on tomorrow's targets were conducted, so all is ready for the attack. Tonight we changed our course, and are headed South, crossing the Equator for the 47th time.

April 21st. D-1 Day. Our squadron was assigned three strikes over the airdromes, Hollandia, Cyclops and Sentani. The first strike, consisting of Lt. Cdr. Miller's and Lt(jg) Kerr's divisions took off at 0615, and raked all Jap planes on the runways that could be located through the mass of clouds that covered the fields. Schmidt and Crockett's divisions were the next to visit the enemy, and carried on with the devastation. While they were coming aboard, the forward elevator broke, with Olin on it. No crack-ups. But the third strike had to be cancelled, which was unfortunate, since a few Jap planes were attempting to escape, and were beautiful targets for our patrolling fighters from a sister carrier. The troop transports are due to arrive tonight, and the landings will be carried on in the morning.

- 24 -

CONFIDENTIAL

D-Day, April 22nd, was uneventful, so far as our expectations were concerned. We sent combat air patrols in over the landing forces, but they were not called on to help in any way whatever. The Japs evidentally moved into the mountains, and will venture forth later. When the planes were returning to base, the weather closed in, and it began to pour. Lieut. Comdr. Miller, Claude Schmidt and Les Kerr were in it, and had a time going through black clouds and with practically a zero ceiling. Our troops landed according to schedule, and were busy building roads as our boys left their patrol sector. Our sector was over Tanahmera Bay, where some of the landings were carried out; the other half of the landings taking place in Humboldt Bay, near the Town of Hollandia.

The 23rd was a quiet, uneventful day. It consisted of routine patrols over our task force and our landing forces. The weather would close in intermittently, which would give the pilots a scare, but the base was always located and all landed safely.

The following day began with an early flight over the landing forces. Jap planes would appear, but leave when our fighters took after them. During the afternoon our boys were called on to strafe ahead of our troops. The Japs had built obstacles along the road, so they were thoroughly strafed. Our planes landed after sundown; it was even necessary for the Signal Officer to use the lighted wands. Just as the boys landed, the Japs appeared over the force, so all hands proceeded to General Quarters. The night fighters shot one down, but the rest of the Japs proceeded on into Hollandia to bomb the landing forces.

April 24th was refueling day for the task group. While the tanker was alongside the balance of the task force was within sight; it was the first time in a few days that we could see them. A Jap bomber came too close, and one of our sister carriers shot him down in a hurry. There were four survivors, who were picked up and delivered to the Admiral. Whether we will stick around or leave is the $64.00 question; everyone is guessing whether we will return to our usual port to go on a raid on the way back. The pilots are all for a direct trip to Pearl. The four pilots we received just before leaving this time, - Tripp, Sprinkle, Farnsworth and Schellenberg, - were permanently transferred to us today.

Not since the Baker Island days has there been more excitement and enthusiasm than today, April 26th, 1944. Lieut.(jg) Webb, Ens. Bledsoe, Ens. J.R. Hill and Ensign Parker took off on a routine combat air patrol at 0610. Lieut.(jg) Tyner's division was also catapulted at the same time, and for the same purpose. Neither Joe Webb or Bob Tyner had at that time shot down any Japs; consequently both boys were hoping for some unsuspecting snooper to appear. It was not long before one did show up; he was near Webb's division. Joe was in luck, and on locating his victim, sent him splashing into the blue Pacific, each of the four boys in the division getting one or more runs on the Nip, so that they each received credit for the kill. All during this time Tyner's division was evidently over the ship, hoping for another Jap to appear. As luck would have it, another one did show up, but he was 20 miles nearer to Webb's division, who were consequently sent out for the intercept. They chased this fellow for a good 70 miles before they finally caught him. It was a new Jap twin-engine fighter, and had the speed, but not enough; since on being overtaken the boys went to work on him, and sent him into the drink.

Having finished up this second Jap, the pilots found themselves a good 100 miles away from their base, and practically out of gas. On hearing of their predicament, Captain Buracker immediately requested permission from the Admiral to be detached from the task group and speed towards our pilots, so as to cut down their distance and take them safely aboard. Permission was granted, so Captain Buracker had them pour the coal on the engines. This consideration won the admiration of the Air Group for the Captain; he really produced when our boys needed help. When the ship met the pilots, Ensign Parker's gas gauge indicated empty. However the ship was already into the wind, and all Parker had to do was head straight in, and with Curtis handling the flags he made a beautiful approach and landing. The other three followed him in, without wave-offs or nervous landings. When the boys were safely aboard, the entire ship roared with three lusty cheers.

CONFIDENTIAL

April 26th (continued).

It looked as though Fighting 23 started something, since in the afternoon the Japs sent in three more snoopers, and each of them went forth to meet his ancestors. We did not get these three, since as luck would have it some other air group had the patrols.

No one mentioned about going home today; everyone wants to get into the air and pick up a Jap or two! This evening the following messages were received:

> TO YOU AND YOUR TASK FORCE, CONGRATULATIONS ON ANOTHER JOB WELL DONE - NIMITZ.
>
> From CTF 58, to PRINCETON:
> WELL DONE. MITSCHER.
>
> From CTG 58.3 to PRINCETON:
> GOOD WORK X YOUR BOYS ARE RIGHT ON THE JOB. REEVES.
>
> From: ComDesDiv 100:
> IF I AM PERMITTED TO SAY QUOTE VERY NICELY DONE UNQUOTE.
>
> From: INGERSOLL, destroyer:
> THE PLEASURE IS OURS X IT GIVES US A CHANCE TO FEEL WE ARE DOING SOMETHING.

April 27, 1944. Yesterday was a day no one mentioned about going home. However, today a new low has been reached, and a pall has been draped over the squadron. An operation order has just been brought aboard ordering a two-day attack on Truk! It has knocked the boys back on their heels, since everyone was practically packed and on their way home for a few days' leave. However the Jap has to be defeated and the complete destruction of Truk is one step further in reaching our goal; so, Japs beware of Fighting TWENTY THREE, the boys are really hot under the collar this time!

After last night's shock of the contemplated attack on Truk, the boys today are resigned to it, and are gathering all the available information obtainable on the target. The forecastle talk has turned to the humorous side, and now it will be a sensational surprise if we are ever relieved.

April 28th, was devoted to last minute lectures and preparations for tomorrow's attack on Truk. The pilots checked their planes thoroughly and are ready for the Japs. A wonderful surprise greeted us today; we received mail, and we are only 300 miles from Truk! It seems a certain battlewagon joined us, and was thoughtful enough to bring our mail along. We say, Well Done.

April 29th. D-Day; our attacks on Truk took off according to schedule, and the great Jap fortress is being reduced to rubble. Two divisions of fighters went in on the first attack. Lt. Cdr. Miller led the group and had McWilliams, Coyer and James in his division. While over the target a Jap fighter closed and was another dead Jap when Miller and McWilliams boresighted the Nip. Kirschke led his division of Darby, Massey and Brugger in on the first attack also. Big John's division is famous for its desire and aptitude in giving ships and boats hell in strafing runs. The boys really wrapped it up today, and despite severe anti aircraft fire and lurking zeros, they gave the Japs hell.

During this first strike Schmidt's and Kerr's divisions drew combat air patrols. Claud's division was sent out to intercept an unidentified plane, and before he realized it, he was in the middle of Truk and A.A. bursting all around him. This certainly was not his job, so he quickly left that particular spot.

The second strike was composed of Lt. Cdr. Miller, Ens. McWilliams, Lt. Tripp, and Ens. James; also of Lt(jg) Crockett's division of Ens. Vaden, Lt(jg) Tynor and Ens. Hendrickson. The aerial opposition had dwindled considerably, and no Jap planes were to be seen airborne, so the grounded planes were the main objective for the boys.

CONFIDENTIAL

April 29th (continued):
The third strike was led by Lieut. Schmidt and his division of Ensign Matlock, Lt(jg) Abell, and Ens. R. T. Hill, along with Lt(jg) Kerr's division of Ens. Weickhardt and Ens. Blyth. When all had landed everyone was in a happy frame of mind, since all were safe. Break out the rations, Doc.!

Sunday, April 30th. The second continuous day that we are attacking Truk. The same schedule was carried on with the Jap fortress receiving one blow after another. The place is in shambles and good targets are difficult to locate. In the midst of all this activity Lieut. Kenyon received orders to report to N. A. S., Bunker Hill, Indiana. About all that can be said about the place is that he may be lucky to have his family with him if a room is to be found.

May 1st, 1944. Word was received that our ship is ordered back to Pearl along with a couple of others, which news was greeted with smiles and great expectations that upon arriving there we will be sent to the States.

May 2nd was another quiet day. Vice Admiral Mitscher sent out the following:
ONCE AGAIN IT HAS BEEN MY PLEASURE TO SERVE WITH THE FINEST ASSEMBLY OF MEN AND SHIPS IN THE HISTORY OF THE UNIVERSE X MY PRIDE IN THEM IS UNBOUNDED X THIS TIME OUR WAY HAS BEEN LONG AND OUR DUTIES TIRESOME X THE LONGING FOR ENGAGEMENTS WITH THE ENEMY FLEET FORCES WAS NOT ACCOMPLISHED DUE TO THEIR TIMIDITY WE CANNOT GUARANTEE A FIGHT EVERY TIME WE GO TO SEA BUT WE CAN ASSURE OURSELVES AND OUR PEOPLE AT HOME THAT WE WILL BE IN THERE HITTING WHEN THE TIME DOES COME ."

May 4th. We entered our usual port at 1000 and immediately speculated on how long we would stay before shoving off for Pearl and points East. Air Group and squadron pictures were taken next to the bridge, and all the Jap flags indicating the squadron's success in the past year. Lieut. Perkins reported aboard; it took him two months to locate and catch up to us.

May 5th was a quiet day; spent the day turning in ship's gear that had been checked out to us. The Langley Air Group gave us a party, a farewell token, and as expected, it turned out to be quite an affair. Everyone came aboard soaking wet, and cheered up the movie audience. The ship is packed with passengers, so anchors aweigh!

Saturday, the 6th, saw us leave our anchorage in the Marshalls, and head toward Pearl Harbor. We weighed anchor at 0900, with everyone in a happy frame of mind, since we were headed in the right direction. We are due to arrive the 11th, and look forward to a short visit there before leaving for California.

So, for the nonce, ends the War Diary of Fighting 23.

Our schedule to date has been as follows:

    May 28, 1943 - sailed from Hampton Roads, Norfolk.

    July 3, - Returned - 36 days at sea (Trinidad)

    July 21, - Sailed - from Philadelphia Navy Yard.

    August 9, - Pearl. 19 days at sea (Panama)
                          16 days ashore (Barbers Point).

    August 25, - Sailed.

    September 23 - Returned. 29 days at sea (Baker-Tarawa)
                              18 days ashore (Ford Island).

    October 11th - Sailed.

    December 7th - Returned. 57 days at sea (Buka-Bonis, in northern
                                Solomons; Rabaul; Espiritu Santo;
                                Nauru, and capture of Tarawa).
                              34 days ashore (Puunene Air Station, Maui).

    January 10th - Sailed.

    January 13th - Returned. Pearl. (qualified new pilots).
                              3 days at sea.
                              6 days aboard ship at Pearl.

    January 19th - Sailed. Capture of Marshall Islands; Majuro;
                              Espiritu Santo; raid on Palau and Woleai;
                              capture of Hollandia; Raid on Truk.

    May 11th, 1944-Returned. Pearl. 113 days at sea.

        Since May 28, 1943, we have been at sea - 257 days.

        Since May 28, 1943, we have been ashore - 92 days.

AIR GROUP TWENTY THREE STATISTICS

41 enemy planes destroyed in aerial combat (4 by VT-23)
3 enemy planes probably destroyed in aerial combat.
11 enemy planes damaged in aerial combat.
1 enemy plane shot down by ship's gun fire.
11 enemy planes destroyed on the ground.
4 enemy planes probably destroyed on the ground.
11 enemy planes damaged on the ground.
2 enemy heavy cruisers torpedoed.
1 enemy destroyer torpedoed.
1 AK destroyed
1 PT boat set on fire.
8 medium AK thoroughly strafed
2 small AK thoroughly strafed.
1 minesweeper thoroughly strafed.
3 large motor launches strafed.
4 barges thoroughly strafed.
18 boats thoroughly strafed.
62 raids.

9,028.51 combat hours flown.

Ship Statistics.

597,640 pounds of bombs dropped, including 14 torpedoes.
661,710 rounds of ammunition expended by aircraft.
4,667 carrier landings - average interval 40 seconds.
1,386 catapult launchings - average interval 55 seconds.
22 barrier and deck crashes.
   (a) 8 major overhaul.
   (b) 2 minor overhaul.
   (c) 2 complete losses.
844,108 gallons of aviation gasoline consumed.
13,990 gallons of motor oil consumed.
80,962 miles travelled by the ship.
8,241,463 gallons of fuel oil consumed by the ship.

Summary of Strikes:

Makin   - 1
Tarawa   - 1
Buka   - 2
Bonis   - 2
Rabaul   - 1 (5 Nov 1943)
Rabaul   - 1 (11 Nov 1943)
Nauru   - 3
Wotje   - 16 (9 were CAP over Wotje)
Taroa   - 4 (1 was CAP over Taroa)
Eniwetok - 27 (13 were CAP over Eniwetok)
Palau   - 4
Hollandia - 9 (7 were CAP over Hollandia)
Truk   - 5

76
7 (CAP over task force resulting in action)

Total - 83

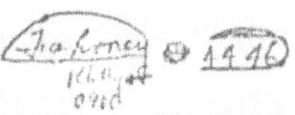

CONFIDENTIAL

Strikes per pilot

Pilot	Strikes	CAP over enemy territory
Miller, H. L., Lt. Cdr.	26	16 CAP; 3 Air Coordinator
Schmidt, C.C., Lieut. 129507	21	15
Crockett, S.K., Lt(jg) Stanley 5-01-43	12	10
Kerr, L.H., Lt(jg)	14	10
Abell, J.M., Lt(jg)	20	16
Kirschke, W.J., Lt(jg)	15	9
Tynor, R.S., Lt(jg)	13	13 (took pictures 16 times)
Olin, D.H., Lt(jg)	10	10
Webb, J.L., Lt(jg)	13	10 CAP; 2 Air Coordinator.
Syms, J.W., Lt(jg)	17	13
Massey, D.E., Lt(jg) 156706 1-01-44	12 Eugene	11
Coyer, P., Jr., Lt(jg) 158105 1-01-44	15	13
Darby, G.J., Lt(jg) 156972 3-01-44	10	10
Muhlfeld, F.B., Lt(jg) 156961 3-01-44	8 Bearss	11
Pupillo, C.S., Lt(jg)	12	4
Vadon, F.W., Ens. 251392 5-01-44	12 William	11
Hill, J.R., Ens. 263466 5-01-44	12 Roland	11
Whitlock, G.J., Ens. 63544 5-01-44	10 Joseph	17
Williams, L.F., Ens. 263598 5-01-44	18 Francis	16
James F., Ens. 263532 5-01-44	18	18
Hendrickson, H.E., Ens.	14	11
Brugger, L.O., Ens. 273044 4-16-43	7 Otis	8
Nickum, T., Ens. 283077 6-16-43	3	9
Reickhardt, C.E., Ens.	8	9
Hill, R.T., Ens.	2	4
Blyth, R.I., Ens.	2	1
Tripp, D.K., Lieut.	1	3
Sprinkle, C.I., Ens.	0	2
Bledsoe, I.T., Ens.	0	0
Parker, W.E., Ens.	0	0
	325	291

5 Air coordinator
16 photographic missions.

CHANGE of COMMAND

31 August 1971

Naval Air Systems Command
Test and Evaluation Coordinator

Commander
Naval Air Test Center

Commander
Fleet Air, Patuxent

Naval Air Station
Patuxent River Maryland

REAR ADMIRAL HENRY L. MILLER, USN

Rear Admiral Henry L. MILLER will terminate a distinguished 37-year Naval Career when his flag is hauled down in formal ceremonies here today. Rear Admiral MILLER is leaving the Naval Air Test Center after three years as Naval Air Systems Command Test and Evaluation Coordinator, Commander, Naval Air Test Center and Commander Fleet Air, Patuxent.

A native of Fairbanks, Alaska, our 49th state, Rear Admiral MILLER entered the U. S. Naval Academy on appointment from Alaska in July 1930. He was graduated with the Class of 1934, was designated Naval Aviator at the Naval Air Station, Pensacola, in June 1938, and subsequently completed the Bombardiers' Course at Sandia Base and the All Weather Flight Course at Corpus Christi, Texas.

His early service included three years' duty at sea in the battleship TEXAS and engineering and gunnery duties in Fighting Squadron 3, based on the aircraft carrier SARATOGA. From November 1940 until October 1942, he was a Flight Instructor and Personnel Officer at the Naval Air Station, Ellyson Field, Florida, and while there during the early period of World War II, trained General Jimmy Doolittle's "Tokyo Raiders" in carrier takeoffs, then accompanied them to within 700 miles of their destination, on board the USS HORNET in April 1942.

From November 1942 to May 1944, he commanded Air Group 23, based on the USS PRINCETON, and during the remainder of the war had command of Air Group 6, based on the USS HANCOCK. He was "recalled" from an air strike on Tokyo when hostilities ceased in August 1945. For World War II service he holds the Legion of Merit with Combat "V"; the Distinguished Flying Cross with four Gold Stars in lieu of additional awards; the Air Medal with five Gold Stars; the Army Commendation Ribbon; and the Navy Unit Commendation Ribbon (USS HANCOCK).

He had duty in the Navy Department during the period December 1945 until July 1948, first assigned to writing Air Operations Instructions, later serving as Executive Officer, Air Branch, Office of Naval Research. For two years he served as Public Information Officer on the Staff of Commander in Chief, Atlantic Fleet, and from June 1950 to August 1952, served successively as Executive Officer of Composite Squadron 7, and of the USS LEYTE (CV-32).

After graduation from the Industrial College of the Armed Forces in July 1953, he returned to the Office of the Chief of Naval Operations for a tour of duty in the Strategic Plans Division. In August 1955 he assumed command of the U. S. Naval Station, Sangley Point, Luzon, P. I., and on September 1, that year, became Commander Fleet Air, Philippines, and Commander Naval Air Bases, Philippines. He left this "three-hat" job in May 1957, to become Assistant Director, later Director, of the Progress Analysis Group, Office of the Chief of Naval Operations. In January 1959, he assumed command of the USS HANCOCK.

Selected for Rear Admiral on July 22, 1959, he reported on March 3, 1960, as Chief of Staff and Aide to the Commander Naval Air Force, Pacific. He commanded Carrier Division FIFTEEN, an Anti-Submarine Hunter-Killer Task Group, from May 1961 to June 1962. He served as Assistant Chief of Staff for Plans, Joint Staff, Commander in Chief, Pacific, during the time when the situation in Southeast Asia began to escalate. In September 1964, he assumed command of Carrier Division THREE, a Heavy Attack Carrier Task Group, and at the same time took command of Task Force 77, the Carrier Striking Force of the SEVENTH Fleet.

In February 1965, as CTF 77, he launched the first of a succession of aircraft carrier strikes on North Vietnam from the decks of the USS RANGER, CORAL SEA and HANCOCK. In October of 1965, he took the nuclear-powered Task Group, the USS ENTERPRISE and USS BAINBRIDGE from Norfolk, Virginia, to Subic Bay, P. I., and subsequently, on December 2, 1965, he engaged the first nuclear-powered Task Force in Combat with the enemy in Vietnam.

From April 13, 1966, until October 4, 1968, he served as Chief of Information, Navy Department, and on October 8, 1968, he became Commander, Naval Air Test Center, Patuxent River, Maryland, with additional duties as Commander Fleet Air, Patuxent, and Naval Air Systems Command Test and Evaluation Coordinator.

Admiral MILLER is married to the former Miss Lucille Dean of Opp, Alabama. They have two children, Henry L. Miller, Jr., presently residing in San Francisco, California, and Richard B. Miller, who will begin his freshman year at the University of Virginia this fall.

Rear Admiral and Mrs. MILLER will begin their retirement by travelling throughout the United States.

PROGRAM

Music by the
United States Navy Band

Commander Donald W. Stauffer, USN
Leader

Master Chief Musician, Larry Kreitner, USN
Conducting

★ ★

Arrival Honors

Rear Admiral Arthur G. Esch, USN

Rear Admiral Albert H. Clancy, Jr., USN

Rear Admiral Henry L. Miller, USN

Rear Admiral Roy M. Isaman, USN

Vice Admiral Robert L. Townsend, USN

★ ★

Post the Colors

★ ★

Inspection of the Honor Guard

★ ★

National Anthem

★ ★

Invocation
Captain J. H. Carnes, CHC, USN

★ ★

Sound Off

★ ★

Presentation of Legion of Merit
Rear Admiral Albert H. Clancy, Jr., USN

Remarks and Reading of Orders
Rear Admiral Henry L. Miller, USN

★ ★

Full Honors Rendered to
Rear Admiral Henry L. Miller, USN

★ ★

Presentation of Personal Flag

★ ★

Reading of Orders
Rear Admiral Roy M. Isaman, USN

★ ★

Full Honors Rendered to
Rear Admiral Roy M. Isaman, USN

★ ★

Remarks
Rear Admiral Roy M. Isaman, USN

★ ★

Presentation of Retirement Certificate
Vice Admiral Robert L. Townsend, USN

★ ★

Benediction
Commander J. X. Bergeur, CHC, USN

★ ★

Retire the Colors

★ ★

Rear Admiral Henry L. Miller, USN
Piped Ashore

★ ★

Departure of Distinguished Guests

REAR ADMIRAL ROY M. ISAMAN, USN

Rear Admiral Roy M. ISAMAN will assume the duties of Naval Air Systems Command Test and Evaluation Coordinator, Commander, Naval Air Test Center and Commander Fleet Air, Patuxent when his flag is broken in formal ceremonies today. He is reporting to the Test Center from the Staff of Commander in Chief, U. S. Pacific Fleet, where, since May 1970, he served as Deputy Chief of Staff for Operations and Plans.

Rear Admiral ISAMAN was born in 1917 in Lewiston, Idaho. He attended Idaho State Normal School and the University of Idaho. He entered the Naval Reserve on 10 July 1940 and in September was appointed Aviation Cadet, USNR. Completing flight training at Naval Air Station, Pensacola, Florida, in April 1941, he was designated a Naval Aviator and received his commission as an Ensign, USNR. He transferred from the Naval Reserve to the Regular Navy on 12 January 1944.

After receiving his wings in 1941, he joined Bombing Squadron THREE to serve as Personnel and Operations Officer. While attached to that squadron, he participated in the Doolittle Raid, the Battle of Midway, and Guadalcanal operations. For outstanding service with Bombing Squadron THREE, he was awarded the Navy Cross and the Air Medal.

In September 1943, he reported to the Staff of Commander, Fleet Air Quonset at Quonset Point, Rhode Island, and served as Fleet Bombing Training Officer. In October 1944, he became Executive Officer of Bombing Squadron EIGHTY-NINE. He attended the General Line School at Newport, Rhode Island, from June 1946 to June 1947, when he became Head of the Airborne Early Warning Department on the Staff of the Fleet Airborne Electronics Training Unit, Atlantic, at Norfolk, Virginia.

From September 1948 until May 1949, he served as Operations Officer of Composite Squadron TWELVE. He then served as Anti-Submarine Warfare Officer and Attack Squadron Officer in the Office of Naval Research, Navy Department, Washington. In October 1951, he joined Attack Squadron FIFTEEN, stationed in Jacksonville, Florida, as Executive Officer, and later became Commanding Officer. In January 1953, he became Assistant Training Officer on the Staff of Commander, Fleet Air Jacksonville.

He served as Assistant Head, and then Head, of the Attack Weapon System Section, Office of the Chief of Naval Operations, from February 1955 until July 1957. In November 1957, he reported for duty in the Bureau of Naval Personnel. While there, he additionally served in the Office of the Chief of Naval Operations. He was a student at the Industrial College of the Armed Forces, Washington, D. C., from July 1958 to June 1959, and then became Operations Officer on the Staff of Commander, Carrier Division SIX.

He assumed command of the USS SHASTA (AE-6) in January 1961, and from April 1962 to January 1963, commanded the USS MIDWAY (CVA-41). He then became Head of the Special Weapons Plans Branch, Office of the Chief of Naval Operations.

His selection for the rank of Rear Admiral was approved by the President on 1 June 1965, and in August he reported as Commander, Patrol Force Seventh Fleet/Commander, U. S. Taiwan Patrol Force/ Commander, Fleet Air Wing One.

Prior to reporting as Commander Carrier Division SEVEN, Rear Admiral ISAMAN was assigned as Director of the Strike Warfare Division, Office of the Chief of Naval Operations, Navy Department.

On 18 April 1969, he became Commander Carrier Division SEVEN in ceremonies conducted on the flight deck of the USS BON HOMME RICHARD (CVA-31) steaming in the Gulf of Tonkin.

In addition to the Navy Cross, the Legion of Merit with three gold stars in lieu of third and forth awards, the Air Medal and the Presidential Unit Citation Ribbon with two stars, Rear Admiral ISAMAN has the American Defense Service Medal, American Campaign Medal, Asiatic-Pacific Campaign Medal, World War II Victory Medal, Navy Occupation Service Medal, China Service Medal (extended), the National Defense Service Medal, Republic of China Medal of the Special Order of Cloud and Banner, and the Vietnamese Navy Distinguished Service Order First Class.

Rear Admiral ISAMAN is married to the former Nancy Mower Taylor of Roanoke, Virginia. He has two children, Roy Larkin and Gail Elizabeth Isaman, and four stepchildren, Nancy Lurton, Christie Mackall, Susan Smythe and Bruce Mackall.

More than an airport...

testport is the Naval Air Test Center, pulsing hub of the Navy's aircraft appraisal. In a mere quarter century, testport has saved millions of American defense dollars and untold numbers of American lives. Its proof or disproof of an air system's safety and efficiency is the case for its approval or disapproval.

Raw cliff banks of the Patuxent River tremble as the newest patrol plane in the fleet swoops to a concrete strip cut through Southern Maryland woodland. A sea gull hovers in bay skies mimicking man's whirly gulls as they practice recoveries of astronauts or downed pilots. Colonial plantation walls hear the talk of admirals discussing a national defense where British lords once conferred on the defense of their struggling province.

Nature and history have hospitably received testport. And testport has helped defend them through the Second World War, Korea and now Vietnam.

In the last three years, testport has looked southeast with the rest of America. But she has not neglected a vigilant scan of other compass points and her own shores. Under the command of Rear Admiral Henry L. Miller, testport has appraised, protected and grown. This is the story of testport's last three years ... the Naval Air Test Center 1968 to 1971.

aircraft are transitory objects of testport's attention as they stop and then pass on from this point of trial between the draftsman's line and the flight line of the fleet.

OV-10A

October 1968, the OV-10A Bronco faced carrier suitability trials aboard USS Kennedy. Lacking both tailhook and catapult fittings, the Bronco fully depends on reversible pitch propellers for landings.

This observation aircraft, used in Southeast Asian combat before the Board of Inspection and Survey trials were completed, provides close air support for ground troops as well as aerial reconnaissance.

The North American Rockwell-built OV-10A is acclaimed for its maneuverability and defense capabilities.

AH-1G

The Huey Cobra, fastest and most maneuverable helicopter in production to date, arrived at the Test Center in May 1969. At that time, this AH-1G was urgently needed in Southeast Asia by United States Marine Corps forces and was introduced in Vietnam one month before trials began at Patuxent River.

The Cobra, a Bell helicopter, is the only rotary wing gunship built specifically for attack missions. It carries a two-member crew——pilot and gunner.

In September 1970, the AH-1G's sister, the AH-1J, made its appearance at the Test Center. The J-bird, slightly longer and heavier than the G, sports twin engines. It is armed with one of the largest automatic guns in the Marine Corps and can forward fire ordnance or drop either bombs or night flares. The AH-1J completed Board of Inspection and Survey trials late summer 1971.

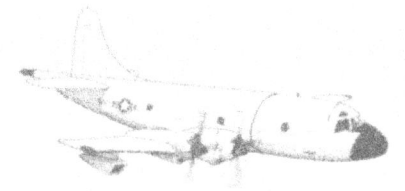

This three-year period marked the Navy's transition to the P-3C patrol aircraft. The Lockheed-built plane arrived at Patuxent River, June 12, 1969.

On January 22, 1971, a Naval Air Test Center P-3C recorded the world's longest non-refueled flight for its class——Atsugi, Japan, to Patuxent River, 7,010 miles, in 15 hours, 21 minutes. In later weeks the same aircraft bettered seven more world records formerly held by Soviet aircraft:

It flew 502 miles per hour over a 9.3 to 15.5 mile course;

Climbed to 44,900 feet for a record altitude in horizontal flight;

Soared still higher to 46,100 feet for a maximum altitude record;

Bolted from brake release on the ground to 9,843 feet in 2 minutes, 59 seconds;

Continued from that point to 19,685 feet in 5 minutes, 48 seconds;

Pushed on to 29,528 feet in 10 minutes, 31 seconds

And topped off at 39,370 feet in 19 minutes, 53 seconds.

A-7E

The A-7E was catapulted to new records with Test Center pilots at the stick in fall 1969 when it left the aircraft carrier USS Independence with nine and one half tons of ordnance. This payload weight exceeded that carried by any other single-engine aircraft launched from a ship.

The Vought Aeronautics-built attack bomber includes an intricate avionics package. A projected map system stores charts of one million square miles of the earth on 35 mm film. Governed by a digital computer, the display scope shows the pilot where he is flying. The A-7E also boasts a Head-Up Display (HUD) at eye level to give the pilot constant navigational data and attack solutions.

A-6

In spring 1970, the EA-6B arrived at the Test Center for Board of Inspection and Survey trials. Designed to jam hostile radar, the four-seat aircraft protects air strike forces.

During contractor demonstrations and structural tests of the Grumman-built EA-6B, a cost and timesaving system of in-flight refueling was used. And by late winter that year, the plane was approved for the fleet.

Summer 1970, the A-6C, a night attack aircraft, passed acceptance trials of its low light level television and advanced infrared systems.

And shortly afterward, a modified A-6A, the KA-6D tanker, arrived at

Patuxent River for four and one half months of testing. This carrier-based plane is primarily used for air-to-air refueling missions.

AV-8A

British-born, the AV-8A Harrier was purchased in 1970 by the United States Marine Corps for advanced base, light attack missions. It was subsequently tested at the Naval Air Test Center and evaluated aboard aircraft carrier USS Guadalcanal.

The vertical take off and landing aircraft has a single seat, high wing design.

tomorrow

At the frontier of Naval aviation, the Naval Air Test Center thrives on tomorrowness.

As early as March 1969, a meeting was convened at the Test Center by Rear Admiral Henry L. Miller, Test and Evaluation Coordinator for Naval aviation, to plan for testing of the F-14.

This Grumman fighter/interceptor is distinguished by swing wings which automatically move backward or forward in flight. Thus, the F-14 is capable of dashes at twice the speed of sound or slow speed flight necessary for aircraft carrier landings.

The F-14 is manned by two—pilot and missile control officer. Its ordnance includes three types of missiles and a 20 mm cannon.

An S-3A Test and Evaluation conference was held in 1970 at Patuxent River to coordinate the trials schedule. The jet-engined S-3A, capable of speeds twice those of the propeller-driven S-2 Tracker, will be the Navy's primary anti-submarine warfare plane based on a carrier.

A P-3A Orion is being reconfigured as a flying avionics test bed for the Lockheed-built S-3A and should make its first flight late summer 1971.

Projects in support of aviation are collateral dimensions of testport.

IR-100 award

The first Navy laboratory to receive an IR-100 Award, the Naval Air Test Center strode forward with innovation in 1970. The award recognized the work of Test Center civilians who developed a transparent photo-diode, an instrument used to calibrate extremely sensitive devices which measure acceleration.

The photo-diode was developed under the FR-IED, Foundational Research-Independent Exploratory Development, program and was selected by Industrial Research, Inc., as one of the 100 most significant developments of the year.

VAST

April 1970, the first Versatile Avionic Shop Test (VAST) system was delivered to the Naval Air Test Center. Before its introduction to the fleet, VAST is undergoing tests at Service Test and Weapons Systems Test Divisions. A later model of the VAST system is due for evaluation at the Test Center in December 1971.

VAST automatically checks sophisticated aeronautical electronics systems and serves as a general purpose, computer-controlled test station for a wide range of evaluations.

surface effect ships

Late spring 1971, it was announced that Navy testing of two surface effect ships would begin the following year at the Test Center. A $1.7 million test facility will be built.

Though weighing 100 tons, the ships are capable of speeds of more than 80 knots as they ride on a cushion of air which reduces drag.

This initial test phase is an important part of a program to determine the suitability of 4,000 to 5,000-ton, high-speed surface effect ships. The future design of all Navy vessels may rest on the outcome of these tests.

programs revitalize testport's zeal and contemporary insight.

test and evaluation coordinator

Four hundred test aircraft, which involve 11 Naval test bases and 22 civilian contractors, were placed in late 1968 under the administration of Rear Admiral Henry L. Miller, Naval aviation Test and Evaluation Coordinator.

The first Test and Evaluation conference met on December 2 that year at the Naval Air Test Center. Subsequent conferences were convened at such places as Albuquerque, New Mexico; Point Mugu, California; Warminster, Pennsylvania and China Lake, California.

Through the last three years, the Coordinator has dealt with the demands of the Navy's technical evaluations and Board of Inspection and Survey trials.

weapons systems test

In 1968, the Weapons Systems Test Division was selected by Naval Air Systems Command to manage all problems of electromagnetic compatibility.

Also in 1968, the Tactical Support Center of Weapons Systems Test was founded. The Support Center is a land-based element which underlies the air wing forces of anti-submarine warfare. An organizational concept developed at Patuxent River, the Center instantly provides the anti-submarine warfare command facts derived from computers within aircraft so that full attention might be given the decision making rather than information gathering process.

automatic carrier landing system

Aircraft now land on carriers, guided to the point of arrestment by fully automatic controls. In June 1969, the USS Saratoga became the first aircraft carrier certified for this operation. Since then, Flight Test Division has certified four more carriers and two field installations.

Work is continuing to provide greater compensation for carrier deck motion, to widen the range of landing ability with wind-over-the-deck velocities and to analyze the effect of turbulence resulting from the ship's movement.

Today, the F-4J and F-4B, if properly configured, are certified for the fully automatic carrier landing system. Tests are continuing on the A-7E, A-6A and RA-5C.

service test reorganization

As a result of reorganization and a more technological philosophy, Service Test Division has grown in the last three years from a simple organization testing whether a sailor might service an aircraft, to a complex division with a scientific approach.

The branches of the division reflect its growth. Ground Support Equipment Branch was reorganized in spring 1969, in recognition of the fact that complex weapons systems require complex support. In January 1970, all Service Test Division aircraft came under the newly formed Aircraft Systems and Propulsion (ASAP) Branch.

masters degree test pilots

A joint masters degree/Test Pilot School diploma program is sought for the future.

Test Center officials feel that the technical knowledge of Naval test pilots should adequately support dialogues with contractors and that the learning reflected by a masters degree would bolster that technical knowledge.

If approved, the proposed masters program would be affiliated with the

Naval Postgraduate School at Monterey, California. Increasing the present three-year test pilot tour to four years, the curriculum would require fifteen months at the Postgraduate School, eight months at the Test Pilot School and two years at work with a Test Center division.

figures of world fame and local recognition are profiled in testport history.

Burdette award

In memory of a Flight Test Division engineer who died in a helicopter crash, the John E. Burdette Award was established in 1968 to recognize the outstanding young project engineer at the Naval Air Test Center.

Three annual presentations have since been made by the Society of Engineers and Scientists who instituted the award.

students of the year

One test pilot, one flight officer and one project engineer are honored annually by three Test Pilot School best-of-the-year awards.

School officials review the three graduating classes of the fiscal year and select representatives of excellence in academics, flight reports, flight performance and motivation.

The first Student Test Pilot of the Year Award was made 1969. Naval Flight Officers were recognized in 1970 and project engineers in 1971.

reunion and symposium

Annual traditions, the Test Pilot School reunion and symposium have grown in the last three years to involve more returning graduates and extended lists of celebrity speakers. The 1969 guest speaker was Vice Admiral Thomas F. Connolly, Deputy Chief of Naval Operations for Air. Apollo 12 moon walkers, Captain Charles Conrad, Jr. and Alan Bean, attended the 1970 symposium which was addressed by guest speaker, Robert A. Frosch, Assistant Secretary of the Navy for Research and Development.

Admiral Elmo R. Zumwalt, Chief of Naval Operations, and Captain James A. Lovell, Apollo 13 commander, took turns at the speaker's podium in 1971.

and the demands of testport's growing task effect demands for new construction.

hospital

A 50-bed Naval Hospital was opened at Patuxent River in late spring 1969. Housing both medical and dental facilities, the building cost nearly $2 million.

A far cry from the first infirmary built at Patuxent River in 1943, the hospital is manned by approximately 30 doctors, nurses and Medical Service Corps officers.

new housing

Ground was broken in February 1969 for 300 housing units at Patuxent River. The three and four-bedroom units were constructed under a $5.5 million contract to augment the 508 existing quarters.

Enlisted families occupy 272 of the units while 28 officer families occupy the others.

chesapeake range building

The Chesapeake Test Range Building, a facility housing instruments which track aircraft, was opened in late October 1969. The Theodolite and Radar Range Branch of Technical Support Division moved in.

Their instruments——radars, a computer system and central cine-theodolite control equipment——gather data used to evaluate weapons systems, testing systems and navigational traffic control devices.

academic building

An annex adjacent to the Test Pilot School Building was opened in May 1970 to house academic facilities.

This modular unit provides the school additional classroom and faculty office space as well as a computer center.

computer services division building

The Computer Services Division Building was opened in July 1970.

A modular unit of 14 trailers, the potentially mobile complex is rented by the government. Computers are housed in a permanent structure nearby.

aircraft electrical evaluation facility

A $6.5 million home for the Electrical Evaluation Branch of Weapons Systems Test was opened in March 1971. The single-story building boasts high altitude chambers and endurance test stands. Special air conditioning and ventilation systems protect delicate equipment.

With the opening, electrical evaluation performed in six separate buildings was at last centralized. The branch's mission is to test project aircraft electrical systems.

www.ingramcontent.com/pod-product-compliance
Lightning Source LLC
Chambersburg PA
CBHW080620170426
43209CB00007B/1473